"Taking teaching and learning outside of the traditional classroom into urban and/or rural settings, has the potential to provide academic, personal and professional development benefits for both students and staff in higher educational settings. This book is a great platform into past, current and future directions of theory, research and applied practice related to this dynamic pedological approach. It also explores aspirational methods and opportunities to further develop and enhance current outdoor learning opportunities in HE and may just inspire you to take it outside!"

Sally-Ann Starkey, *Senior Lecturer, Liverpool John Moores University*

"Outdoor learning, such as field trips, have been around in higher education for many years but recently I have become more interested in learning outside, not only in terms of curriculum content but also introducing alternative pedagogic approaches and considering the wellbeing of my students. Much of the current literature has focused on outdoor learning in the school environment, so for me this is a much-needed book bringing the spotlight to outdoor learning in higher education."

Dr Isobel Gowers, *Associate Professor, Anglia Ruskin University*

"For university lecturers and students, outdoor learning opens up a wide range of creative possibilities for subverting and transcending traditional approaches to teaching and university education more broadly. The innovative pedagogies and real-world examples presented in this volume not only break down the walls of academia but also create a bridge that connects learners to the natural world and diverse ways of thinking. As someone deeply invested in humanistic pedagogies, inclusivity and the holistic development of my students, I found this book to be an invaluable resource for reimagining the possibilities of higher education in the great outdoors."

Tabban Betts, *Lecturer in Higher Education Pedagogy, University of Sussex*

"The book comes at a time when the insightful exploration of outdoor learning and its impact on HE couldn't be needed more."

George Robinson, *Senior Learning Technologist, University of Sussex*

Outdoor Learning in Higher Education

Outdoor Learning in Higher Education is essential reading for educational developers and academic teachers of all disciplines interested in the theory behind, and benefits of, learning outdoors. Filled with practical case studies and backed by recent research, it provides educators with the tools needed to create an effective yet inclusive learning experience for their students beyond the lecture hall or seminar room.

In chapters which offer analysis, discussion of current debates and advice for good practice, the book is structured around five key themes:

- Theoretical perspectives and research supporting outdoor learning.
- Health and wellbeing benefits for learners and educators.
- Tools and techniques for teaching outdoors, including new technology.
- Examples of effective fieldwork.
- Crossing educational borders and implementing sustainability and the natural world into the curriculum.

This key book covers issues which are relevant across all disciplines in higher education, including: experiential learning, sustainability, diversity and inclusion, and incorporating new technology. *Outdoor Learning in Higher Education* develops perspectives on these and other themes, while encouraging the creation of inspiring and effective learning environments.

Wendy Garnham is Professor of Psychology at the University of Sussex, UK. She is also co-founder of the Active Learning Network and has won several awards for innovative teaching. Currently, Wendy also acts as Director of Student Experience for the Central Foundation Year programmes.

Paolo Oprandi is a Doctor of Digital Pedagogy which he attained from the University of Sussex. He is a Senior Fellow of the Higher Education Academy and is currently the co-chair of the Active Learning Network. He has a research background and currently leads the implementation and operations of numerous digital environments and CPD programmes within the charity sector. He is a nature and wildlife enthusiast, Wikipedia editor and proponent of active learning pedagogies.

The Staff and Educational Development Series

Series Editor: James Wisdom

Written by experienced and well-known practitioners and published in association with the Staff and Educational Development Association (SEDA), each book in the series contributes to the development of learning, teaching and training and assists in the professional development of staff. The books present new ideas for learning development and facilitate the exchange of information and good practice.

Titles in the series:

For more information about this series, please visit: https://www.routledge.com/SEDA-Series/book-series/SE0747

Outdoor Learning in Higher Education

Educating Beyond the Seminar Room

Edited by
Wendy Garnham and Paolo Oprandi

Routledge
Taylor & Francis Group

LONDON AND NEW YORK

Designed cover image: Getty Images

First published 2025
by Routledge
4 Park Square, Milton Park, Abingdon, Oxon OX14 4RN

and by Routledge
605 Third Avenue, New York, NY 10158

Routledge is an imprint of the Taylor & Francis Group, an informa business

© 2025 selection and editorial matter, Wendy Garnham and Paolo Oprandi; individual chapters, the contributors

British Library Cataloguing in Publication Data
A catalogue record for this book is available from the British Library

ISBN: 978-1-032-56738-9 (hbk)
ISBN: 978-1-032-56737-2 (pbk)
ISBN: 978-1-003-43692-8 (ebk)

DOI: 10.4324/9781003436928

Typeset in Galliard
by Taylor & Francis Books

Contents

PART 5
Crossing educational borders

Contributors

Editors

Wendy Garnham is a Professor of Psychology at the University of Sussex and a National Teaching Fellow. As co-founder of the international Active Learning Network, her scholarly interests are dominated by active learning pedagogy. Wendy is a Senior Fellow of Advance HE, a Fellow of SEDA and jointly hosts a regular community of practice for academics interested in transition into, through and out of higher education. She has edited open access books on active learning as well as two SEDA special publications on transitions into higher education and contributed a case study to an Advance HE publication on action research. Wendy writes from first-hand experience in research and teaching.

Paolo Oprandi is a Doctor in Education with over 20 years' experience in pedagogic research and learning technologies. An advocate for change in educational practices, he promotes curricula that require active participation by students, produce memorable learning experiences and involve the creation of student artefacts which can be added into their portfolios. His research has focused on curriculum designs that welcome diversity into the academic disciplines and value, above all else, student contributions. He is co-editor of two open access publications – Disrupting Traditional Pedagogy: Active Learning in Practice and 100 ideas for Active Learning. He has been a regular contributor to a number of blogs including the Sussex Technology Enhanced Learning blog, the Dare to Transform blog, the Sussex E-learning team blog and the Active Learning Network blog.

Authors

Agnes Bosanquet is an Associate Professor, academic developer and higher education researcher. Her current role is Director, Learning and Teaching Staff Development at Macquarie University in Sydney, Australia. She has over 20 years' experience teaching in face-to-face, blended and online learning environments and her research focuses on critical university studies and changing academic roles and identities. She blogs as the *Slow Academic*.

Aled Singleton is a Postdoctoral Research Fellow in Human Geography based at Swansea University, Wales, UK. Before starting his PhD, Aled spent over a decade in local government and the voluntary sector, working at a street and neighbourhood level to develop and implement community and urban regeneration projects. He uses walking interview techniques and mobile outdoor groups to explore the relationships that people have with place over the lifecourse. Aled is a psychogeographer who works closely with performers and theatre makers to engage with the public in creative and disarming ways. He follows Rebecca Solinit's recommendation in *A Field Guide to Getting Lost* (2017, p. 5) that: "It is the job of artists to open the doors and invite in prophesies, the unknown, the unfamiliar..."

Alexander Sabine is course leader for Early Childhood Studies at the University of Portsmouth. Living on the Isle of Wight, Alex has worked in education since 2006 and has always had a passion for experiential learning in outdoor environments, of which the island has plenty to offer! Alex is also a qualified Forest School and Beach School practitioner and is currently engaged in doctoral research into the potential benefits of open source civic mapping for schools and the wider community. He has also visited outdoor settings in Norway on several occasions and has taught principles of outdoor education to kindergarten leaders in China. Alex also has a lifelong interest in technology and its cutting edge use in education.

Andrew Middleton is Deputy Head of Anglia Learning & Teaching at Anglia Ruskin University where he is responsible for promoting academic innovation and leading curriculum enhancement, digital fluency, and media-enhanced teaching and learning. As a National Teaching Fellow and PFHEA, he is Chair of the UK Media-Enhanced Learning Special Interest Group and a leader within the international Active Learning Network. Andrew researches and publishes on spaces for learning, co-operative pedagogy, and studio-based learning. He blogs at Tactile Learning (https://tactilelearning.wordpress.com/) and co-leads the Exquisite Education podcast (https://exquisiteeducation.podbean.com/).

Beth Hammond is a Senior Digital Learning Designer in the Digital Learning Service at the University of the West of England, based in the College of Arts, Technology and Environment. Having previously studied Careers Guidance, she has an interest in personal and professional development within the curriculum and the tools and pedagogies that support this. She is also interested in designing education for a future of social, environmental and technological change, questioning what, how and where we teach to allow students to thrive.

Carrie Winstanley has taught in schools and higher education for thirty years. She is currently Professor of Pedagogy at Roehampton University, London, with a particular responsibility for learning and teaching, and is working on a range of student programmes (undergraduate, Masters, Doctoral) and with faculty. Carrie is particularly committed to encouraging all learners to embrace museum and gallery visits and outdoor activities as an essential aspect of their education, and she is interested in informal as well as formal learning. She is fascinated by ideas around challenges in education, with an emphasis on broadening inclusion and diversity in all phases of education, and with a particular reference to social justice.

Cathy Elliott is Associate Professor in the Political Science department and interdisciplinary Arts and Sciences department at UCL, as well as Vice Dean (Education) for the UCL Faculty of Social and Historical Sciences. She is also Co-Convenor of the Political Studies Association Teaching and Learning Network and a Co-Director of the UCL Centre for the Pedagogy of Politics. She is a Senior Fellow of the Higher Education Academy. She has an interest in active and experiential learning, engaging students' emotions and imaginations in their learning, and has previously written about education in art galleries and about simulations. She has also co-produced research with students and worked with student activists to promote inclusive, anti-racist and queer pedagogies and curriculums.

Chris Barlow is an ex-primary school teacher who has been a senior lecturer at the University of Cumbria for twenty years. Chris teaches predominantly on primary and postgraduate teaching courses and is a geography specialist who has previously conducted work on behalf of the Geography Association. Chris has a passion for creative teaching and works closely with schools in the Morecambe Bay area as they develop a bespoke place-based curriculum inspired by the prospect of Eden Project North and is involved in the development of nature-inspired, place-based learning ideas with schools and Lancaster University, work which was recently recognised as the Education Faculty's showcase activity of the year for 2023. Chris has recently established an Environmental and Experiential Primary Postgraduate specialism, also inspired by the prospect of Eden Project North, and operates a think tank of students from different routes into primary teaching who meet regularly to discuss and contribute ideas to the Morecambe Bay Curriculum. Chris is currently undertaking research into student involvement in curriculum design.

Colin Wood is course leader for the MA in Outdoor Education at the University of Worcester, supporting outdoor professionals to study in their workplaces. He is a Senior Fellow of the Higher Education Academy and is an active researcher in both outdoor learning and teaching and learning in higher education. Previously, Colin had a long career in Outdoor Education, working in senior posts around the world. Colin's work spanned corporate development, outdoor recreation, sail training and expeditionary learning, including leading numerous jungle expeditions.

Gustavo R. Espinoza-Ramos is the module leader of Sustainable City Economies, a second-year undergraduate module, and the course leader for the MA Management (online) at the Westminster Business School. He is a Senior Fellow of the Higher Education Academy (SFHEA). He is the digital champion at the school of Management and Marketing, with his current interests being in active learning and the use of online tools and simulation games to promote student engagement.

Heather Prince is Professor of Outdoor and Environmental Education in the Institute of Science and Environment at the University of Cumbria. She designs, develops and teaches undergraduate and postgraduate programmes in outdoor studies at the university and is interested in the development and efficacy of pedagogic practice in higher education. She is a Principal Fellow of Advance HE. Her main research interests are in school-based outdoor learning, sustainability and adventure. Recently, she has been engaged on projects developing nature-based and place-based curricula in north-west England. She has published widely and is co-editor of the *International Handbook of Outdoor Studies* (2016), *Research Methods in Outdoor Studies* (2019) and *Outdoor Environmental Education in Higher Education: International Perspectives* (2021).

Jamie Heywood is an Associate Professor and Academic Lead for Academic Development & Recognition at Anglia Ruskin University (ARU). Jamie leads on initiatives and opportunities across the university to support academic development and recognition, working in partnership with faculties, teams, and individuals. Jamie's work aims to celebrate and showcase practice and support development and progression, to empower and encourage colleagues and to enhance teaching excellence and the student experience.

Jo Peat is Head of Educational Development at the University of Roehampton. Jo's research interests include innovative pedagogies, retention and success in higher education and academic professional development. Jo is a Fellow of SEDA, a member of the SEDA Executive and a Principal Fellow of the HEA. Jo has contributed to publications and blogs on aspects of teaching and learning in higher education and has been involved in nationally and internationally funded projects on Black and minority ethnic students and attainment, gender and pedagogic relations and professional accreditation and recognition.

Jonathan T. Schulte is the Education Evaluation manager at LSE's Eden Centre for Education Enhancement, working across a range of projects to deliver and support evaluation of education activities and policies. His recent work ranges from projects on environmental education, to research on the impact of admissions policies on widening participation, or the role of social class in shaping student experiences. Outside of these projects, Jonathan mainly works on evaluation theory, thinking about approaches to evaluation that support building a culture of critical reflective practice across the institution.

Julie Peacock is an Associate Professor in Ecology and Director of Student Education in the School of Geography at the University of Leeds and holds Senior Fellowship status with Advance HE. Julie has developed novel approaches towards learning outside of the classroom in order to make fieldwork more inclusive. Alongside Karen Bacon, Julie developed a model for teaching on-campus urban ecology with social media to enhance student employability and professional development skills early in their degree. Julie came to Leeds from the Higher Education Academy, where she promoted learning and teaching in higher education nationally across STEM subjects.

Karen Bacon is a Lecturer in Plant Ecology in the School of Natural Sciences at the University of Galway. Karen has developed new approaches towards teaching plant ecology and botany in higher education and in schools outreach, such as using virtual field trips to complement in-person fieldwork skills learning and address the problems surrounding plant awareness in undergraduate students. Karen leads the fieldwork stream of the digilego project, which is developing open educational resources for digital methods training in Geography and Environmental Sciences in higher education.

Kate Lloyd is in Geography and Planning where her research, learning and teaching experiences focus on Indigenous and Development Geographies, University-Community engagement and practice-based learning. She is a Principal Fellow of the Higher Education Academy and takes an applied, action-oriented and collaborative approach to research and teaching characterised by community partnerships, co-construction of knowledges and an ethics of reciprocity. As a result, at the heart of her life-work are innovative co-authored and co-created projects that focus on learning, nurturing, healing and sensing.

Kath McLachlan is an experienced community practitioner committed to advancing education and research in higher education. Her extensive background encompasses a passion for outdoor learning environments and fostering nature connections. Kath's multifaceted portfolio includes teaching, research, and engagement activities, informed by relational approaches with a central emphasis on reflective and contemplative practices. She firmly believes that a relational approach is essential for comprehending, coexisting with, and addressing our social-ecological systems. She leverages her expertise to conduct workshops on creativity and reflective practice at both national and international levels.

Liam Taylor is a Lecturer in Extended Reality and Digital Pedagogies in the School of Geography at the University of Leeds. Liam's work involves using digital technologies and social media to make fieldwork more accessible and inclusive across the Geography curriculum. Liam uses 3D models and immersive media to create digital twins of undergraduate fieldwork sites to improve student understanding of physical landscapes. Outside of pedagogical research, Liam uses virtual reality in schools and outreach programmes to show students the impacts of climate change on the natural world.

Miles Holmes is Co-Founder and Director of The Connective and is a professional facilitator, anthropologist and nature connection mentor, who has been working with groups in the outdoors for over 25 years. He has been mentored in deep nature connection, wilderness survival and meditation by leading experts in Australia and the USA and holds a PhD in anthropology completed in partnership with Warlpiri people from Central Australia. Through this work and research he has developed a deep understanding of the processes through which humans become connected to nature, and an insight into the knowledge that Aboriginal peoples can offer in the practice of nature connection and environmental stewardship.

Oliver Haslam is currently a Senior Digital Learning Designer at the University of the West of England. He has worked in digital education for over 20 years and first discovered the benefits technology can bring to learners whilst teaching international students in the UK and overseas. He joined UWE Bristol in 2011, initially as a learning technologist, and in recent years he led the Learning Innovation Unit, a faculty-based team of learning technologists. His professional interests lie in exploring and enabling the use of web and mobile technologies to support active and authentic learning at scale.

Patrick Boxall is a lecturer at Queen Margaret University, Edinburgh with primary interests in how critical and creative pedagogies can forward human and eco-centred conceptions of social justice. At QMU he is Project Lead for the creation of the Outdoor Learning Hub. Building on MRes inquiry, he is working towards a PhD by publication that is focused on the importance of creative pedagogy in outdoor learning as enacted by leaders and practitioners. He spent much of his career as an English and Drama teacher working in England, the USA and Scotland; later running a social enterprise and working in Adult Education. He is an experienced Forest School leader and, while at Newbattle Abbey College, developed the Forest and Outdoor Learning Awards.

Russell Crawford is Director of Learning and Teaching and Associate Professor of Education at Falmouth University. With an interest in gamification for learning, a background in bioscience and academic development experience in implementing high impact pedagogies, he is a Senior Fellow of Advance HE, won the Times Higher Education Awards "Most Innovative Teacher of the Year" in 2017 and was awarded a National Teaching Fellowship in 2018. In his role as DLT, he has created a range of curriculum innovations such as the "Hitchhiker's Guide to Curriculum Design", The Falmouth Formative Feedback Cycle and the 9 Domains of Collaboration.

Sabiha Iqbal is serving as the Muslim Chaplain to the University of Roehampton. Sabiha has worked for over 18 years in the HE sector with roles in recruitment, international student support, and most recently in a multi-faith chaplaincy. Over the years, she has continued professional development from studying geography to business and currently is completing a second Masters degree in Theology and Religious Studies. She uses her work and learning to further enhance the co-curricular experience for students and staff at university, and this in the past has included organizing UK and EU excursions for students and staff to provide opportunities of learning in multi-cultural social contexts. As Muslim Chaplain to the University of Roehampton, she has set up a variety of spaces for worship, reflection spaces promoting coexistence, as well as organizing activities that invite members of the community to venture into altruistic works, learning or sharing a skill, or just exploring their outdoor environment. Collaborating with colleagues and students, Sabiha has set up a partnership between the University of Roehampton and the London Wetland Centre (Barnes) to explore how barriers to accessing green spaces can be lowered for the university community.

Suzie Dick was the deputy head teacher on the Isle of Arran, Scotland, and is now Lecturer in Education at Queen Margaret University, Edinburgh. She is the instigator of the Scottish Island Schools Network and current vice chair of International Professional Development Association Scotland. Additionally, Suzie has worked for over 20 years on youth expeditions, is qualified as an international mountain leader and is the Scotland rep for the British association of International Mountain Leaders. Her key research interests include outdoor learning, rural education and practitioner enquiry.

Thomas E. L. Smith is Associate Professor in Environmental Geography at the LSE. He teaches on a number of environmental courses, focusing on innovative technology-enhanced experiential learning and field-based education in geography. He joined LSE in 2018, having previously been a Lecturer at King's College London. He holds a PhD in Physical Geography from King's College London and has held Visiting Fellow posts at the National University of Singapore, Monash University Malaysia, the University of Wollongong (Australia) and Universiti Brunei Darussalam. Tom is a geographer and environmental scientist, specialising in interdisciplinary approaches to understanding the role of biomass burning in the Earth system. Tom enjoys highly-collaborative research focusing on greenhouse gas and reactive emissions from wildland fires in savannas and tropical peatlands. He is particularly interested in complex interactions between agricultural practices, land degradation, fire emissions characteristics and their associated impacts.

Tom Langston is a Learning Designer at the University of Portsmouth and has worked in a variety of roles within the university for the past 16 years. Over that time Tom has worked in TEL and Academic departments, looking at creating environments for student engagement. When his children started at a local school, the idea of forest schools became an interesting notion as it was a much more practical approach to engagement than Tom had seen before in HE. While the activities in HE are not the same as in primary school, the idea that students in HE are constrained to fixed classrooms and computer screens was one that Tom felt could and should be challenged. Tom is now working on a London Campus project looking at blending the learning environment (both physical and digital) with green spaces flowing between taught and shared spaces on campus and how learning in this space can be utilised.

Waminda Parker is Co-Founder and Director of The Connective (NatureFix) and has over 25 years of strategic planning, operations and project management experience. Waminda has a high-end capacity to build transdisciplinary networks across government, land managers, industry groups, community and research and as aligned to legislative frameworks, policy and planning instruments. As a Director of Programmes, Waminda has successfully established a range of large, long-term and complex projects, alliances, networks, consortiums and programmes addressing holistic models of sustainability, community resilience and conservation, and is an Infrastructure Sustainability Accredited Professional.

Introduction

Wendy Garnham

Sometimes the world conspires to create pedagogical paradigm shifts, and the current move towards considering outdoor learning as a valuable tool, not just for developing learning but also for promoting healthy learners, feels very much like one of these. Concerns about climate change, the global health concerns of recent years and the pressure on institutions to grow student numbers whilst maintaining restricted teaching space have all contributed to practitioners exploring the value of outdoor learning afresh. In recognition of this, the first section of this volume contains contributions that explore the recent theoretical underpinnings of outdoor learning, exploring the ideas of pedagogical biomes, heutagogy and the creativity associated with outdoor learning experiences.

Coming from a psychology background, it is clear that the benefits of the great outdoors are numerous. For example, Tifferet and Vilnai-Yavetz (2017) point to the way in which natural environments can reduce negative emotions, something that they refer to as the phytophilic effect. Berman et al. (2008) identified the beneficial effects of walking in nature on cognitive performance, specifically a backwards digit span task, and Gascon et al. (2018) suggested access to green spaces reduced the need to take anti-anxiety medications. With regards to the COVID-19 pandemic, Soga et al. (2021) reported a decrease in loneliness as people used the green spaces around their homes more often. Similarly, Corley et al. (2021) pointed to the improvement in sleep quality linked with spending time in the garden during the COVID-19 pandemic.

Combined with commonly reported difficulties experienced by students of poor sleep, anxiety issues and loneliness, it is clear that the great outdoors can offer valuable boosts to their wellbeing, something which Groenewegen et al. (2006) claim is equivalent to the effect of a vitamin. Learning outdoors enables individuals to feel a sense of belonging, not just to their university groups but to their communities, something which is a key message emanating from chapters in the second section of this volume looking at health benefits.

As this volume illustrates however, it is not just wellbeing that has fueled the recent increase in interest in outdoor learning. Technological advances have enabled

DOI: 10.4324/9781003436928-1

practitioners to embrace learning in new and innovative ways, for example using newly developed apps that use GPS to guide students' learning in new environments or using social media to immerse students in their learning environments. The rapid change in pedagogical resources ensures the continual development of practice which helps to avoid the stale repetition of well-rehearsed dissemination of knowledge and instead provides students with a dynamic and interactive opportunity to apply their learning in and to the environments around them.

The ability to take students out into the "field" is not without its challenges; however in the third section of this volume, these are explored alongside consideration of the unique value of fieldwork to students' understanding and appreciation of the natural world. Whether this is through the use of newly available tools such as air pollution monitors to actively engage students in environmental projects in their community or using virtual and actual field trip experiences alongside each other to promote inclusivity, the fieldwork experience can help to create memorable and lasting educational experiences that promote reflection as well as knowledge creation.

Whilst outdoor learning is nothing new, and is particularly well established for younger age groups, the crossing of educational borders has remained an ill-achieved objective. In the final section of this volume, this barrier becomes the focus as ideas about how to maximize the affordability of outdoor environments across different phases of the educational journey are presented.

My own interest in outdoor learning was inspired by colleagues who introduced me to the ideas of walking seminars, nature identification apps and even community projects such as "Toad Patrol" as ways of taking learning into natural environments. I hope that in reading the contributions contained within this book, you too will be inspired to take learning outdoors and experiment with the variety of pedagogical ideas presented herein.

References

Berman, M. G., Jonides, J., & Kaplan, S. (2008). The cognitive benefits of interacting with nature. *Psychological Science*, 19(12), 1207–1212.

Corley, J., Okely, J. A., Taylor, A. M., Page, D., Welstead, M., Skarabela, B., & Russ, T. C. (2021). Home garden use during COVID-19: Associations with physical and mental wellbeing in older adults. *Journal of Environmental Psychology*, 73, 101545.

Gascon, M., Sánchez-Benavides, G., Dadvand, P., Martínez, D., Gramunt, N., Gotsens, X., & Nieuwenhuijsen, M. (2018). Long-term exposure to residential green and blue spaces and anxiety and depression in adults: A cross-sectional study. *Environmental Research*, 162, 231–239.

Groenewegen, P. P., Van den Berg, A. E., De Vries, S., & Verheij, R. A. (2006). Vitamin G: Effects of green space on health, wellbeing, and social safety. *BMC Public Health*, 6 (1), 1–9.

Soga, M., Evans, M. J., Tsuchiya, K., & Fukano, Y. (2021). A room with a green view: The importance of nearby nature for mental health during the COVID-19 pandemic. *Ecological Applications*, 31(2), e2248.

Tifferet, S., & Vilnai-Yavetz, I. (2017). Phytophilia and service atmospherics: The effect of indoor plants on consumers. *Environment and Behavior*, 49(7), 814–844.

Part 1

Theoretical perspectives

Chapter 1

Contextual learning and the great outdoors

Pedagogic biomes!

Russell Crawford

Engaging learners has an almost eternal flavour to it. Pedagogists from time immemorial have grappled with trying to elicit that elusive spark of interest in the academic discipline itself, rather than just focus on the necessities of "progression" to the next step or stage of learning. Dress it up in the jargon of "tactical learning" or, if you prefer, the ever-familiar refrain from students of *"just tell me what I need to know to pass"*, and even as far back as the late 1970s, pedagogists were looking at behaviour where students' motivation was focused on passing their course rather than learning from a position of disciplinary passion (Mathias, 1978). It is ironic then, that so many higher education (HE) student interviews and applications to HE, cite drivers like "passion", "interest" and "a love of..." as their primary motivational starting point for joining a course. To this author, it seems almost criminal that these positive attitudes are promptly dispensed with once the course has been started, a situation that is compounded, in many cases, by a group consumerist or transactional mindset (Marshall et al., 2015).

This is not to denigrate strategic learning as a way to meet objectives, especially as that is a great way to instil healthy learning behaviours and encourage genuine interest in students, as they often hark back to Ramsden's classic rationale of using exam strategies to aid academic performance. The caveat I would mention is that this can get in the way of gaining true comprehension of academic materials, and it remains to this day a challenge that educators face (Ramsden, 1992).

Students frequently use this sort of "exam strategy" early in their academic careers, mostly as a survival tool, which might therefore mean its use leads to some passive academic understanding over time, or at the very least, suggest some level of active engagement with learning by proxy of adopting a strategy of any sort in the first place.

Certainly, for most higher education courses (especially where skills or core competencies are essential), it is patently impossible for students to finish a course of study without developing a deeper understanding of those elements of the wider materials and/or the development of key skills and knowledge.

Conversely, Gibbs' idea of personalised learning describes the need for teachers to be cautiously aware that their advice is framed clearly as advice because it may

DOI: 10.4324/9781003436928-3

not be supported by either pedagogic or scientific benchmarks. Interestingly, this idea further postulates that teachers should be clearly differentiating between "necessary" study skills and their own opinions of the "right" approach to assimilating information and skills (Gibbs, 1981). From a pedagogic, archaeological perspective, this early-1980s point still resonates with this author, and speaks in similar beats to the more contemporary personalisation of learning ethos that has been emerging post-pandemic (Tzavara et al., 2023).

Ramsden defines "teaching" as the integration of curriculum aims, transmission methods, assessment and self-evaluation, taking the view that effective teaching is also about learning a series of skills and/or knowledge, and coining the phrase "content over method" (Ramsden, 1992). Whilst the sentiment is laudable, if the aim of higher education study is to maximise student learning with each encounter, this author now postulates that for effective contextual learning, *the method and environment of teaching is at least as important as the content*. This goes doubly so when considering learning outdoors, where method and environment are very tightly linked and contextual learning truly comes to the fore.

Contextualism: Know your roots

Colliver convincingly articulates his treatise on educational theory, warning against using educational theory as a justification for practice (Colliver, 2002). He postulates that many educational theories originate from four main sources: constructivism, adult learning theory, grounded theory and cognitive science (Schuwirth & Van Der Vleuten, 2004; Appleton & King, 2002; Kaufman, 2003; Kennedy & Lingard, 2006; Leigland, 2000). Of these, it is the last one that is more interesting historically, as it led directly to the development of the branched theory this chapter positions as THE way to approach learning outdoors: contextualism (Bakken, 2002; Clough & Lehr, 1996).

Contextualism: So what is it?

By way of an example often cited in the literature, a perfect exemplar of contextualism in action is a study where scuba divers were able to recall a memorised list better underwater if they learned the list underwater in the first place, rather than on dry land, and vice versa (Koens et al., 2003). The core take-away from this work is that environmental cues encoded during learning aid in recall (Thompson et al., 2001) and it should immediately become apparent why this suits learning outdoors so well. The many arguments of E. Eich, J. M. Eich and others over a clear decade (from 1985–1995) add layers of complexity by positing that one of the confounding factors in Godden and Baddeley's original work might be that differing environments can result in differing moods, which are themselves known determinants of learning and memory performance (E. Eich, 1995, E. Eich et al., 1994, E. Eich et al., 1985, J. M. Eich, 1985).

Current thinking in this area and something to consider for outdoor pedagogists looking for effectiveness, is the need for a match in "learning mood" and "recall mood" to maximise performance, always with the caveat that high levels of stress are accepted to negatively affect learning (Laney & Loftus, 2005, Paz-Alonso & Goodman, 2008). These "moods" therefore will heavily feature in the core ways through which contextualism can be applied to learning outdoors. It was this idea, when amalgamated with the brilliant view of the "*environment as the third teacher*" from Wurm (2005), that triggered this author's own thinking around characterising and exploring "Pedagogic Biomes" to inform learning outdoors.

Pedagogic biomes!

A biome is a natural area containing a community of plants and animals that share commonalities specific to that area. Extending that apt metaphor to learning outdoors, there are three "Pedagogic Biomes", with thematic commonalities of style, success, design and implementation of the educational experience offered within each biome and thereby, drivers of success. Table 1.1 presents them in summary.

Table 1.1 Summary of the three pedagogic biomes, each grouped with their respective contextual elements and key considerations.

BIOME: *Learning...*	CONTEXTUAL ELEMENTS	KEY CONSIDERATIONS
1 - **Actively**	• Macro education of large groups or populations • Driving behavioural change • Authentic assessment through active pedagogies • Person-centric academic social transformation	Designing macro educational intervention(s) that change perceptions, behaviours and cultures through motivation and innovative practices. 　Narrative and story-telling as a way to build on previous learning experiences to make sense of new learning.
2 - **On the job**	• Participative by nature • Learning by becoming • Authenticity	Developed pre-existing collaborative skills and mitigation of negative experience.
3 - **On location**	• Time as a key variable • Affective learning • Experience-based learning • Accounting for disciplinary biases • Cross-cultural immersion	Integration of learning design with learning outcomes on location. 　Interdisciplinary learning using "just-in-time" pedagogic design contexts and participative elements.

Each pedagogic biome has its own character and educational context to consider, especially when explored through a contextual learning lens.

Biome 1: Learning actively

"Active" learning has become almost synonymous in recent years with health and psychological wellbeing, with clear correlates between participation in learning and emotional wellbeing emerging since 2016 (Brame, 2016). Beyond the obvious health and safety concerns, as well as the team working and engagement skill development opportunities that an active learning approach to outdoor pedagogy fosters, more complex applications can be also be found in the form of gamification and playful learning that allow educators to explore activity-based (*and if you are still with me, contextualist*) learning to authentically develop the learners' sense of "self" and spark interest, engagement and motivation (Aynsley et al., 2022).

Core to this first pedagogic biome are outdoor educational design elements which speak to action-centric and experiential-driven creativity, where outdoor participants typically engage in action-reflection cycles to make meaning. The underpinning philosophy for adopting this approach is firmly grounded in the educational literature of "belonging", an especially contemporary topic in HE. Active learning is rapidly re-becoming a critical aspect of the modern student experience and contextual outdoor pedagogues would do well to start working from the base assumption that "belonging" is a core human trait that encompasses a sense of respect, being valued, feeling supported and experiencing inclusion and personal/professional validation, each in linked but distinct ways, and each of which is in play in learning outdoors (Gravett and Ajjawi, 2022).

Often equated with gaining "deeper" understanding of knowledge and skills, active engagement outdoors comes with unique responsibilities for curriculum design where outdoor environments must be carefully accounted for in the overall experience (Fullan and Langworthy, 2013). This has particular resonance when educators are meeting their obligations and indeed, aspirations around designing active outdoor learning that is both accessible and equitable (Thurber and Bandy, 2018).

This pedagogic biome encompasses teaching design related also to learning gain (Evans et al., 2018), defined as the educational "distance travelled" and enticingly made possible through the application of outdoor contextual learning. There are clear collaborative elements to consider, chiefly "motivation" and "innovation", as active outdoor learning establishes a causal link between outdoor activity and the transferability of knowledge and skills to enhance learning, creating outdoor-based active learning cultures and innovative contextual education as a result.

Biome 2: Learning on the job

Work-based or "employer-based" learning is inherently participative in nature within "real world" environments where productivity, established norms and socially constructed hierarchies are ever-present (Ajala, 2012). Taking a contextualist view, it is the highly authentic nature of the "work" environment (*by definition outside of the classroom*) that both equally drives and places learning at some risk. This biome represents the most "at the coalface" experience for learners to enter, meaning that once in "real" work or industry environments, they irrevocably become part of that living culture and part of the wider shared "work" experience.

This has tremendous potential to positively impact outdoor learning, with placement year opportunities reliably shown in the wider literature to be as close to an employability magic bullet as it is possible to get (Auburn, 2007). It is notable that students who take up placement year work find employment success more frequently than those who do not (Mansfield, 2011). Part of this is down to the networks and connections that simply being in those environments offer, but within that there is also a key element of "learning through becoming", where the learner essentially joins a living, breathing culture and conforms to its professional and more importantly, social "rules".

Whilst you might correctly argue that collaborative skills are integral to all learning, it is within this biome where "collaboration as a skill" is more keenly required than elsewhere. To survive and thrive in the workplace environment, the learner must have a pre-existing collaborative skill set to draw upon, as the challenges faced day-to-day in these environments require agility and resilience. This author's previous work has described nine discrete collaborative domains in terms of skills, and for this pedagogic biome, "participation", "awareness" and "reciprocity" are of particular importance when organising workplace-based experiences and pre-arming learners as they enter these sometimes unpredictable environments (Crawford, 2022). Learners in the work environment also require an advanced understanding of what "participation" means as it crosses professional-social boundaries and links tightly with self- and group-awareness, touching on living hierarchies, fluid group and personal dynamics and the "reciprocity" of what is expected of the group from the individual and logically, what is then expected from the group of the learner.

Whilst useful from an educational perspective, negative experiences in the workplace can risk disproportionately impacting perceptions, as it can discolour perceptions of a whole sector, discipline or environment, something that is especially risky when the learning experience was participative in the first instance, as any negative experiences must have mitigation built into and accounted for in the pedagogic design (Scholtz, 2020). Offering a debrief post-experience can go a long way towards rationalising negative experiences. In tandem, absolute clarity that associated assessments are contextual to the learners' personal experience means that rather than any "output" or "product" of a given workplace experience, it is the reflective and highly personal journey that represents the learning distance travelled for the individual. It is this that should therefore inform assessment at all costs, so that even negative experiences are able to have positive assessment outcomes.

One of the central benefits of this pedagogic biome is the opportunity for the learner to "become" in the sense of both a work-based identity and a personal identity fostered in a professional environment, removing them from more role-based boxes that can sometime be prevalent in educational environments. Upon losing the legacy "teacher" and "student" labels, the individual seeks and develops personal meaning (self-efficacy) to learn from their experiences and see their emergent holistic identity as a gestalt of professional, personal, social and individual characteristics that require constant awareness to successfully manage. Getting this intricate balance right is essentially "professionalism" made writ, where the elusive skill of "probity" can be learned and acquired by the individual and is highly transferable. Perhaps the selling point to educators in offering this biome for your learners is the usefulness of its "try-before-you-buy" style of learning and the benefits a well-designed outside "on the job" opportunity underpinned by mitigations for negative experiences, can have on the learner in a uniquely transformative and very "real" way.

Biome 3: Learning on location

Fundamentally different from the previous biome, learning outdoors "on location" has a strong bias towards the disciplinary experience. It carries with it a degree of scaffolding that enhances the application of specific learning outcomes outdoors and offers a high degree of flexibility-with-structure to define the learning gains from the location-based experience and critically, to contextualise them upon return to the classroom (Robertson, 2018; Ballantyne et al., 2010). Learning outdoors "on location" is a useful way to safely and iteratively build disciplinary identity though targeted, timed, designed and ideally, sustained exposure to relevant outdoor environments provided you use and apply your learning outcomes to integrate that learning back into the core curriculum (Ferns and Moore, 2012).

Learning outdoors "on location" involves collaborative elements of "engagement" and "participation", where there are practical/disciplinary aspects to "how" the learning outdoors will take place, as well as an inherent reflective lens on learner expectations. The participative element of learning outdoors in this biome cannot be overstated, where engagement with the "on location" learning promotes understanding of how the individual works and their experience of participation, engagement and disciplinary "place" (Al-Hmouz & Freeman, 2010). From the nine discrete collaborative domains, "knowledge" and "reflection" are also of relevance here as "knowledge" gained is refined and contextualised from the outdoor learning environment, making sense of the "bigger picture" of the "on location" experience, thereby adding value and perspective to it (Crawford, 2022).

With this in mind, the outdoors "on location" biome carries with it a fundamental opportunity to foster cross-cultural and/or interdisciplinary learning, more so than the other pedagogic biomes, by proxy of the design of outdoor learning "on location" as well as implementation of its other hallmark, "just-in-time" learning. Just-in-time learning, offering relatability and relevancy through quickly accessible content, should not be underestimated as a go-to for many students as a learning preference when faced with new, often outside, learning environments (Riel, 1998). In this way, looking at just-in-time learning as a time-limited version of experience-based learning means educators have a whole new way of approaching curriculum design for outdoor learning, where design pedagogy comes to the fore. Unlike the other biomes, the strong disciplinary bias of learning outdoors "on location" allows for a transformative learning experience to be highly contextualised to the personal interests of the learner.

A critical aspect of learning in this biome is therefore linked with "affective learning", the development of attitudes, beliefs and emotions in the learner that help the learner understand their own relationship outdoors "on location" and through that, their discipline (Picard et al., 2004). When combined with the point above, a new flavour of learning outcome emerges, termed "affective learning outcomes". This better captures the language that elevates the learning outcome itself to articulate the interests, attitudes and beliefs of the learner, triggered by the outside environment(s).

There you have them, each of the pedagogic biomes outlined above along with how they can be considered to aid planning outdoor educational activities. Whilst each biome is distinct, there is however a common thread across them all.

Enter: Person-centric academic social transformation

More than just being about reducing distress, this approach is rooted in the application of established social- and activity-informed practice that enhances the outdoors experience. It offers an environment where participants can model and encourage development in a psychologically safe space to enhance academic, social and personal wellbeing and possibly even resilience through person-centric academic social transformation (Valls-Carol et al., 2022). If that all sounds too theoretical or removed from the outdoors coalface, just consider that the world's best example of this is also its most common in education, i.e., creating narratives and storytelling in the educational setting (McDowell, 2022; Aynsley et al., 2018).

With clear cross-pollination with playful learning, narrative as a technique in outdoor education is perhaps our greatest weapon in the next decade against the rise of the machines and the avalanche of artificial intelligence (AI) that is emerging. As AI forces a renaissance in modes of assessment, outdoor learning is quite possibly the safest place to be these days. In this, contextualist learning pedagogy is very well suited to authentic assessment practices, many of which are also active in nature (McArthur, 2023). It may be early days for AI in assessment, which is always when the negative case studies disproportionately emerge, but already there are multiple opportunities to personalise and thereby, transform assessment and feedback. The most exciting aspect of this is that it offers educators with a contextualist mindset and those who incorporate learning outdoors into their design, an almost limitless buffet of ways to uniquely apply these tools to advance accessibility and equality of learning (Kelly et al., 2022).

Wherever your learning happens, however your learners benefit and no matter how fantastic the environments you might take that learning into, the core concepts of contextual learning will surely follow. It is simply a matter of being aware of which biome you are working within and allowing for deeper appreciation of the possibilities those biomes offer. If our imaginations are the only limit to effectively designing and planning learning outdoors then we are in a great position because educators are, if nothing else, imaginative to our core.

References

Ajala, E. M. (2012). The influence of workplace environment on workers' welfare, performance and productivity. *The African Symposium*, 12, 141–149.

Al-Hmouz, A., & Freeman, A. (2010, June). Learning on location: An adaptive mobile learning content framework. In *2010 IEEE International Symposium on Technology and Society* (pp. 450–456). IEEE.

Appleton, J. V., & King, L. (2002). Journeying from the philosophical contemplation of constructivism to the methodological pragmatics of health services research. *Journal of Advanced Nursing*, 40(6), 641–648.

Auburn, T. (2007). Identity and placement learning: student accounts of the transition back to university following a placement year. *Studies in Higher Education*, 32(1), 117–133.

Aynsley, S. A., Ball, V., Berry, J., Hancock, A., Harrison, R., Maddock, K., & Crawford, R. (2022). Pedagogic development of a gamified approach to enhancing engagement in interprofessional education. *Compass: Journal of Learning and Teaching*, 15(1).

Aynsley, S. A., Nathawat, K., & Crawford, R. M. (2018). Evaluating student perceptions of using a game-based approach to aid learning: Braincept. *Higher Education Pedagogies*, 3 (1), 478–489.

Bakken, L. L. (2002). Role of experience and context in learning to diagnose Lyme disease. *Journal of Continuing Education in the Health Professions*, 22(3), 131–141.

Ballantyne, R., Anderson, D., & Packer, J. (2010). Exploring the impact of integrated fieldwork, reflective and metacognitive experiences on student environmental learning outcomes. *Australian Journal of Environmental Education*, 26, 47–64.

Brame, C. (2016). Active learning. Vanderbilt University Center for Teaching.

Clough, R. W., & Lehr, R. P. (1996). Testing knowledge of human gross anatomy in medical school: An applied contextual-learning theory method. *Clinical Anatomy: The Official Journal of the American Association of Clinical Anatomists and the British Association of Clinical Anatomists*, 9(4), 263–268.

Colliver, J. A. (2002). Educational theory and medical education practice: a cautionary note for medical school faculty. *Academic Medicine*, 77(12 Part 1), 1217–1220.

Crawford, R. M. (2022). Advance HE blog: Is it possible to measure collaboration? Advance HE.

Eich, E. (1995). Mood as a mediator of place dependent memory. *Journal of Experimental Psychology: General*, 124(3), 293.

Eich, E., Macaulay, D., & Ryan, L. (1994). Mood dependent memory for events of the personal past. *Journal of Experimental Psychology: General*, 123(2), 201.

Eich, E., Reeves, J. L., Jaeger, B., & Graff-Radford, S. B. (1985). Memory for pain: relation between past and present pain intensity. *Pain*, 23(4), 375–380.

Eich, J. M. (1985). Levels of processing, encoding specificity, elaboration, and CHARM. *Psychological Review*, 92(1), 1.

Evans, C., Kandiko Howson, C., & Forsythe, A. (2018). Making sense of learning gain in higher education. *Higher Education Pedagogies*, 3(1), 1–45.

Ferns, S., & Moore, K. (2012). Assessing student outcomes in fieldwork placements: An overview of current practice. *International Journal of Work-Integrated Learning*, 13(4), 207.

Fullan, M., & Langworthy, M. (2013). *Towards a new end: New pedagogies for deep learning*. Seattle: Collaborative Impact.

Gibbs, G. (1981). *Teaching students to learn: A student-centred approach*. Open University Press.

Gravett, K., & Ajjawi, R. (2022). Belonging as situated practice. *Studies in Higher Education*, 47(7), 1386–1396.

Kaufman, D. M. (2003). Applying educational theory in practice. *BMJ*, 326(7382), 213–216.

Kelly, O., Buckley, K., Lieberman, L. J., & Arndt, K. (2022). Universal Design for Learning: A framework for inclusion in outdoor learning. *Journal of Outdoor and Environmental Education*, 25(1), 75–89.

Kennedy, T. J., & Lingard, L. A. (2006). Making sense of grounded theory in medical education. *Medical Education*, 40(2), 101–108.

Koens, F., Cate, O. T. J. T., & Custers, E. J. (2003). Context-dependent memory in a meaningful environment for medical education: In the classroom and at the bedside. *Advances in Health Sciences Education*, 8, 155–165.

Laney, C., & Loftus, E. F. (2005). Traumatic memories are not necessarily accurate memories. *The Canadian Journal of Psychiatry*, 50(13), 823–828.

Leigland, S. (2000). On cognitivism and behaviorism. *American Psychologist*, 55(2), 273–274. https://doi.org/10.1037/0003-066X.55.2.273.

Mansfield, R. (2011). The effect of placement experience upon final-year results for surveying degree programmes. *Studies in Higher Education*, 36(8), 939–952.

Marshall, J. E., Fayombo, G., & Marshall, R. (2015). I paid for it, so I deserve it! Examining psycho-educational variables and student consumerist attitudes to higher education. *International Journal of Higher Education*, 4(4), 73–80.

Mathias, H. (1978). *Science students' approaches to learning*. Lancaster 4th International Conference on Higher Education.

McArthur, J. (2023). Rethinking authentic assessment: Work, wellbeing, and society. *Higher Education*, 85(1), 85–101.

McDowell, K. (2022, October). Many narratives: Storytelling as epistemological bridge. In *Proceedings of the ALISE Annual Conference*.

Paz-Alonso, P. M., & Goodman, G. S. (2008). Trauma and memory: Effects of post-event misinformation, retrieval order, and retention interval. *Memory*, 16(1), 58–75.

Picard, R. W., Papert, S., Bender, W., Blumberg, B., Breazeal, C., Cavallo, D., & Strohecker, C. (2004). Affective learning: A manifesto. *BT Technology Journal*, 22(4), 253–269.

Ramsden, P. (1992). *Learning to teach in higher education*. Routledge.

Riel, M. (1998, May). Education in the 21st century: Just-in-time learning or learning communities. In *Fourth annual conference of the emirates center for strategic studies and research, Abu Dhabi*.

Robertson, S. L. (2018). Spatialising Education (or, the Difference that Education Spaces Make). In E. Glaser, H.-C. Koller, W. Thole & S. Krumme (Eds.), *Räume für bildung–räume der bildung: Beiträge zum 25. Kongress der deutschen gesellschaft für erziehungswissenschaft* (pp. 43–54).

Scholtz, D. (2020). Assessing workplace-based learning. *International Journal of Work-Integrated Learning*, 21(1), 25–35.

Schuwirth, L. W., & Van Der Vleuten, C. P. (2004). Changing education, changing assessment, changing research? *Medical Education*, 38(8), 805–812.

Thompson, L. A., Williams, K. L., & L'Esperance, P. R. (2001). Context-dependent memory under stressful conditions: The case of skydiving. *Human Factors*, 43(4), 611–619.

Thurber, A., & Bandy, J. (2018). Creating accessible learning environments. Vanderbilt University Center for Teaching.

Tzavara, A., Lavidas, K., Komis, V., Misirli, A., Karalis, T., & Papadakis, S. (2023). Using personal learning environments before, during and after the pandemic: The case of "e-Me". *Education Sciences*, 13(1), 87.

Valls-Carol, R., de Mello, R. R., Rodríguez-Oramas, A., Khalfaoui, A., Roca-Campos, E., Guo, M., & Redondo, G. (2022). The critical pedagogy that transforms the reality. *International Journal of Sociology of Education*, 11(1), 58–71.

Wurm, K. B. (2005). Andragogy in survey education. *Surveying and Land Information Science*, 65(3), 159.

Chapter 2

Heutagogy and outdoor learning

Designing postgraduate studies that support self-determined learners

Colin Wood

This chapter argues that the concept of heutagogy (or self-determined learning) provides a strong educational rationale for postgraduate study of outdoor learning in its recognition of the primary agency of the learner. It argues that the formal structures of postgraduate study can be used to scaffold and validate the learners' explorations of their professional experience in the outdoors and of academic theory. By recognising the primacy of the learner, heutagogic approaches to course design challenge both the effectiveness and the legitimacy of teacher power over both the formal curriculum and the hidden curriculum in postgraduate study of outdoor learning. This approach to the provision of postgraduate courses recognises the ability of adult learners to make decisions about their learning, but beyond this, it recognises that the learner has the right to determine their own learning. Whilst heutagogic study can be challenging for learners, it is closely aligned to the ethos of many people working in outdoor learning whose careers are often driven by personal values and a sense of mission, and whose navigation through a patchwork career structure means that they expect to have considerable agency over their work and studies.

Background

Courses leading to postgraduate awards in outdoor learning have existed for over 50 years and typically support career development as well as advanced academic study. In their curricula and their approaches to teaching, they address the twin issues of an unbounded field of study and a highly segmented workplace. The first of these issues is problematic for the development of the curriculum. Many authors have sought to define outdoor education, but with little success; indeed Nicol (2002) suggests that outdoor education defies definition. Dyment and Potter (2015) attempted to define it through its shared knowledge base. They found some evidence of a traditional knowledge base around technical skills development, social and interpersonal development, development of a connection to nature and risk management. However, they also noted that there was no consensus on this knowledge base, and that it was evolving into other areas such as social justice, sustainability and place attachment.

DOI: 10.4324/9781003436928-4

Without agreed definitions or consensus on the boundaries to the field of study there is no canonical guidance on what should be included or excluded. Indeed, it has been argued that the outdoor field also lacks an agreed core to the body of theory (Brown, 2009) and has a stubborn adherence to discredited concepts of character building (Brookes, 2023). Consequently, postgraduate courses engage with a wide knowledge base and tread carefully through disputed theoretical underpinnings.

The second issue is the segmented and unstructured nature of employment in outdoor education. Wagstaff (2016, p. 76), referencing Allin and Humberstone (2004), encapsulates this issue as follows: "with the diverse job possibilities and career options, a clearly defined career structure within the outdoor industry remains elusive ... This is problematic for academic institutions preparing professional outdoor leaders and for students interested in this career path."

Furthermore, Allin and West (2015) suggest that many careers in the outdoors can also be considered as "boundaryless", with no clear division between employment and personal life. Consequently, the sector appears to be a convoluted area of employment in which many people pursue patchwork careers. This presents problems for the design of postgraduate courses in outdoor learning, as learners arrive with a diversity of prior experiences and with very different learning needs. In response, courses tend to address the issues by focusing on optionality, flexibility and reflexivity rather than on tight adherence to a specified curriculum.

People tend to apply for a postgraduate course in outdoor learning when they are established professionals and mid-career. This differs from other fields where postgraduate study often follows directly after undergraduate studies. This means that outdoor learning applicants tend to have considerable experience of making decisions about their own careers and their own learning. Indeed, it could be argued that the ubiquity of patchwork careers in outdoor education means that most mid-career outdoor professionals have faced more career turning points than those in other fields. This may make them more aware of their career directions, and their control over their careers, than other postgraduate applicants. In addition, the predominance of established professionals within postgraduate courses means that their motivations for study usually relate to aspirations for career development and a desire for a deeper understanding of theory and/or practice. Thus, the principal reasons for application to postgraduate study in outdoor learning can be seen to reside within the career aspirations and personal development aims of the applicant.

Consequently, postgraduate courses in outdoor learning have developed to address the diverse needs of mid-career professionals who are navigating complex career paths, and who are accustomed to having considerable autonomy over their own professional development. The courses do this within a field of academic study that is unbounded and where there are significant disagreements about theory and evidence. The result of this is that postgraduate course design and course delivery leans away from prescriptive teaching and tends towards reflexivity and individualised learning.

Andragogy and outdoor learning

Malcolm Knowles introduced the concept of *andragogy* into modern teaching, suggesting that adult education is different from the education of children and is characterised by learner control and self-responsibility in learning (Knowles, 1968). He suggested that the adult learner enters education for a reason and has prior experience on which to make decisions about their learning. Thus, the learner develops their own learning objectives in relation to their reasons for studying. Effective adult education within this perspective usually adopts a problem-solving approach to learning. This is based on assumptions of intrinsic learner motivation and recognition that the learner is self-directed in how to learn. Thus, the delivery of courses that support andragogic learning is expected to include opportunities for the conscious recognition and incorporation of the learner's experience.

However, Blaschke (2012) suggests that Knowles' focus on learner motivation was a product of its time and does not align with more recent ideas about lifelong learning. She argues that, whilst the learner has control and self-responsibility, this exists within a curriculum and an approach to learning that are both determined by the educator. Thus, Blaschke (2012) concludes that the andragogic learner is self-motivated but does not normally have the ability to determine the direction of their learning.

Although this approach to adult learning is the bedrock of postgraduate course design, it can be seen to have a number of significant limitations for postgraduate study in outdoor learning. Firstly, the curriculum content is based on the assumption that the educator's judgement is more valid than that of the learner. This is usual in most fields where educators bring specialist knowledge and understanding, and where the learners are generally limited in their theoretical and professional understanding of the subject. In these situations, the decisions about what subjects, topics and approaches are included in the curriculum tend to be made by the educators and thus prioritise academic knowledge. By contrast, mid-career professionals are more likely to define the curriculum in relation to the practices of themselves and those that they recognise as professionals. As such their decisions about what they want to learn tend to prioritise professional utility and personal interest. If the educator has sole agency in determining the curriculum, then it seems likely that this will devalue professional knowledge and understanding.

Secondly, the diversity of outdoor learning students means that educators' decisions about the curriculum and the approach to learning are often based on an assumption of best fit. Whilst such diversity has significant benefits it means that some aspects of the course will have little relevance.

As a third consideration, outdoor students often struggle to incorporate prior experiences into their studies because there is little literature to support critical analysis. This tends to limit opportunities for the conscious recognition and incorporation of the learner's experience, and thus reduces their autonomy and direction over their learning. Once again, the andragogic model does not seem to appropriately represent the nature of postgraduate study in outdoor learning.

An alternative model: Heutagogic learning

Perhaps, a better model of postgraduate outdoor learning is found within heutagogic learning. The concept was originally explored by Hase and Kenyon (2000). Heutagogic learning is often termed *self-determined learning* and is seen as a progression from andragogic learning. It is characterised by the recognition that adult learners have the ability to make decisions about their learning, and furthermore that they have the right to determine their own curriculum and their approach to learning. As such, it challenges the effectiveness and the legitimacy of teacher power over both the formal curriculum and the hidden curriculum in adult education. Indeed, it suggests that effective learning should be based on human agency, the development of self-efficacy, reflection and metacognition (Blaschke & Hase, 2015).

Kerry (2013) suggests that heutagogy is an extension of, rather than a replacement for, pedagogy and andragogy, and that it displays certain principles about learning/educating which are absent from pedagogy, and often from andragogy. She lists the following eight characteristics of heutagogic programmes (pp. 72–73):

1   Learning when the learner is ready: the learner largely controls the process of learning, making their own decisions about pace and activity according to need and interest.
2   Learning is seen as a complex process requiring the learner to move beyond knowledge and skills – it is not regurgitation, copying, modelling (though these things may happen). It requires new connections and more inventive insights to be made.
3   Learning does not depend on the teacher and can be triggered by an experience beyond the control of the teacher, that is, it becomes self-directed.
4   Learning is focused on the student not on a syllabus: it is about what the student wants to know and chooses to explore. Learning results in an expanding capability to learn for one's self: to direct and control one's own learning and its directions, which in turn leads to:
5   Self-sufficiency in learning: the confidence to explore avenues, take risks and know how to find things out.
6   Reflexivity: the ability to take on board the implications of learning, absorb these into one's own situation, to change ways of thinking and ways of acting as a result of learning.
7   Applicability of what is learned: so that connections are made with professional and other lives beyond "theory alone".
8   Positive learning values: so that learning becomes a pleasurable experience to be indulged in for its own sake.

These characteristics provide a framework to support learning that is determined by the learner. Within this, Blaschke (2012) identifies as a key concept in heutagogy the importance of self-reflection, often linked to Argyris and Schön's (1996) "double-loop learning". Here the learner considers a problem and the resulting action and outcomes, in addition to reflecting upon the problem-solving process and how the reflection influences the learner's own beliefs and actions. Blaschke (2012) points out that this approach develops autonomy as the learner's reflection and action increasingly determine their own definitions of their field of study, their own learning aims and tasks, and even their own assessment criteria. As such the heutagogical approach can be seen as developing maturity and autonomy.

The difference in the approach to teaching and facilitation is significant. In andragogy, the curriculum, the questions, the discussions and any assessments are designed by the teacher according to their evaluation of the learner's needs. By contrast in heutagogy, Hase (2009) suggests that the learner sets their own learning course, designing and developing the map of learning. Thus, Blaschke (2012) suggests that the key design elements of heutagogic education are: learner-defined learning contracts; flexible curriculum; learner-directed questions; and flexible and negotiated assessment. However, like any postgraduate course, there is also an educational imperative to support the learner to develop both competency and capability. Here, competency is the "proven ability in acquiring knowledge and skills", whilst capability is characterised by learner confidence in his or her competency. The combination of these is thus the ability "to take appropriate and effective action to formulate and solve problems in both familiar and unfamiliar and changing settings" (Cairns, 1996, p. 80).

Thus, the heutagogical approach emphasises the learners' control and responsibility whilst also providing a framework for the development and assessment of competency and capability. This provides a role for the educator, as a compass for the learner, guiding them towards using and developing their competence and capabilities, whilst recognising that the learner is the driver in creating a flexible curriculum, which is defined by the student (Hase & Kenyon, 2007; Hase, 2009).

Heutagogy in practice: A case study

The preceding discussion of learning theory and its convergence with post-graduate study in outdoor learning under-represents the complex and varied experiences of learners. Thus, we now consider the experiences of six graduates of a Masters programme in outdoor education, and their own understanding of the learning process. Like many, the postgraduate course that they completed was designed on heutagogic principles of human agency, self-efficacy, reflection and metacognition. However, the course differs from most in that it is only offered as a part-time online programme of study. As such it embodies the methods explored by Kerry (2013) in its use of learning contracts, reflexivity and self-determined projects as a framework for learning.

The graduates included four men and two women. All were working as outdoor professionals at the time of studying. Their specialisms at the time included youth work, forest school leadership, adventure therapy and expeditionary learning. Five of them had management or supervisory roles within organisations during the time they were studying, and three worked for periods as expatriates. Since completing the Masters, five had changed employment and two were no longer predominantly working in outdoor education. They were interviewed three to five years after completing their studies. The semi-structured interviews were based on the five principles of heutagogic learning (Hase and Blaschke, 2021) and thematically analysed using Hase (2009). As such, they explored their learning experiences during the Masters course, their agency and power whilst studying, changes in capabilities and competence, and changes in their approaches to learning.

When asked about their agency, there was consensus that the *locus of control* lay with the learner. The responses centred around the terms "ownership" and "control", with both presented as positive aspects.

> It was all my own learning and so I had a lot of control. And it was up to me with quite a few of the modules as to what I did the subject in, so again that was a lot of control.

This was a double-edged sword for many, who struggled to define their own field of study without a fixed curriculum or pre-determined endpoints. This was particularly notable in the discussion of project working.

> That was very scary because you had complete control over where you took it. That was probably the most frightening part of it, because actually it was down to you. You decided the pathway that you went, and you determined the way that you went down that pathway.

However, four participants related their ownership and control over their studies to the value that their learning would bring to their employers and to the sector. This perhaps suggests that their understanding of their ownership and control was intertwined with their *professional identity* and *career aspirations*: "It gave me enough autonomy to choose areas that were both interesting to me and actually made progress within the organisation." Thus, the agency and control of learners in determining the curriculum and the ownership of the outcomes may be partially subsidiary to their organisational and sectoral context.

It is interesting to note that there was little discussion of the agency or control of the educator. However, two themes emerged: *the tutor as a resource* and *becoming less reliant*. These are both exemplified by the following quotation which shows the tutor as a source of guidance and support with areas relating to competency and capability rather than having control over the direction of the studies or of the content.

> [I had] complete control, and it was obviously wonderful having the tutor to bounce ideas off and [advise] in terms of direction of travel and with regards to specific research to target, with regards to not overestimating the data, and alike. But ultimately, I had complete control.

Also, there was exploration of the difference between their *experiences* of undergraduate and postgraduate study. Four of the participants discussed how their earlier studies contributed to their Masters study, with prior knowledge being contextualised into theory and professional practice.

> One of the things I've reflected on most, is that it isn't the learning necessarily on the Masters itself, but it was the learning that I did in my undergraduate studies, because suddenly [the Masters] brought some of the things which I thought were OK, it made them much more relevant... so they went from "kind of OK" and I'd gone through a process to "actually that's useful!"... It was worth putting in that little bit of work then, because now at Masters level I'm actually able to start to build on that and use that.

Thus, postgraduate study is seen as a proactive *use of existing knowledge* in order to develop original and highly personal outputs. However, much of the discussion of undergraduate study related to a lack of agency and depth within their under-graduate work. This was seen as highly descriptive and largely based on other people's ideas. As such it was negatively contrasted with the active engagement required on the Masters programme.

> I felt like I was just regurgitating what was already there at undergrad, whereas now I really had to challenge myself and piece together the puzzle and theories, to take that next step in the academic field. So, the first key learning for myself was realising that I can't just read the information and pass it on. I need to critique it and look at new opportunities, and start to for-mulate myself in a position as an academic.

As well as supporting a more critical approach to learning, the participants also explored the ways that autonomy and empowerment led to a validation of their professional experience and their opinions. This was considered through a *growth in capability* and a *growth in confidence*. Whilst these were coded separately, they are clearly connected concepts in the minds of the participants.

> So, in the past it was very much, "this is what he said" and "this is what she said" and that's their opinion. But it was never my opinion. And I think as time goes on, you learned that actually you do have a wealth of knowledge. So, your opinion does count and that is why you're writing, and you are sharing your own opinions and that is OK and is allowed.

These two concepts are also described as reinforcing each other and leading to further empowerment:

> I think the confidence grew and I remember getting into the middle of [the degree] and being surprised that I was managing. And I remember, I'd often

ruminate during expeditions, and then it would become like a bit of a state of flow because when I got back, I did have things to write, and I did have focus.

Again, the growth of capability and confidence are both related to the individual's organisational context, professional development and career. Thus, the concept of connectionism appears to have been very important, with significant synergy between work and study appearing throughout the discussion of agency, learning and outcomes. This appears in two forms throughout the interviews. Sometimes studying was described as a method for exploring workplace issues through a theoretical lens, and at other times it was seen as a way to bring conceptual understandings into the professional domain. In all cases the perceived benefits were described as greater than the utilitarian value of the degree and having benefits that related to understanding and professional development.

I focused [the projects] on topics that I was struggling with at work. And it did give me an outlet to explore those issues. In a setting where I couldn't pragmatically change much, I could change my own approach.

Finally, the research explored the proposal that learners would change the way they study as a result of greater autonomy. This was resoundingly rejected by most participants, who felt that their approach to learning was largely unchanged and that the principal gains came in changes to knowledge and understanding. This is nicely explained by one participant who had identified numerous personal and professional benefits from studying: "Towards the end you get a little bit more finesse, and you get a little bit of sort of more confidence towards the end of it as well." Thus, the data shows that the course approach of agency and autonomy was recognised and valued; that the intersection between professional and academic domains required active learner engagement; that learners felt empowered by studies that they felt ownership of; and that approaches to learning were largely unchanged by the progression to postgraduate learning.

Discussion and implications for practice

This case study suggests that mid-career outdoor professionals are capable of studying within a form of higher education that allows them to define their own curriculum, to create their own learning map and to use academic support as a compass for their learning. Their comments show that heutagogic study was not easy as it was characterised by fear, a heightened sense of personal responsibility and concerns about imposter-syndrome. As the course progressed these morphed into a sense of pride and ownership, and a validation of their professional experience and embodied understandings of outdoor learning. Despite this change, the students did not feel that their own approach to learning was altered; those who were familiar with reflective learning continued to use this approach; those who were familiar with project working continued to use this approach.

The case study also shows that the students saw studying as a way of integrating prior learning. This prior learning was largely derived from professional experiences and from undergraduate study, with little coming from connections within the cohort. The course then provided opportunities for exploration, evaluation and theoretical deconstruction of the prior learning and as such this became a highly-personalised, and self-determined, curriculum for their studies. However, the students felt that their own determination of the curriculum meant that their studies sometimes lacked breadth.

The case study makes no claims about the relative effectiveness of andragogic and heutagogic course design. However, it does highlight that mid-career professionals in outdoor education embrace educational autonomy and seem to appreciate the opportunity to determine the scope and range of their studies, and to align it to their professional context. Although the participants often found the opportunities to determine their own curriculum were "scary", they were able to design studies that were relevant to their learning needs, built on their prior experiences of work and study, and fitted with their own ideas about their careers.

Thus, the study provides some evidence for the appropriateness of heutagogic course design in the postgraduate study of outdoor education, and of allowing students to determine the curriculum and approaches that suit them. However, the study does not justify, or advocate, simply passing all educational responsibility to the learner. Indeed, the responses of the participants reinforce the importance of expert support in the development of competency and capability through graduated projects that allow students to develop competency (and confidence) in key postgraduate skills such as article reading, critical analysis and project management, so that they can expand their own capability to explore issues and practices in a systematic and critical manner and produce meaningful outcomes. In addition, the responses suggest that the educator has a key role in supporting reflective self-analysis and in providing support in developing competency and capabilities. As such, the case study seems to point to the value of formal structures of postgraduate study as a scaffold to workplace learning, and as a framework for combining personal opinions and professional understandings about outdoor learning into the body of academic theory.

References

Allin, L., & Humberstone, B. (2004). Transitions and turning points: Understanding the career decision-making of outdoor professionals. In *Proceedings from the International Conference in Outdoor Education, Bendigo, Australia.*

Allin, L., & West, A. (2015). Careers in the outdoors. In B. Humberstone, H. Prince & K. A. Henderson (Eds), *Routledge international handbook of outdoor studies* (pp. 159–167). London: Routledge.

Argyris, C, & Schön, D. (1996). *Organizational learning* II. USA: Addison-Wesley.

Blaschke, L. M. (2012). Heutagogy and lifelong learning: A review of heutagogical practice and self-determined learning. *The International Review of Research in Open and Distributed Learning*, 13(1), 56–71.

Blaschke, L. M., & Hase, S. (2015). Heutagogy, technology, and lifelong learning for professional and part-time learners. In A. Dailey-Herbert & K. S. Dennis (Eds), *Transformative perspectives and processes in higher education* (pp. 75–94). USA: Springer.

Brookes, A. (2023). A paradigm shift that never was. (A critique of Neo-Hahnian outdoor education theory part three). *Journal of Outdoor and Environmental Education*, 26(2), 153–165.

Brown, M. (2009). Reconceptualising outdoor adventure education: Activity in search of an appropriate theory. *Journal of Outdoor and Environmental Education*, 13 (2), 3–13.

Cairns, L. (1996). Capability: Going beyond competence. *Capability*, 2(2), 79–80.

Dyment, J. E., & Potter, T. G. (2015). Is outdoor education a discipline? Provocations and possibilities. *Journal of Adventure Education and Outdoor Learning*, 15(3), 193–208.

Hase, S. (2009). Heutagogy and e-learning in the workplace: Some challenges and opportunities. *Impact: Journal of Applied Research in Workplace E-learning*, 1(1), 43–52.

Hase, S., & Blaschke, L. (2021). So, you want to do heutagogy: Principles and practice. In S. Hase & L. Blaschke, *Unleashing the power of learner agency* (pp. 13–33). EdTech Books.

Hase, S., & Kenyon, C. (2000). From andragogy to heutagogy. *Ultibase, RMIT*. https://webarchive.nla.gov.au/awa/20010220130000/http://ultibase.rmit.edu.au/Articles/dec00/hase2.htm (accessed 21 June 2023).

Hase, S., & Kenyon, C. (2007). Heutagogy: A child of complexity theory. *Complicity: An International Journal of Complexity and Education*, 4(1).

Kerry, T. (2013). Applying the principles of heutagogy to a postgraduate distance-learning programme. In S. Hase & C. Kenyon (Eds), *Self-determined learning: Heutagogy in action* (pp. 69–83). London: Bloomsbury.

Knowles, M. S. (1968). Andragogy, not pedagogy. *Adult Leadership*, 16 (10), 350–352.

Nicol, R. (2002). Outdoor education: Research topic or universal value? Part one. *Journal of Adventure Education & Outdoor Learning*, 2(1), 29–41.

Wagstaff, M. (2016). Outdoor leader career development: Exploration of a career path. *Journal of Outdoor Recreation, Education, and Leadership*, 8(1), 75–95.

Chapter 3

A good stick

An inquiry into creativity in Forest School

Patrick Boxall

Creativity? Outdoor learning? Aren't they always 'good things'? Creativity and holistic approaches to learning outdoors such as Forest School are often discussed with an implicit assumption that one is contained in the other.

The literature suggests that person-centred progressive philosophies within traditions of social constructivism provide a philosophical rationale for both areas. Yet, little has been written about creativity as an aspect of outdoor learning, nor is there empirical evidence that has tested these assumptions, beyond experience and pragmatic observation. To assume that creativity is inevitably part of outdoor learning leaves both concepts under-theorised, poorly understood and with less potential positive impact for learners.

In this chapter, I will problematise both concepts by showing how they are open to multiple definitions and interpretations. I explore how approaches to creativity and outdoor learning are interconnected and go on to argue that a framework for creative pedagogy within outdoor learning could be profoundly positive for people, place and planet. I present 'A Description of Creativity' to address this need. I argue that creative pedagogies outdoors are essential aspects of hopeful solutions to some of the deep problems we are grappling with in education today.

A word on methodology

To address the problems and connections between creativity and outdoor learning I used the tools of Constructivist Grounded Theory (Charmaz, 2014; 2016) as the basis of an approach to research design, synthesising theory with data, and undertaking analysis.

First, the existing literature on creativity and outdoor learning were analysed to create 'A Description of Creativity', to act as a theoretical framework to support pedagogical practice. This framework positions creativity as grounded in person-centred progressive philosophies within traditions of social constructivism and critical pedagogy. Then, 'A Description of Creativity' was tested with eight Forest School leaders in Scotland through semi-structured interviews. Participants were initially invited to describe creativity in their own practice, and then were given the

DOI: 10.4324/9781003436928-5

'Description' to comment on. This data was then analysed using 'A Description of Creativity' as a framework for thematic coding.

Problems

Conceptions of outdoor learning have developed in recent years, with strong criticisms of traditions of hyper-masculine, Euro-centric and racialised narratives of the outdoors (Beames & Brown, 2016; Dyment & Potter, 2014; Potter & Dyment, 2016; Warren et al., 2014). A robust rationale for progressive outdoor learning is emerging, grounded in concepts of social justice and person-centred pedagogies (Beames et al., 2012; Ross et al., 2014; Warren & Breunig, 2019)

Forest School itself has been problematised in recent criticism, as needing a clear philosophical rationale and becoming a commodity within the education system (Leather, 2018), or as being seen as an add-on to existing curricula rather than being embedded in the learning (Lloyd et al., 2018). However, when Forest School (Harris, 2017; Knight, 2011; 2018) is considered within a wider articulation of 'outdoor learning' (Beames et al., 2012; Dyment & Potter, 2014; Potter & Dyment, 2016) then it can be seen as a form of holistic person- and eco-centred pedagogy.

Creativity too is a contested term. The definitions are either simplistic and serve political narratives (Scot. Gov., 2012; Robinson, 1999) or are so complex and multi-faceted (Banaji & Burn, 2007; Pope, 2005) that they can become impractical to work with in education. The most convincing definitions of creativity in learning are ones that are inclusive and accessible for all people. One powerful conception is 'possibility thinking' (Craft, 2010; 2013). Possibility thinking is the act of generating imaginative options when approaching a problem or stimulus. The accessibility of possibility thinking for all people has been positioned and explored as an aspect of social justice (Cremin, 2015; Gardner, 2008; Hempel-Jorgensen, 2015). Another persuasive conception is 'cultural improvisation' (Hallam & Ingold, 2007), which describes the imaginative choices that a person makes as they move through life, both in the daily challenges humans face, and in terms of more purposeful acts of making. Hallam and Ingold (2016) further explore the relationship of humans to the creative process in a discussion of 'making and growing', describing the complex relationship between people as they interact with their environment.

An approach that has gained international recognition by the Organisation for Economic Cooperation and Development (OECD) is the 'Dispositions of Creative Thinking' (Spencer et al., 2012), which are presented as being Imaginative, Inquisitive, Persistent, Disciplined and Collaborative. This is of practical use as it is flexible, maps to pedagogical practice and supports an inclusive approach. However, being adapted into a tool for measurement of creative thinking by the Programme for International Student Assessment (PISA) seems antithetical to the centrality of creativity for human flourishing. The concern for measurement is highly problematic as it begins to encode creativity within global neo-liberal agendas of performativity (Ball, 2013; 2016; Loveless and Williamson, 2013).

Working from an analysis of this literature, 'A Description of Creativity' was developed to synthesise theory to give a framework for practice.

Possibilities

A Description of Creativity:

1. All conceptions of creativity describe a process of 'making' meaning or product.

Throughout definitions of creativity there is a description, or assumption, of making as central to creative acts. Making includes as creative the most accomplished original artistic acts, spontaneous or naïve expression (Pope, 2005), highly crafted performances (Csikszentmihalyi, 1996), posing and solving problems (Freire, 1970), possibility thinking (Craft, 2010; 2013) or improvisation (Hallam & Ingold, 2007). The making process may produce a physical object, meaningful idea or an experience bounded in time and place.

The centrality of making is an assumption throughout conceptions of creativity that have been adopted in political and societal contexts in Scotland (Scot. Gov., 2012) England (Robinson, 1999), Europe (Punie et al., 2010) and globally (OECD, 2019).

2. Agency: In all creative processes agency is exerted by a 'maker' to use imagination to make meaning or product.

Within the 'making' process, agency is exerted by a 'maker' who uses imagination to make choices over the form and purpose of what is being made, whether it is physical, linguistic, social or abstract. 'Imagination' is central to this process where the maker makes an idea, a connection or a motif that has some significance. The imaginative process is a recurring descriptor in discussions of creativity. It is also explicitly referenced by leaders in political and societal arenas: Ken Robinson (1999; 2001), the Scottish Government (2012) and the OECD (Lucas et al., 2013; Spencer et al., 2012).

The agency of individuals has been shown to be fundamental to creativity within the learning process (Cremin, 2015; Hempel-Jorgensen, 2015) and becomes an enactment of 'learner identity' (Jeffrey, 2008). This significance of agency within learning is reinforced by a range of critics (Beames & Brown, 2016; Priestley et al., 2015; Mercer, 2011). Learner agency is strongly grounded in discourses of social justice (Darder et al., 2017; Freire, 1970; 1998; Hempel-Jorgensen, 2015; Smith, 2012, Thrift & Sugarman, 2019).

3. Creativity is 'situational' and 'relational'.

A 'maker' is the agent of learning, so the 'voice' of the 'maker' has primacy and is connected to the social space through a dialogic process (Alexander, 2008; Custodero, 2015; Freire, 1970). Therefore, the 'making' process is grounded in the 'situation' (Lave and Wenger, 1991; Rogoff, 1990). The 'maker' navigates the situation and makes decisions to make meaning or product. Creativity can become an improvisation grounded in experience of life (Hallam & Ingold, 2007). In the outdoor environment the 'situation' is rich with the 'affordances' (Sharma-Brymer et al., 2018) of natural materials that are aspects of the making process.

The centrality of active and empirical experience within a situation places creativity within a social constructivist tradition. This notion has been implicit within the work of lead thinkers (Bruner, 1960; 2000; Daniels, 2007; Dewey, 1964; Rogoff, 1990; Vygotskiĭ, 1962) and has been made more explicit in recent years (Craft, 2013; Cremin, 2015; Hempel-Jorgensen, 2015). The cooperative and social aspect of creativity have been highlighted in many works (Gardner, 2008; Jeffrey & Craft, 2010; Jeffrey, 2008; Spencer et al., 2012) and adopted by the OECD (OECD, 2019).

4. The process of creativity is about 'problem posing' and 'possibility thinking'.

Within the creative process, a person uses their voice to engage in 'problem posing' (Darder et al., 2017; Freire, 1970). This is reinforced and extended by the concept of 'possibility thinking' (Craft, 2010; 2013). Craft convincingly argues that 'possibility thinking' is central to this 'creative' process; her research has been built on with explicit reference to the social constructivist tradition (Cremin, 2015; Cremin et al., 2015; Hempel-Jorgensen, 2015).

Both concepts are based on the 'maker' as central to the creative process: posing problems, thinking of multiple possibilities, using 'voice' to make meaning and product in response to the problems posed. The meanings and products raise new questions, problems and invite new possibilities within the situation. It is less about 'solving' problems than engaging in an iterative process. The process becomes cyclical and generative.

This process of posing problems, and making possibilities, is grounded in human experience, and involves risk. The 'making' may not work or may not be valued by the 'maker' or the audience (Jeffrey & Craft, 2010; Jeffrey, 2008; Sternberg & Lubart, 1998). However, it is the engagement and enactment of the process itself that makes it meaningful, that makes it 'creative'. Ultimately the processes of 'problem posing' and 'possibility thinking' become actions of 'learner agency' (Hempel-Jorgensen, 2015) or 'learner identity' (Jeffrey, 2008).

Findings

1. All conceptions of creativity describe a process of 'making' meaning or product.

The data showed consistent evidence that 'making' is a core aspect of creativity. In the sense used here, making involves building or constructing an object, product, idea, or experience. The word making and associated forms of the verb were used consistently by the participants: making shelter, making stories, making up games. The emphasis was on the process of making, rather than product. The data suggested that the making process may lead to a 'product' that was just as likely to be intangible, part of an iterative process, or bounded by time and space as it was to be an object. For example, all participants saw 'play' as being a key aspect of Forest School and related to the idea of making. This related to both children and adults, but in slightly different forms of language. Participants described children as 'making up' or 'inventing' games or stories. The data resonates with pedagogical approaches from other disciplines such as 'learning through imagined experience' developed in educational drama (Neelands, 1992). The process of making contributed to situations where agency could be exerted by learners through such self-directed learning.

The data reinforced the idea that making something that had significance to the maker was central to creativity. The idea of 'new' with the suggestions of original had no place in the data. The process may have been new to the maker, but that concept was not mentioned by any of the leaders. This is supported by the more complex definitions of creativity in the literature (Banaji & Burn, 2007; Munday, 2014; Pope, 2005).

2. Agency: In all creative processes, agency is exerted by a 'maker' to use imagination to make meaning or product.

Participants used a wide variety of language that supported conceptions of agency, where a person can exert autonomous choice within the framework of the learning (Mercer, 2011). There was explicit reference by every participant to learners in language that suggested the making process was about individual empowerment: choices; freedom; self-direction; autonomy; freedom to fail; empower; voice. There were explicit links made between play, lack of rules and ideas of empowerment.

The autonomy of individual humans was put at the core. The open choices of Forest School were described and how the situation became conducive to dialogic pedagogy, with the voices of each person described as being valued within the learning. Evidence for the significance of agency was closely related with evidence for the situational and relational aspects of creativity.

The findings suggest that learner agency is fundamental to creativity in learning within Forest School. It also suggests that creativity within Forest School as an aspect of learning outdoors can provide an antidote to the concerns of critics of the neo-liberal policy set because it can facilitate learner 'subjectification' (Priestley et al., 2015). The implication is that nurturing creativity is a key element of developing socially just pedagogies.

3. Creativity is 'situational' and 'relational'.

The descriptor that creativity is 'situational and relational' was supported through emphasis on the connection to the natural environment and the relationship of the learner to others in the group. This descriptor was illustrated by many examples of the freedom of interaction with the environment. This led to the title of this study: 'A good stick...'. This was a phrase that recurred in the data, sometimes word for word, sometimes in phrases such as 'a funny stick', 'a knobbly stick', or by general description of natural materials. All participants in the study referred directly to the importance of natural objects in the outdoor space as conducive to creativity in learning. This connected to other themes of 'A Description of Creativity': the making process involved natural materials; agency was exerted by autonomously interacting with the environment; and problems were posed and possibilities were explored through interaction with the material in the environment. The data led to the descriptor of how in the outdoor environment the 'situation' is rich with the 'affordances' (Sharma-Brymer et al., 2018) of natural materials that are aspects of the making process. The data also suggested that the 'emotional intelligence' of a person and their relationship with other people in the situation, especially leaders or mentors, significantly supports the making process.

The relationship between the person and the place is key to making creative pedagogies within outdoor learning distinct. It supports conceptions of place responsive learning (Gruenewald, 2003; Mannion et al., 2013; Smith & Sobel, 2010). This relationship between creativity and response to place could be an area of further inquiry.

4. The process of creativity is about 'problem posing' and 'possibility thinking'.

This descriptor of creativity being about 'problem posing and possibility thinking' was the most strongly supported of the descriptors. The empirical evidence suggests that dialogic learning, the collaborative interaction of the participants through using their voices to exert agency, underpins discussions of creativity and Forest School. This evidence consistently supports creativity as an aspect of pedagogy that contributes to discourses of social justice. This was illustrated repeatedly by the participants in the research giving examples of individual learners who were struggling to engage through conventional educational contexts. One participant told an entertaining anecdote of a child who was dyslexic, and struggled in classrooms, managing to avoid returning to class and staying with the Forest School for double the time. This point is reinforced by the way Forest School is often offered to learners who are disadvantaged or harder to reach. The evidence suggests that conceptions of agency (Beames & Brown, 2016; Hempel-Jorgensen, 2015; Mercer, 2011), problem posing pedagogies (Darder et al., 2017; Freire, 1970) and possibility thinking (Craft, 2010; Craft & Jeffrey, 2004) are significant aspects of creative learning.

Other insights

In addition to conclusions that relate to 'A Description of Creativity', several other key themes recurred in the findings.

The idea that *not defining something as creative* within a learning experience helped free up learners and leaders. The word creative could lead to barriers, whereas more open or 'loose' language, lack of specific direction, providing resources and open activities led to creative practice. In relation to adults there were accounts of people who described themselves as 'not creative' or 'not arty', but when just asked to 'mess about' or 'do what you want' or 'try it out' – effectively to self-direct activity within the outdoor situation – then creative things happened. Indeed, two participants said of themselves that they were 'not creative', that they were scientists, and then they proceeded to describe multiple examples of creative learning experiences that they had participated in or had led.

These included narrative approaches to teaching tree identification, innovative use of clay, and examples of play using natural materials.

Participants used a variety of non-literal language to describe the process of creativity, including images, onomatopoeic words and physical gestures. This range of descriptions included: 'sparkle'; 'sparks fly'; 'psh pshh'; 'whirr'; 'fizz'; 'buzz'; and physical gestures such as whirling hands near their head and physically illustrating getting 'hands on'. This non-literal expression was used in conjunction with the phrase 'flow' to describe individual learners who were involved in the act of 'making'.

The findings suggested that the role of the leader is important in the creative process for a learner. The emotional support a leader gives to build the confidence of a learner was described as having a key positive effect. The motivation of the leader was clearly significant – the level of commitment, even passion, to make life better for the learners and have a positive effect on the environment was consistently strong. Participants explicitly commented that Forest School has a contribution to make to social justice because of the inclusive approach to pedagogy. The discussion of creativity led, unprompted, to critical comments about the 'mainstream' educational system – that it did not suit everyone, that it is too academic and restrictive. They also all showed an awareness of the pressure of performativity within education, with the focus on attainment being prioritised over outdoor learning. The data suggests that leaders working in this context could be described as activists, who are in different ways seeking social change through their actions as educators.

The idea of outdoor leader as activist, with the pedagogical practice being grounded in ethical motivation invites the proposition that this kind of practice address some of the deep-seated criticisms of our current educational culture (Ball, 1993; 2008; 2013; Misiaszek, 2020; Munday, 2014; Loveless and Williamson, 2013). This insight suggests that creative pedagogies in the context of outdoor learning are important aspects of critical pedagogy (Darder et al., 2017; Freire, 1970) and can contribute to developing concepts of 'eco-pedagogy' (Darder, 2011; Kahn, 2010), that increasingly accounts for our place within the global ecology as a core aspect of social justice. The message growing from the evidence is that creative learning outdoors can be an expression of an eco-pedagogical approach to education.

Recent criticism (Bainbridge, 2020) articulates a 'metabolic rift', a fundamental gap between the 'real' value and the exchange value of education. Bainbridge sees signs of hope through development of pedagogies that build on the relationship between humans and the 'more than human' – the natural world. Evidence from this study suggests that creative pedagogies in outdoor learning could be one way to build a bridge across this rift.

Final reflections

Creativity matters. Learning outdoors matters. The climate crisis shows that the relationship with community, the environment and generative learning are essential. The position taken in this chapter is that creativity and outdoor learning have a special positive contribution to make to education. All the leaders interviewed for this study consider themselves as making a creative and positive contribution to making lives better for the people they work with.

The positive evaluation of 'A Description of Creativity' by these leaders suggests that it may be a useful framework to support pedagogy outdoors. However, it can be developed further to show a greater focus on what makes creativity distinct within outdoor learning. There is also the potential for the description to be applied to other areas of education. Further inquiry would also give insight into the role of the outdoor leader as an activist motivated to make a difference to people, place and planet.

The findings suggest that practitioners are seeking to cut through such debate and consider what is best for their learners. They speak consistently and enthusiastically of great creative learning experiences outdoors. All folk need is a good stick.

References

Alexander, R. J. (2008). *Essays on pedagogy*. Routledge.

Bainbridge, A. (2020). Digging our own grave: A Marxian consideration of formal education as a destructive enterprise. *International Review of Education*, 66(5–6), 737–753.

Ball, S. J. (1993). Education policy, power relations and teachers' work. *British Journal of Educational Studies*, 41(2), 106–121.

Ball, S. J. (2008). *The education debate: Policy and politics in the twenty-first century*. Policy Press.

Ball, S. J. (2013). Foucault, power, and education. *British Journal of Sociology of Education*, 35(6), 933–945.

Banaji, S. & Burn, A. (2007). Creativity through a rhetorical lens: Implications for schooling, literacy and media education. *Literacy*, 41(2), 62–70.

Beames, S. & Brown, M. (2016). *Adventurous learning: A pedagogy for a changing world*. Routledge.

Beames, S., Higgins, P. & Nicol, R. (2012). *Learning outside the classroom: Theory and guidelines for practice*. Routledge.

Bruner, J. S. (1960). *The process of education*. Harvard University Press.

Bruner, J. S. (2000). *Acts of meaning*. Harvard University Press.

Charmaz, K. (2014). Grounded Theory in global perspective. *Qualitative Inquiry*, 20(9), 1074–1084.

Charmaz, K. (2016). The power of Constructivist Grounded Theory for critical inquiry. *Qualitative Inquiry*, 23(1), 34–45.

Craft, A. (2010). Possibility thinking and wise creativity: Educational futures in England? In R. A. Beghetto & J. C. Kaufman (Eds.), *Nurturing creativity in the classroom* (pp. 289–312). Cambridge University Press.

Craft, A. (2013). Childhood, possibility thinking and wise, humanising educational futures. *International Journal of Educational Research*, 61, 126–134.

Craft, A. & Jeffrey, B. (2004). Learner inclusiveness for creative learning. *Education 3-13*, 32(2), 39–43. https://doi.org/10.1080/03004270485200201.

Cremin, T. (2015). Perspectives on creative pedagogy: Exploring challenges, possibilities and potential. *Education 3–13*, 43(4), 353–359.

Csikszentmihalyi, M. (1996). *Creativity: flow and the psychology of discovery and invention.* HarperCollins.

Custodero, L. (2015). Ubiquitous creativity, imagination in dialogue, and innovative practice-in-action. *Teachers College Record: The Voice of Scholarship in Education,* 117.

Daniels, H. (2007). Pedagogy. In H. Daniels, M. Cole & J. V. Wertsch (Eds.), *The Cambridge Companion to Vygotsky* (pp. 307–331). Cambridge University Press.

Darder, A. (2011). It's not nice to fool mother nature: Eco-pedagogy in the pursuit of justice. *Counterpoints,* 418, 327–342.

Darder, A., Torres, R. D. & Baltodano, M. (Eds.) (2017). *The critical pedagogy reader* (3rd Edition). Routledge.

Dewey, J. (1964). *John Dewey on education: Selected writings.* Modern Library.

Dyment, J. E., & Potter, T. G. (2014). Is outdoor education a discipline? Provocations and possibilities. *Journal of Adventure Education and Outdoor Learning,* 15(3), 193–208.

Freire, P. (1970). *Pedagogy of the oppressed.* Seabury Press.

Freire, P. (1998). *Pedagogy of freedom: Ethics, democracy, and civic courage.* Rowman & Littlefield.

Gardner, H. (2008). Creativity, wisdom, and trusteeship. In A. Craft, H. Gardner & G. Claxton (Eds.), *Creativity, wisdom, and trusteeship: Exploring the role of education* (pp. 49–65). Corwin Press.

Gruenewald, D. A. (2003). Foundations of place: A multidisciplinary framework for place-conscious education. *American Educational Research Journal,* 40(3), 619–634.

Hallam, E., & Ingold, T. (2007). *Creativity and cultural improvisation.* Berg.

Hallam, E., & Ingold, T. (2016). *Making and growing: Anthropological studies of organisms and artefacts.* Routledge.

Harris, F. (2017). The nature of learning at Forest SSchool: Practitioners' perspectives. *Education 3–13,* 45(2), 272–291.

Hempel-Jorgensen, A. (2015). Learner agency and social justice: what can creative pedagogy contribute to socially just pedagogies? *Pedagogy, Culture & Society,* 23(4), 531–554.

Jeffrey, B., & Craft, A. (2010). Teaching creatively and teaching for creativity: Distinctions and relationships. *Educational Studies,* 30(1), 77–87.

Jeffrey, B. (2008). Creative learning identities. *Education 3–13,* 36(3), 253–263.

Kahn, R. V. (2010). *Critical pedagogy, ecoliteracy & planetary crisis: The ecopedagogy movement.* Peter Lang Publishing.

Knight, S. (Ed.) (2011). *Forest School for all.* Sage.

Knight, S. (2018). Translating Forest School: A response to Leather. *Journal of Outdoor and Environmental Education,* 21(1), 19–23.

Lave, J. & Wenger, E. (1991). *Situated learning: Legitimate peripheral participation.* Cambridge University Press.

Leather, M. (2018). A critique of "Forest School" or something lost in translation. *Journal of Outdoor and Environmental Education,* 21(1), 5–18.

Lloyd, A., Truong, S., & Gray, T. (2018). Place-based outdoor learning: More than a drag and drop approach. *Journal of Outdoor and Environmental Education,* 21, 45–60.

Loveless, A. & Williamson, B. (2013). *Learning identities in a digital age: Rethinking creativity, education and technology.* Routledge.

Lucas, B., Claxton, G., & Spencer, E. (2013). Progression in Student Creativity in School: First Steps Towards New Forms of Formative Assessments. *OECD Education Working Papers,* 86(86), 45. https://doi.org/10.1787/5k4dp59msdwk-en.

Mannion, G., Fenwick, A. & Lynch, J. (2013). Place-responsive pedagogy: Learning from teachers' experiences of excursions in nature. *Environmental Education Research*, 19(6), 792–809.

Mercer, S. (2011). Understanding learner agency as a complex dynamic system. *System*, 39 (4), 427–436.

Misiaszek, G. W. (2020). Ecopedagogy: Teaching critical literacies of 'development', 'sustainability', and 'sustainable development'. *Teaching in Higher Education*, 25(5), 615–632.

Munday, I. (2014). Creativity: Performativity's poison or its antidote? *Cambridge Journal of Education*, 44(3), 319–332.

Neelands, J. (1992). *Learning through imagined experience: The role of drama in the National Curriculum*. Hodder & Stoughton.

OECD (2019). *PISA 2021 Creative Thinking Framework (Third Draft)*. OECD, 53(9), 1689–1699.

Pope, R. (2005). *Creativity: Theory, history, practice*. Routledge.

Potter, T. G. & Dyment, J. E. (2016). Is outdoor education a discipline? Insights, gaps and future directions. *Journal of Adventure Education and Outdoor Learning*, 16(2), 146–159.

Priestley, M., Biesta, G. & Robinson, S. (2015). *Teacher agency: An ecological approach*. Bloomsbury Academic.

Punie, Y., Ferrari, A., Cachia, R. & Ala-Mutka, K. (2010). *Creative learning and innovative teaching: Final report on the study on creativity and innovation in education in the EU member states*. Publications Office. https://data.europa.eu/doi/10.2791/52913.

Robinson, K. (1999). *All our futures: Creativity, culture and education*. National Advisory Committee on Creative and Cultural Education.

Robinson, K. (2001). Out of our minds: Learning to be creative. *Order: A Journal On The Theory Of Ordered Sets And Its Applications*, 2. Retrieved from http://www.amazon.co. uk/dp/1907312471.

Rogoff, B. (1990). *Apprenticeship in thinking: Cognitive development in social context*. Oxford University Press.

Ross, H., Christie, B., Nicol, R. & Higgins, P. (2014). Space, place and sustainability and the role of outdoor education. *Journal of Adventure Education & Outdoor Learning*, 14 (3), 191–197.

Scottish Government (2012). What is creativity? Retrieved from http://www.sociology. org/media-studies/what-is-creativity/.

Sharma-Brymer, V., Brymer, E., Gray, T. & Davids, K. (2018). Affordances guiding Forest School practice: The application of the ecological dynamics approach. *Journal of Outdoor and Environmental Education*, 21(1), 103–115.

Smith, E. (2012). *Key issues in education and social justice*. SAGE.

Smith, G. A. & Sobel, D. (2010). *Place- and community-based education in schools*. Routledge.

Spencer, E., Lucas, B., & Claxton, G. (2012). *Progression in creativity: Developing new forms of assessment*. Centre of Real World Learning.

Sternberg, R. J. & Lubart, T. I. (1998). The Concept of Creativity: Prospects and Paradigms. In R. J. Sternberg (Ed.), *Handbook of creativity* (pp. 3–15). Cambridge University Press.

Thrift, E. & Sugarman, J. (2019). What is social justice? Implications for psychology. *Journal of Theoretical and Philosophical Psychology*, 39(1), 1–17.

Vygotskiĭ, L. S. (1962). *Thought and language*. (E. Hanfmann & G. Vakar, Eds.). M.I.T. Press.

Warren, K. & Breunig, M. (2019). Inclusion and social justice in outdoor education. In M. Peters (Ed.), *Encyclopedia of teacher education* (pp. 1–7). Springer.

Warren, K., Roberts, N. S., Breunig, M. & Alvarez, M. A. G. (2014). Social justice in outdoor experiential education: A state of knowledge review. *Journal of Experiential Education*, 37(1), 89–103.

Chapter 4

The great equalizer

Learning in the outdoors

Paolo Oprandi

Education throughout the world follows a similar model and comes from a similar heritage. The model is one of education happening indoors in lecture theaters and classrooms. For students it is a process of being talked at, taking notes, reading books, writing essays and answering questions (Freeman et al., 2014). The model came about during the Enlightenment era when a belief had erroneously grown that we should prioritize abstract, analytical and rational thinking. Weber (2013, p. 15) said of the period, that they saw "no use for notions of life, sentience, experience, subjectivity, corporeal embodiment and agency". It is true to say that since then our ideas have moved on, but the methods of teaching that established themselves during that era are maintained through the buildings, teaching time-tables and the ease of repeating methods that have gone before, compared to doing something new (Dewey, 1938). Whether these methods are truly the best environment for learning the topic in hand is largely left unquestioned in public discourse. Even from a personal perspective, as a researcher I have found tradi-tional teaching methods hard to challenge because of the shared experience it has provided us and questioning its merit has required me to question our childhoods.

Why should we question traditional teaching models?

The ubiquity of the indoor traditional model of education is almost complete. It has largely gone under the radar that in many parts of the world this model of education might be a legacy of our imperialist past. This is mainly because of the much-touted idealist view of education as "a good thing" and something that allows students "to reach their full potential". However, few would argue this idealist view is the whole story (Biesta & Säfström, 2011). Some have suggested that education is a filtering system for identifying and developing only the best students and condemning our less good students to menial lowly-paid jobs (Bourdieu, Passeron & Nice, 1977; Apple & Apple, 2018; Reay, 2012). Others have argued that it is an instrument of control to get young people used to the authority of the workplace and 9-to-5 workdays (Freire, 1970; Hooks, 2000). Yet others contend that student fees and loans tie them further into a life of debt and paying back the state (Sandel, 2020). The decolonizing of the curriculum agenda

DOI: 10.4324/9781003436928-6

has noted that on a global stage, education can work to pedestal Western, white, male, heteronormative knowledge and scholars (Mohanty, 2003; Oprandi and Crossouard, 2022).

There is no doubt that the vast majority of teachers want the best for their students and believe that education is an instrument to allow students to learn the skills they need in later life. However arguments such as those made by the scholars mentioned above mean that we have to be cautious about some of the things we take for granted. The insightful and key work of the anthropologists Lave and Wenger (1993) described how learning happens outside of educational institutions. They studied learning in seven traditional, occupational settings, including those of midwives, meat-cutters and tailors. They described the pathway to coming to "know" in these environments as "situated learning" because learning was situated within the place where experts were authentically "doing". Becoming an expert in these settings is a process of "legitimate peripheral participation" and slow immersion into "communities of practice" through witnessing, doing and slowly being given increased responsibilities.

There is little doubt that much can be learned through ethnographic research, such as the advantages to students of having authentic experiences with real needs, but even if "situated learning" theory were deemed an improvement to current schooling methods, bringing it into the classroom would be a challenge. Apart from the cultural forces at work that encourage the reproduction of teacher-centric, indoor teaching methods, there are a number of practical reasons for traditional teaching to happen the way it does. Teacher-led instruction allows one person to teach many students at a time, and indoor spaces allow us to speak to our students without competing with external noises, or being limited by weather conditions. In the indoors students can comfortably capture notes through jotting them down on a page or computer. Furthermore, the learning experiences and environments within the professions of traditional communities are quite different to the learning that students experience. In the comparatively engineered learning environment of the classroom the students do not spend the majority of the time watching the expert doing or doing themselves. Instead they participate in the "community of practice" of the classroom, with one teacher teaching and many other students learning. Nevertheless, Lave and Wenger's research does give us reason to question some things about our teaching methods, including where our students learn best. While there are efficiencies to classroom learning, there are undoubtedly things we have lost. In an age where education is so important, we must question whether indoor environments always translate into the best spaces for learning.

New spaces for learning

Education has many functions. On one hand it informs the student about a topic so they have knowledge about it, and on the other hand, students need to use the knowledge. There are many ways in which indoor learning restricts the way in which knowledge can be known and used. For one thing, much knowledge can only be understood in its entirety when immersed in the environment we are learning about. Authentic usages for the knowledge can sometimes only be found when in particular environments. Books and other media can help us imagine, but being in the environments we are studying gives us new and personal insights. Teaching in classrooms often has to be abstract. We talk about things happening "out there", whilst not being in the environment we are learning about at all. Outdoor learning, in situ, can often allow students to engage with the subjects they are studying physically and give them personal tangible experiences and memories to learn firsthand from.

Some scholars point out that some of the factors that make the indoors a good space for concentration, are also factors that make learning within them static and staid (Thomas, 2013). Indoor environments, while safe, are often uninspiring and inauthentic. The outdoors creates an atmosphere with bodily memory, often including a physical journey more likely to be remembered, cared about and referenced in the future (Macfarlane, 2012). When we are inside and "plugged in", it is difficult to take a step back and understand the onslaught of information presented to us. Nietzsche (2005) believed that the sights and sounds of one's environment, particularly when seen in motion, inspire original ideas. Sherrington (2020) talks about the importance of nature in producing the radical openness necessary for learning. Wallace Stevens (2011) questioned whether finding the truth depended upon "a walk around the lake", suggesting only time in nature could clear our thoughts in order to make sense of the information presented. Beavington (2021) argues that the outdoors gives us enough of a gap between one thought and the next to make the necessary connections between complex concepts and ideas. He describes outdoor learning as "engaging, enlivening, enveloping" and asks if it is "not a recipe for transformative pedagogy?"

Pedagogists have made a distinction between learning that is convergent and learning that is divergent, both of which are important to students (Pryor & Crossouard, 2010). Convergent learning revolves around understanding a known solution to a problem, for example that one plus one equals two. It is learning that requires students to converge and agree with the teacher's understanding. For convergent learning to happen personal experience is less important. In contrast, divergent learning requires thinking outside the box, using personal experience and creativity, and often finding multiple solutions and exposing nuances. Deep learning requires students to engage in both convergent and divergent learning, but the more complex the task, the deeper the learning required and the more the need for divergent thinking. A curriculum solely dedicated to convergent learning has little value for 21st-century living; students need to be able to think for themselves (Robinson & Aronica, 2016). It has been argued that divergent thinking is catalyzed when using the outdoors as a teaching space. The outdoors provides an environment for exciting, eventful and memorable experiences, often revealing unexpected learnings (Beavington, 2021). Goertz (2017) argues that walking outdoors "is an excellent facilitator of original, innovative thinking because the physical act of left-right steps simulates the integration of the two halves of the brain, the logical and the intuitive" (p. 61).

Valuing different ways of knowing

Scientists such as Beavington (2021) point out that "a curriculum that singularly favours the mind also devalues, by its omission, bodily, emotional and spiritual ways of knowing". His argument is in line with the decolonizing of the curriculum agenda, which calls for more recognition and value to be placed on non-traditional knowledge production (Crossouard and Oprandi, 2022). It is argued that ways of knowing within education are all too often Western, white, male and heterosexual, and that the knowledge that universities produce is from a "binary, hetero patriarchal gender system" (Lugones, 2007). It uses the same sources, emerging from the same traditional techniques and values. It is thus repetitive, exclusive and struggles to move forward. More value should be placed on traditional ways of knowledge production. Scholars such as the botanist, Robin Kimmerer, recognize the value of students engaging "all of their human faculties of mind, body, emotion, and spirit which conventional science education practices tend to let atrophy" (2012, pp. 320–321). These scholars, along with many others including the authors in this book, have introduced the outdoors as a space for learning to their teaching curricula. In doing so, these scholars are supporting the "decolonizing the curriculum" agenda, as they introduce personal ways of knowing and coming to know, that are not confined to the classroom, textbook and reciting of the lecturer's notes.

The value of movement

Whilst pedagogical theorists slowly shift their understanding of knowledge from one of being purely a quality of the mind, they start to value the importance of movement and walking, also often absent from our teaching methods. The proposition that cognition is both motion-sensitive and site-specific pre-dates Romanticism, but it was Jean-Jacque Rousseau who made it famous when he said: "I can only meditate when I am walking, when I stop I cease to think; my mind only works with my leg". It is suggested that during muscular activity "creative energy flows". Artists such as Hamish Fulton (2008) contend: "If I do not walk, I cannot make a work of art". Nietzsche (2005) saw walking as a journey with endless possibilities for growth and self-discovery and famously believed that only thoughts which come through walking had any value. He felt sitting or standing still could lead to tunnel vision, and that in contrast, walking provided a holistic experience of reality. Søren Kierkegaard (2002) exclaimed that when walking we can be overwhelmed with ideas and Wittgenstein was well-known for pacing up and down for hours in deep thought (Macfarlane, 2012).

The other factor that movement can bring to a student's experience is deeper and more personal topic-based discussion. The seminar room has traditionally been the place where student discussion is thought to be at its richest, but in modern seminar rooms, discussion is often stilted and overrun with the same, confident student voices, whilst the quieter and more timid students are too shy to raise their voice or in some cases, even come to the classroom at all. Whilst walking people find it easier to talk than in the contrived and staid environment of the classroom (Carpiano, 2009; Evans & Jones, 2011). Eye contact actually increases the pressure of getting the words right and therefore stifles discussion. In contrast, when walking side-by-side, people are primed to talk naturally and without inhibition (Jensen, 2008).

Concluding thoughts

I conclude this chapter with the following thoughts. Education has the potential to be a great equalizer and an opportunity for students to find their strengths and make best use of their skills. However, if not implemented correctly, education can work to increase inequality, exclude and marginalize particular skills and be a negative force to impose and solidify current hegemonies. There are different things we can do as educators. One is to value different skills within our disciplines and give room for participation and contributions from different kinds of knowledge. Many of these are not detectable within the confines of the classroom environment and can only be expressed and found within new teaching spaces, such as "the great outdoors". The authors in this book all encourage you to make use of the outdoors and the great learning potential it has for your students.

References

Apple, M., & Apple, M. W. (2018). *Ideology and curriculum*. Routledge.

Beavington, L. (2021). Walking pedagogy for science education and more-than-human connection. *Journal of the Canadian Association for Curriculum Studies*, 18(2), 163–178.

Biesta, G., & Säfström, C. A. (2011). A manifesto for education. *Policy Futures in Education*, 9(5), 540–547.

Bourdieu, P., & Passeron, J. C. (1977). *Education, society and culture*. Trans. Richard Nice. London: SAGE Publications, 15–29.

Carpiano, R. M. (2009). Come take a walk with me: The "Go-Along" interview as a novel method for studying the implications of place for health and well-being. *Health & Place*, 15(1), 263–272.

Crossouard, B., & Oprandi, P. (2022). Decolonising formative assessment. *Theory and Method in Higher Education Research*, 8, 181–196. Emerald Publishing Limited.

Dewey, J. (1938). *Experience and education*. New York: Macmillan.

Evans, J., & Jones, P. (2011). The walking interview: Methodology, mobility and place. *Applied Geography*, 31(2), 849–858.

Freeman, S., Eddy, S. L., McDonough, M., Smith, M. K., Okoroafor, N., Jordt, H., & Wenderoth, M. P. (2014). Active learning increases student performance in science, engineering, and mathematics. *Proceedings of the National Academy of Sciences of the*

United States, 111(23), 8410. https://www.pnas.org/doi/full/10.1073/pnas. 1319030111.

Freire, P. (1970). *Pedagogy of the oppressed.* Continuum.

Fulton, H. (2008). *El camino: rutas cortas por la Península Ibérica.* Fundación Ortega Muñoz.

Goertz, K. K. (2017). Walking as pedagogy. In C. M. Hall, Y. Ram & N. Shoval (Eds), *The Routledge international handbook of walking* (pp. 55–64). Routledge.

Hooks, B. (2000). *Feminist theory: From margin to center.* New York; London: Routledge. (Original work published 1984.)

Jensen, E. (Ed.) (2008). *Super teaching: Over 1000 practical strategies.* Corwin Press.

Kierkegaard, S. (2002). *Provocations: Spiritual writings of Kierkegaard.* Plough Publishing House.

Kimmerer, R. W. (2012). Searching for synergy: Integrating traditional and scientific ecological knowledge in environmental science education. *Journal of Environmental Studies and Sciences,* 2, 317–323. Lave, J., & Wenger, E. (1991). *Situated learning: Legitimate peripheral participation.* Cambridge University Press.

Lugones, M. (2007). Heterosexualism and the colonial/modern gender system. *Hypatia,* 22(1), 186–219.

Macfarlane, R. (2012). *The old ways: A journey on foot.* Penguin.

Mohanty, C. T. (2003). *Feminism without borders: decolonizing theory, practicing solidarity.* Durham, NC: Duke University Press.

Nietzsche, F. W. (2005). *Nietzsche: The anti-Christ, ecce homo, twilight of the idols: And other writings.* Cambridge University Press.

Pryor, J., & Crossouard, B. (2010). Challenging formative assessment: disciplinary spaces and identities. *Assessment & Evaluation in Higher Education,* 35(3), 265–276.

Reay, D. (2012). What would a socially just education system look like?: Saving the minnows from the pike. *Journal of Education Policy,* 27(5), 587–599.

Robinson, K., & Aronica, L. (2016). *Creative schools: The grassroots revolution that's transforming education.* Penguin.

Sandel, M. J. (2020). *The tyranny of merit: What's become of the common good?*Penguin.

Sherrington, T. (2020). *Learning rainforest: Great teaching in real classrooms.* John Catt Educational.

Stevens, W. (2011). *The collected poems of Wallace Stevens.* Vintage.

Thomas, K. (2013, May 14). A classroom for the 21st century: Where are the best places for learning? *The Guardian.* https://www.theguardian.com/teacher-network/2013/may/14/best-places-for-learning-21st-century-classroom#:~:text=In%20summary,to%20help%20schools%20to%20innovate.

Weber, A. (2013). *Enlivenment: Towards a fundamental shift in the concepts of nature, culture and politics.* Heinrich-Böll-Stiftung.

Part 2

Health benefits

Chapter 5

More than a walk in the park

Enhancing campus green space for student and staff learning and wellbeing

Agnes Bosanquet, Miles Holmes, Kate Lloyd, Kath McLachlan and Waminda Parker

This chapter explores a university staff and student collaboration with a nature-wellness trail through the bush and waterways of Wallumattagal Campus. Located in what is now known as Sydney, Australia, Macquarie University comprises 113 hectares built on the homelands of the Wallumattagal clan, the Wullamai (black snapper fish) people, of the Dharug nation whose cultures and customs have cared for and continue to care for this land. We pay our respects to Dharug Elders past, present and future, and the wisdom and knowledge passed down through their generations. We are mindful of our responsibilities to connect with and care for the Country. In this chapter we build on these foundations and share scholarly evidence for the benefits of nature-connection on wellbeing and stress regulation. We draw on the philosophy of the "placeful" university (Nørgård and Bengtsen, 2016) and its role in promoting connection and care for Country: humans, other-than-humans and environments.

The nature connection advantage

Spending time in nature has a positive impact on mood (Gilbert, 2016), facilitates physical activity and encourages socialisation (Keskinen et al., 2018). Time in nature can improve performance in reading, writing, maths, science and social studies (Chawla, 2015; Williams & Dixon, 2013). It also enhances creativity, critical thinking and problem solving, improves attention restoration and focus (Mårtensson et al., 2009) and promotes motivation to learn (Rios & Brewer, 2014).

Research shows that the benefits of nature are amplified when connection occurs. It is not just the contact with nature, but the nature of the contact that counts. Nature connection (or connectedness) is a measurable construct that broadly describes a person's cognitive, affective and experiential relationship with nature, including worldview (the extent that one sees themself as being a part of the rest of nature) (Zylstra et al., 2014). Connecting with nature is recognised as an important mediating pathway for emotional-nervous system regulation, mental resilience, eudemonic wellbeing (life satisfaction and the sense of a worthwhile life) and greater overall happiness (Sheffield et al., 2022). It is also correlated with an increased desire to care for the natural environment (Barragan-Jason et al., 2022).

DOI: 10.4324/9781003436928-8

Mars Creek Nature-Wellness Trail

The Mars Creek Nature-Wellness Trail (Figure 5.1) has been developed by The Connective, a social enterprise that helps rejuvenate communities by creating nature connection experiences. The trail takes approximately half an hour and follows a design flow to maximise experiences with nature that amplify wellbeing benefits. Guided by a NatureFix app, students and staff participate in reflective nature-based sensory activities, connecting with each other and our beautiful campus to care, heal and regenerate people and place. As shown in Table 5.1, the app offers a series of "nature connection routines" to help activate the senses, facilitate mindful attention and engage in reflective nature-based activities.

Taking this nature-wellness trail and participating in the reflective and sensory activities multiple times, the key to connection is noticing and slowing down to absorb the multisensory details of nature: finding beauty, feeling emotions and reflecting on symbolism and meaning. We see colours beyond the green and brown that dominate the landscape, we look up through the canopy, we stand still and listen to each sound, we smell the difference after rain. We learn the names of trees: angophora, bloodwood, ironbark, blackbutt, turpentines, red and blue and grey gums, scribbly and stringybarks. We identify birds: magpies, ravens, ibis, cockatoos, butcherbirds, kookaburras, currawongs, ducks, rosellas and lorikeets.

Connecting with Country as the "placeful university"

The value of the nature-wellness trail goes beyond the individual benefits to learning and wellbeing. The location of the trail on a campus on Dharug Country, embedded in curriculum and research, invites us to consider the role and responsibility of the university. In *Academic citizenship beyond the campus: A call for the placeful university*, Nørgård and Bengtsen (2016) suggest a model of academic citizenship that recognises mutual interest, care and responsibility between universities and the surrounding societies. They call for

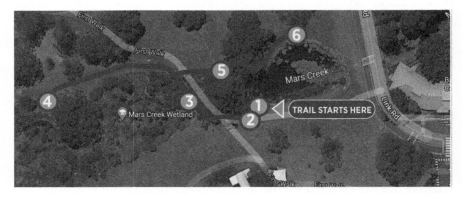

Figure 5.1 Mars Creek Nature-Wellness Trail
Source: NatureFix

Table 5.1 Naturefix stops and benefit summary

Nature Wellness Stop Routine	*Nature Contact Benefits*
Breathe Slowly: Abdominal breathing exercise to increase pleasantness, vigour, alertness, and reduce symptoms of anxiety, depression, anger and confusion (Zaccaro et al., 2018).	Inhaling negative ions from running water and sunlight improves relaxation and boosts immunity and metabolism (Jiang et al., 2018).
Listen Up!: This listening exercise breaks sensory habits to increase connection with nature and includes a placemaking element.	Listening to nature sounds restores attention and reduces muscle tension faster and more effectively than listening to urban sounds (Gould van Praag et al., 2017).
Relax The Eyes: MRI and EEG scans show that peripheral vision stimulates the parasympathetic nervous system, leading to feelings, mindfulness and calm awareness (Nan et al., 2014). Using peripheral vision in nature creates feelings of awe.	Using peripheral vision in nature enhances stress reduction and restoration through "soft fascination", a key component of attention restoration theory (Basu et al., 2019). Experiencing awe of nature increases wellbeing and community spirit (Greater Good Science Center, 2018).
Sensory Switch: This exercise uses sensory experiences to create moments for pausing, stopping and noticing nature in different ways.	Sensory engagement with nature has well-documented beneficial effects on connection, mental restoration, calm and creativity (Franco et al., 2017).
The Tree and Me: This mimicry exercise is used to trigger mirror neurons to create empathy and compassion. This exercise helps to create a stronger connection between the person and the place.	Standing near trees increases access to phytoncides, adiponectin and anti-cancer T-cells (Twohig-Bennett & Jones, 2018). Looking up and out on nature has a range of neurological benefits (Kerr & Maze, 2019). Mimicking nature activities activates body senses that increase our connection and empathy with nature.
Five Beautiful Things: This exercise helps individuals to notice and enjoy beautiful things.	Noticing the beauty of nature has a particular effect on increasing pro-community behaviours such as agreeableness, friendship and helping behaviours (Zhang et al., 2014b); it is also a driver of nature connection which is linked to overall increases in life satisfaction (Zhang et al., 2014a).

Source: NatureFix/The Connective

us to consider the university, not as "physical architectural spatiality (concrete) or imagined articulated space (concept)" but as place, with its own being "imbued with significance, belonging and commitment" (Nørgård and Bengtsen, 2016, p 5).

Station 1: Breathe Slowly

Abdominal breathing exercise designed to increase relaxation and alertness

Figure 5.2 Breathe Slowly
Source: NatureFix

Indigenous scholars at our university remind us that a connection to Ngurra or Country and caring-for-Country practices have always been and continue to be important to human and other-than-human wellbeing. Dharug scholar Jo Anne Rey urges us to see what can be achieved through recognition of humanity's need to connect to places and presences (humans and other-than-humans) to care for the biodiversity on which we all depend. With that caring, together we build a sense of belonging (Rey, 2019). Gamilaroi scholar Michelle Bishop's work on Indigenous education sovereignty explores other ways of "doing" education, which pre-date the university and prompt us to look beyond the classroom and institutional learning (Bishop, 2021).

Our student and staff reflections show that the nature-wellness trail contributes to physical and mental health and social wellbeing. We acknowledge, however, that our claim that the most effective learning environment in the university is outdoors, is by no means a new one. As Bishop says:

> in a sterile classroom environment, we put trust in books and computers to tell us all we need to know ... Country can help all people to remember. Take a moment to be outside, what can you see, hear, smell, feel, learn?
>
> (Bishop, 2022)

Over the past five years The Connective has worked with First Nations custodians, Macquarie researchers (urban planners, anthropologists, social ecologists, environmentalists), students and staff to explore the role of nature connection in enhancing wellbeing for students and staff (see https://www.naturefix.life/diversity-inclusion). Structured through a research project on socio-ecological regenerative approaches to liveability and sustainability, the research team engaged with a range of different student cohorts from across the university to gather evidence of the benefits of the trail.

Students' connection with nature

Geography and Planning students undertook the nature-wellness trail multiple times over a 7-week period and (during each trail experience) responded to an anonymous online survey that asked questions about perception of nature, experiences in engaging with various environments, and the impact this has had on their physical and emotional wellbeing. An analysis of the results indicated increases in positive mood and attention restoration, greater resilience to anxiety and a deeper sense of care for and enjoyment of place. Students doing the nature-wellness trail improved on average their digit span test (testing cognition) by 7.7%, while those that just walked around the green spaces of the campus improved 1.4%. For many students, being able to enjoy the greenery and the natural setting of the campus was one of the features that drew them to Macquarie University. Being able to immerse themselves in nature through mindful activities means students are rewarded through improved wellness and better learning experiences.

Students' connection with nature (INS nature connectedness score) increased by 30%. Even with an average of 13 minutes three times a week, students felt 50% more relaxed, 36% happier, 20% less negative, 31% more connected and 20% more appreciative of place. The qualitative measures show an almost 100% positive experience. Indicative comments include:

> I personally came away with an increased appreciation of the incredible power that nature can have on my wellbeing – lowering my stress levels, increasing relaxation. It had a profound effect on me, and I would encourage anyone to just try it *(Medical Student)*.
>
> My initial thought to hearing about this activity was pretty adamant and arrogant – I felt that this is not going to do anything. But after the first couple of days, I really did really start to feel something towards everything around me. So, you really develop an appreciation for what you have around you *(Medical Student)*.
>
> For me experiencing the wellness trail and how good I've been feeling has been amazing. How I felt at the start of the start of the week to now – I feel a lot more relaxed and connected with nature. I would definitely encourage students to come with an open mind to this as I have really felt the benefit *(Geography and Planning Student)*.
>
> Acknowledging the five beautiful things in front of around me enabled to be grateful of my relationship with nature. It made me relaxed and happy *(Geography Student)*.

> This activity really encouraged me to look at the finer details of the environment. I noticed things which I wouldn't have noticed if I hadn't looked hard enough *(Geography Student)*.
>
> It is beneficial in a way that a university is not just a place to study but also a place to improve wellness. At Macquarie we are so lucky to have a campus with so much nature – and would encourage that we come out and use the space that we have got *(Geography Student)*.

The staff and student collaboration with the nature-wellness trail affirms the value of outdoor connection for learning and wellbeing. It often took individuals three walks before they saw the benefits. Fleeting "feel good" states with nature have value in themselves, but the long-term goal for a flourishing society is to transform transient states of connection into durable traits of connection with nature. This relies on deepening our relationship with nature in a way that reinforces a life-affirming approach. For this reason, it was important that students were given permission to regularly spend time connecting with nature and to learn from repetition and routine with nature. In addition to wellbeing outcomes, students were able to apply the insights they discovered to their practice in environmental science, medicine, psychology, human and physical geography and planning as professionals and researchers.

Concluding remarks

Mars Creek has long been a site for learning and wellbeing. We invite staff and students to renew their connection with the university by immersing their senses in the bush and waterways of the campus. The Mars Creek Nature-Wellness Trail embodies a different idea of the university, a "formation of dwelling, being and becoming on the placeful university" (Nørgård and Bengtsen, 2016, p. 4). The vision and values of the nature-connection trail promote ongoing connection and care for humans, more-than-human and environments. Our findings are unequivocal: the green spaces of the campus provide more than a walk in the park. The most effective learning environment in the university is outdoors.

References

Barragan-Jason, Gladys, Claire de Mazancourt, Camille Parmesan, Michael C. Singer, and Michel Loreau. 2022. Human–nature connectedness as a pathway to sustainability: A global meta-analysis. *Conservation Letters*, 15 (1).

Basu, Avik, Jason Duvall, and Rachel Kaplan. 2019. Attention restoration theory: Exploring the role of soft fascination and mental bandwidth. *Environment and Behavior*, 51 (9–10): 1055–1081.

Bishop, Michelle. 2021. A rationale for the urgency of indigenous education sovereignty: Enough's enough. *The Australian Educational Researcher*, 48: 419–432.

Bishop, Michelle. 2022. Indigenous education sovereignty: Another way of 'doing' education. *Critical Studies in Education*, 63 (1): 131–146.

Chawla, Louise. 2015. Benefits of nature contact for children. *Journal of Planning Literature*, 30 (4): 433–452.

Franco, Lara S., Danielle F. Shanahan, and Richard A. Fuller. 2017. A review of the benefits of nature experiences: More than meets the eye. *International Journal of Environmental Research and Public Health*, 14 (8): 864.

Gilbert, Natasha. 2016. Green space: A natural high. *Nature*, 531 (7594): S56–57.

Gould van Praag, Cassandra D., Sarah N. Garfinkel, Oliver Sparasci, Alex Mees, Andrew O. Philippides, Mark Ware, Cristina Ottaviani, and Hugo D. Critchley. 2017. Mind-wandering and alterations to default mode network connectivity when listening to naturalistic versus artificial sounds. *Scientific Reports*, 7 (1).

Greater Good Science Center. 2018. The science of awe. https://www.templeton.org/wp -content/uploads/2018/08/Awe-White-Paper_distribution.pdf.

Jiang, Shu-Ye, Ali Ma, and Srinivasan Ramachandran. 2018. Negative air ions and their effects on human health and air quality improvement. *International Journal of Molecular Sciences*, 19 (10).

Kerr, F., and L. Maze. 2019. The art & science of looking up: Transforming our brains, bodies, relationships and experience of the world by the simple act of looking up. www. lookup.org.au.

Keskinen, Kirsi E., Merja Rantakokko, Kimmo Suomi, Taina Rantanen, and Erja Portegijs. 2018. Nature as a facilitator for physical activity: defining relationships between the objective and perceived environment and physical activity among community-dwelling older people. *Health & Place*, 49 (January): 111–119.

Mårtensson, F., C. Boldemann, M. Söderström, M. Blennow, J.-E. Englund, and P. Grahn. 2009. Outdoor environmental assessment of attention promoting settings for preschool children. *Health & Place*, 15 (4): 1149–1157.

Nan, Wenya, Daria Migotina, Feng Wan, Chin Ian Lou, João Rodrigues, João Semedo, Mang I Vai, Jose Gomes Pereira, Fernando Melicio, and Agostinho C. Da Rosa. 2014. Dynamic peripheral visual performance relates to alpha activity in soccer players. *Frontiers in Human Neuroscience*, 8 (November).

Nørgård, Rikke Toft, and Søren Smedegaard Ernst Bengtsen. 2016. Academic citizenship beyond the campus: A call for the placeful university. *Higher Education Research & Development*, 35 (1): 4–16.

Rey, Jo Anne. 2019. Dharug custodial leadership: Uncovering country in the city. *WINHEC: International Journal of Indigenous Education Scholarship*, 1 (November): 56–66.

Rios, José M., and Jessica Brewer. 2014. Outdoor education and science achievement. *Applied Environmental Education & Communication*, 13 (4): 234–240.

Sheffield, David, Carly W. Butler, and Miles Richardson. 2022. Improving nature connectedness in adults: A meta-analysis, review and agenda. *Sustainability*, 14 (19): 12494.

Twohig-Bennett, Caoimhe, and Andy Jones. 2018. The health benefits of the great outdoors: A systematic review and meta-analysis of greenspace exposure and health outcomes. *Environmental Research*, 166 (166): 628–637.

Williams, Dilafruz R., and P. Scott Dixon. 2013. Impact of garden-based learning on academic outcomes in schools. *Review of Educational Research*, 83 (2): 211–235.

Zaccaro, Andrea, Andrea Piarulli, Marco Laurino, Erika Garbella, Danilo Menicucci, Bruno Neri, and Angelo Gemignani. 2018. How breath-control can change your life: A systematic review on psycho-physiological correlates of slow breathing. *Frontiers in Human Neuroscience*, 12 (353).

Zhang, Jia Wei, Ryan T. Howell, and Ravi Iyer. 2014a. Engagement with natural beauty moderates the positive relation between connectedness with nature and psychological well-being. *Journal of Environmental Psychology*, 38 (June): 55–63.

Zhang, Jia Wei, Paul K. Piff, Ravi Iyer, Spassena Koleva, and Dacher Keltner. 2014b. An occasion for unselfing: Beautiful nature leads to prosociality. *Journal of Environmental Psychology*, 37 (March): 61–72.

Zylstra, Matthew J., Andrew T. Knight, Karen J. Esler, and Lesley L. L. Le Grange. 2014. Connectedness as a core conservation concern: An interdisciplinary review of theory and a call for practice. *Springer Science Reviews*, 2 (1–2): 119–143.

Chapter 6

Hope in the garden
Outdoor learning as politics[1]

Cathy Elliott

After our third and final visit to a garden in class time, one of my students proposed the concept of 'slow hope' in response to Rob Nixon's (2011) powerful analysis of the 'slow violence' of climate change, colonialism and toxic pollution, which we had read a few weeks earlier. Slow hope, she explained, was not a disavowal of slow violence or any of the other ills of the world that we explored in the class. Rather, slow hope was:

> the product of small steps, gradual changes and collective dreams for a better future. Hope that thrives regardless of how daunting and overwhelmingly unchanging circumstances may seem. Hope that perseveres. Slowly, but *steadily...*

This chapter is about teaching politics to undergraduates in gardens, in a context not only of climate grief and anxiety, but also of disengagement, withdrawal from politics, and atomisation. I make the argument that it is particularly concerning and dangerous if young people's understandable response to the multiple crises that surround us all is to lose hope. This is particularly the case, I suggest, because hope is the emotion that underpins political and collective action. As Rebecca Solnit (2016) explains, hope is an approach to the world that has two equally dangerous opposites. On the one hand, optimism – the belief that things will work out well, no matter what – can lead to a failure to engage with the scale of the challenges that face us. This can lead to a naive faith in technocratic solutions and a failure to break out of the competitive logics of market societies that structure our education system and offer promises of the comforts of a consumerist lifestyle that our students may aspire to. On the other hand, while despair may be an understandable response, it can lead to dangerous apathy, withdrawal and depression. In its refusal to engage with the world, despair becomes a self-fulfilling prophecy that nothing can change for the better. Hope, on the other hand, as the student quoted above put it so well, asks us to work together collectively to make change happen even against the odds. Hope does not expect a good outcome, but neither does it accept that further disaster is inevitable. It asks us to get together and do the political work of confronting injustice and creating a better future.

DOI: 10.4324/9781003436928-9

For these reasons, hope is deeply entwined with belonging and community. If hope impels us to political and collective work, then, by definition, we cannot be hopeful on our own, any more than the solutions to the problems we face can be found without community. Community is also the building block of everything we do in education. It is fundamental to how students learn (Jacques and Salmon, 2007; Carless, 2015, p. 50), to their ability to feel part of a disciplinary community and to their experience of developing their skills and knowledge through engaging in assessment and feedback (MacKay et al., 2019). It is also key to their happiness and sense of efficacy (Freeman et al., 2007). It is therefore particularly alarming that in the months that followed pandemic lockdowns, we saw so many photographs of deserted classrooms and heard reports of students feeling isolated, alone and lonely (Dickinson, 2023).

Community is also the starting point of politics. Collective action is not only about organisation and the possibilities opened up by persuading large numbers in a democracy. It is also fundamentally about what my student calls 'collective dreams for a better future'. Without the ability to imagine and tell stories about what a just world might look like – a necessarily communal activity – we will be restricted to a future of more of the same.

Meanwhile, hope is about getting beyond the walls – imaginative, social and cultural – that hem us in. For my class, we discovered that we could foster hope and a sense of belonging and community by going beyond the literal walls, too. Using my students' writing about the experience as evidence, I am going to suggest that the act of leaving behind the constraints and assumptions of the traditional classroom and getting outside is a way of fostering both hope and belonging, cultivating dreams and thinking politically.

Hope as politics

I was once told rather sharply at an academic conference that how students *feel* about the climate and biodiversity crisis is none of our concern as educators. By this account, which seems to be rather common, our job is rather to enable students to analyse and argue, not to hold space for sorrow or grief, solace or courage, or indeed hope. As Megan Boler (1999) explains, it is common to demand that classrooms be places of argumentation and objectivity, in which any emotion is understood to be a threat of 'irrationality'. She convincingly argues, however, that this approach ignores the constitutive role that education plays in producing and organising emotional experiences, including the idea that emotions are unwelcome interlopers in certain spaces such as classrooms. If we think that emotion and rationality are not in principle separable – that it is not possible to adjudicate between arguments in the absence of considering how we feel about them – then it is appropriate to engage with emotions as a core element of our work as educators.

However, this is not to say that our classrooms could or should become therapeutic spaces. Rather, as writers in the critical pedagogy tradition have argued for many years (Freire, 2021 [1992]; hooks, 2004; Giroux, 1997), education can enable students to name and recognise emotions and emotional regimes, noting, for example, the emotions produced by harm or injustice and feeling the weight of them. However, simply engaging in a struggle against what is wrong cannot be enough. I have repeatedly been struck by how the way we teach students to critique can leave them feeling disempowered. For example, I was troubled by the way they would offer savage critiques of NGOs trying to do generally unobjectionable, useful work. They later confessed to feeling guilty about such arguments, but told me that they did it to please me with their incisiveness. Cynicism, dressed up as critical thinking, is rewarded and modelled in our classrooms even as it becomes increasingly obvious that these are not the skills or dispositions that are going to help us in the face of crisis (Siperstein et al., 2017).

Meanwhile, it is unsurprising that in a time of multiple crises, many writers have asked the question about what approaches might be more fruitful. Ideas about hope seem promising: Freire (1998) argues that hope is central to efforts to transform the world, whilst the absence of hope can only offer support to the status quo (see also Van Heertum, 2006, p. 46). I asked my students to read work by Rebecca Solnit (2010) and Jonathan Lear (2008), in order to try to understand the complexities of hope as an emotion. Importantly, these authors' respective conceptualisations of hope are more radical than a faith in progress characteristic of market societies (Appadurai, 2007). Hope asks for more of us than to do our recycling, even though students sometimes start out with a faith in individualised solutions that is understandable when perhaps they have been taught little else. Reading Solnit and Lear encourages students to do the challenging work of looking crises full in the face, acknowledging their grief and despair, and asking what they can do, instead of excusing themselves because they feel powerless.

We connected this reading with the living world in embodied ways. One student put it like this:

> Learning in the garden [...] allowed me to directly connect academic theory with the material world. Students are [usually] asked to understand their subject of study whilst spatially detached. [Being outside enables] information to be processed by one's body.

Just as we have become accustomed to thinking of classrooms as abstracted from the embodied emotions, we also sometimes forget that a classroom is itself a *place*. Places become places, rather than abstract spaces (Gieryn, 2000, p. 465), because of the relationships they engender and contain. Thus, when bell hooks (1994, p. 4) writes that,

> the university and the classroom began to feel more like a prison, a place of punishment and confinement rather than a place of promise and possibility,

she is pointing to hierarchical relationships in which ideas are constrained, not allowing for that radical re-imagining which could transform an unjust world.

Such constraint and hierarchy are reproduced by classrooms in which we sit in rows facing the teacher, and in which lively movement and conversation are restricted by architecture. Deep relationship with place and non-human nature is precluded by sitting uncomfortably in stuffy, airless, artificially-lit rooms.

All politics requires us to be in relation with others, human and perhaps also non-human. Robert Macfarlane (2019) recently described protesters against tree felling in Sheffield as working in alliance with their trees, who became 'newly apprised as neighbours and co-citizens', changing our very idea of who may be a legitimate political protagonist. Transformation of the kind required for our planet and our non-human co-inhabitants to thrive will only take place through collective, embodied joint action. Hope is therefore a *political* emotion and one that requires us to get outside some of the walls that constrain us and be in relationship with the non-human world that lives outside our buildings. In order to engage in hopeful learning, I therefore took my class outdoors.

The politics of nature class

For context, the class was an undergraduate Level 6 class, designed and taught for the first time in 2022 at UCL in London. There were 38 students in the class in total, of whom 28 were women. The class was diverse, with white students making up just over half the number. There were several students who were originally from London (many of them students of colour), others from other parts of the UK, and a large number of international students. The module was advertised as offering ideas about gender and queer theory: probably not coincidentally, a number of LGBTQ+ students took the class.

Although everyone in the class had voluntarily signed up to study a class on the politics of nature, I was surprised and interested to discover that hardly any of them knew much about non-human nature. I realised this when I asked them to meet me beside 'that silver birch over there' and a look of terror entered many of their eyes! One student later made a podcast about the political catastrophe represented by this kind of 'plant awareness disparity' and her experience of overcoming it (Wowra, 2023). There were no avid bird or wildlife watchers in the class and only a few gardeners, though a good number did already enjoy walking, hiking or wild swimming.

I wanted students to develop their own relationships with the non-human world, and the assessment was therefore a weekly portfolio which asked them to notice the world around them and make links with the week's reading and ideas. We also visited three different gardens together. In October, we went to Chelsea Physic Garden in London on a bright sunny day to learn about Queer Botany with the expert help of Sixto-Juan Zavala. In November, on a cool but dry day, we went to Kew Gardens and spent time in the magnificent, Victorian Palm House to think about the colonial history of gardens with academic historian, Dr Caroline Cornish. Finally, in early December, on a freezing cold day, we visited the UCL Institute of Education (IoE) garden with the help of the garden coordinator, Susan McGrath, who explained how she gardens with volunteers in ways that give non-human nature decision-making power. We had hoped to plant some bulbs that day, but nature had other ideas, so instead we learned how to propagate some baby spider plants, as an act of faith in the future.

I chose gardens rather than other spaces where we might find non-human nature for mainly practical reasons. Most obviously, we are based in London and therefore there are some world-renowned gardens, along with their knowledge-able staff, on our doorstep, whereas national parks, rural areas and the coast would be more challenging to get to. All public gardens must also be compliant with disability anti-discrimination legislation, so I was confident that they would be accessible and safe for all students. The history and politics of gardens were also a core element of the syllabus. It is notable, however, that between them students wrote about a huge range of encounters with non-human nature in their portfo-lios, from houseplants and culinary herbs, to coastal hikes, wild swimming, work-ing in agriculture, the abandoned lands of the demilitarised zone on the Korean Peninsula and much more. Therefore the invitation to think outdoors was not restricted to the particular places we visited: just the fact of valuing the outdoors was also generative.

In terms of logistics, I made two separate trips to each garden to keep the groups of a manageable size. For the visits to both external gardens, UCL paid the students' fares and entry, if applicable, out of a departmental budget. However, lots of students made return visits out of their own pockets as and when they could. Within these garden visits, there was a combination of scaffolded free-range small group work, plenary listening and conversation with the external facilitator and me, and opportunities just to sit on a bench with me or each other and talk about the ideas and feelings that had arisen, or wander and have a look round at leisure.

For the other classes over the course of the term, we also visited the UCL Object-Based Learning Lab one week to see how nature has been represented in UCL's incredible art collection. For the remaining six weeks, we sat in a circle in a basement classroom with no natural light but with our thoughts and memories about the outdoors. We chatted in small groups or in plenary about ideas, con-cepts, our reading, our own work and non-human nature. The final assessment was a self-reflective questionnaire and a selection of work from the weekly port-folios. All the students without exception ticked a box to say that I could have their permission to use their work for scholarly articles and book chapters, which has given me access to an excellent source of data to help me understand their learning and particularly how outdoor learning affected it.

Belonging, community and hope

On the basis of all this data, I can confidently say that students loved learning outdoors. Almost all the portfolios included pictures of our trips to gardens, dis-cussions of how much they enjoyed it and a deep engagement with their learning.

Examples of their engagement included anti-racist politics as they wrote letters to the Director of Kew Gardens with suggestions for how to decolonise and arguments about why they should, or passionate newspaper articles in defence of the rights of Gypsy, Roma and Traveller communities, or reflexive writing challenging their own ableist assumptions about access to the countryside (having read Antonelli (2020), Kabachnik (2014) and Kafer (2013)). However, I want to focus on two aspects of their hopeful engagement here. First, I will highlight the enhanced sense of belonging, and related political efficacy, that the module produced. Second, I will look briefly in a bit more detail at an example of a student's work which provided a hopeful prefigurative politics that was made possible by the module and demonstrated how its themes played out in his life.

The experience of being together outdoors, including walking to and from public transport, was qualitatively different from being in a classroom. There is something about movement that promotes different forms of sociability, including the ability to strike up a conversation with someone new and to talk about the module materials in ways that linked deeply with their immediate surroundings, as well as lightening the mood and creating opportunities for joyful interactions that proved to be bonding. I asked on the module questionnaire whether students had made friends in the class and everyone said either that they had, or at least that they had significantly deepened their friendship with someone. Stories of extracurricular late-night conversations about nature, trips together outdoors or to art galleries and even an open invitation to a module tea party in a student's home abounded. One student, who mentioned that she was commuting to university from her family's home in London, wrote:

> it has been tough to make friendships on other modules which goes back to things like […] all the seats facing forwards towards the professor. […] The field trips added a touch of fun […] that sparks friendship and comradery.

Intriguingly, the module also enabled students to develop deeper relationships with others outside the class. A lot of the students wrote about getting closer to older relatives through discussions about gardening, or family histories related to the land, with one student's mother texting her every week just after our class to ask when she would get home so she could discuss the new ideas with her. Students also described educating their friends about key issues around nature conservation, getting on partners' nerves because they wouldn't stop talking about the problems with industrial agriculture, drawing on their learning from our class in their other modules or assessments, and volunteering to take part in nature conversation or gardening projects. This may all sound rather small in comparison with the scale of crisis, but it is nevertheless necessary. Working together for a common goal and building fellow feeling and community, love, joy and solidarity, as well as persuading others through enthusiasm and passion, rather than tendentious argument, is a starting point for any political action.

This is demonstrated rather nicely in the second little vignette from my students' work. One student was of Greek Cypriot descent and he wrote a policy memo to propose:

> a practical, education programme with the aim of unifying Cyprus's younger generations [...] bringing together Greek and Turkish Cypriot youth to learn about nature [...] The programme seeks to form an emotional connection between the attendees and nature. [The programme will promote] a co-operative future that prioritises social unity and environmental protection.

The proposal went on to suggest various outdoor activities that young people of various ages could do together, and argued that a love of a shared landscape, and the joy of being outdoors and working together would promote both reconciliation among people on opposing sides of a conflict and also between people and the non-human world. These two aspects of peace-making and reconciliation were understood as inseparable and deeply intertwined: if the non-human world is understood as a series of resources, then conflicts between humans will continue, whereas if they can make peace with non-human neighbours, then the difficult work of living regeneratively will, *hopefully*, unite humans and non-humans alike into a complex ecosystem of mutual respect.

What I found particularly important and moving about this student's work was that at no point had I talked about or recommended readings on conservation work in the context of conflict or peacebuilding. He had extrapolated from our own experiences of building community in a context of difference, but not conflict, and his embodied sense of what that might do beyond our class, to imagine how learning outdoors might change the world. This is a prefigurative politics of hope that emerges from a class experience but grows beyond it – organically, resiliently and regeneratively – to allow us to imagine a different, more peaceful, more hopeful politics even in seemingly intractable conflict situations.

Conclusion: Pedagogies of hope

In class, we learned about the colonial histories of gardening and conservation, and the ways in which sterile, regimented environments have been created by attempts to micro-manage nature (Mastnak et al., 2014). In contrast, more recent thinking about gardening focuses on enabling the natural world to thrive in partnership with humans. It is astonishing how quickly nature can bounce back from the harms visited upon it by humans, if only we let it be and give it a chance (Tree, 2019). This means relinquishing strict plans from which we refuse to deviate and instead *trusting the process* and allowing nature to take charge, with uncertain consequences. Many students agreed that seeing this sort of regenerative process in action in the IoE garden was exciting and inspirational, leading to more joyful and beautiful outcomes than a minutely-planned garden, and including all sorts of visiting wildlife, such as kestrels and bats, in the centre of London.

This brings us back to the class reading by Jonathan Lear. Borrowing the concept of 'radical hope' from the Crow Nation, who had witnessed the end of their world, he suggests that we need to hold faith with a 'future goodness' that is currently unimaginable because we *cannot* know what it might look like from within the constraints of where we are. Hope, when everything we used to know no longer works, requires us to focus on 'a granular appreciation of the ways in which people navigate and negotiate crises' (Roy, 2023), when the tools to do so need to be made and remade in the process and the endpoint is uncertain.

I suggest, therefore, that a pedagogy of hope cannot have learning objectives, assessment criteria and lesson plans that are too rigid. Instead we need to *trust the process* of being and working together, with the largest possible biodiversity of humans and non-humans. The Knepp wilding project explains that wild gardening is about 'giving nature more space to evolve, intervening judiciously, always looking for great complexity but trying not to dictate outcomes' (Knepp, nd). These are wise words for any educator: I had not expected my students to engage with outdoor learning in all the myriad ways that they did. I was surprised to find that belonging and community were such powerful themes in our learning together. I don't think the work we did would have happened if I hadn't been there to plant ideas, nurture, scaffold and encourage. But the hopeful community that grew in the marvellous and mysterious ecosystem of the module, including some of the examples described above, was beyond what I could have imagined. As my British Cypriot student intuited, there is just something about being together outdoors that creates something new: a political community that is bigger than the sum of the parts.

My student who proposed the concept of 'slow hope' included some photographs she had taken over the term that she said made her feel hopeful. The two that struck me most were both of humans working to provide water to wildlife in a garden: the coils of a hosepipe over the wild beds at the IoE and a pond at the Chelsea Physic Garden. As every gardener knows, providing water, making a bog or pond, is the thing that can make a hopeful ecosystem out of even the tiniest garden. Similarly, I want to end by suggesting that being outdoors can be the thing that makes a hopeful ecosystem out of a 15 credit module.

Note

1 I am grateful to Roxani Krystalli, Penny Welch, the participants of a Political Studies Association webinar on 20 July 2023 and the editors of this volume for their encouragement and comments on this chapter. I am also particularly grateful to my students for the joyful time we had together in gardens and for their permission to use their words here. Thank you also to everyone who helped us create the garden classes and to my Director of Education, Tim Hicks, for finding a budget for 'the most expensive module in the department'!

References

Antonelli, A. (2020). Director of Science at Kew: It's time to decolonise botanical collections. *The Conversation*, 19 June2020: https://theconversation.com/director-of-science-at-kew-its-time-to-decolonise-botanical-collections-141070.

Appadurai, A. (2007). Hope and democracy. *Public Culture*, 19 (1): 29–34.

Boler, M. (1999). *Feeling power: Emotions and education*. Routledge.

Carless, D. (2015). *Excellence in university assessment: Learning from award-winning teaching*. Routledge.

Dickinson, J. (2023). Can students be bothered to come to campus? *Wonkhe*, 24 March2023: https://wonkhe.com/blogs/can-students-be-bothered-to-come-to-campus/.

Freeman, T. M., Anderman L., and Jensen J. (2007). Sense of belonging in college freshmen at the classroom and campus levels. *The Journal of Experimental Education*, 75 (3): 203–220.

Freire, P. (1998). *Pedagogy of freedom: Ethics, democracy and civic courage*. Rowman and Littlefield.

Freire, P. (2021). *Pedagogy of hope: Reliving pedagogy of the oppressed*. Bloomsbury Publishing.

Gieryn, T. F. (2000). A space for place in sociology. *Annual Review of Sociology*, 26 (2000): 463–496.

Giroux, H. (1997). *Pedagogy and the politics of hope: Theory, culture and schooling: A critical reader*. Westview Press.

hooks, b. (1994). *Teaching to transgress: Education as a practice of freedom*. Routledge.

hooks, b. (2004). *Teaching community: A pedagogy of hope*. Routledge.

Jacques, D. and Salmon G. (2007). *Learning in groups: A handbook for face-to-face and online environments*. Ebook. 4th ed. Routledge.

Kabachnik, P. (2014). 'Where can we put our homes?' Gypsies and Travelers in the English green belt. *Journal of Cultural Geography*, 31 (3): 280–303.

Kafer, A. (2013). Bodies of Nature: The Environmental Politics of Disability. In A. Kafer, *Feminist, queer, crip* (pp. 129–148). Indiana University Press.

Knepp (nd). Walled Garden [online]: https://knepp.co.uk/knepp-estate/gardens/rewild-a-garden/. Accessed 10 July 2023.

Lear, J. (2008). *Radical hope: Ethics in the face of cultural devastation*. Harvard University Press.

Macfarlane, R. (2019). Should this tree have the same rights as you? *The Guardian*2 November2019: https://www.theguardian.com/books/2019/nov/02/trees-have-rights-too-robert-macfarlane-on-the-new-laws-of-nature.

MacKay, J. R. D., Hughes, K., Marzetti, H., Lent, N. and Rhind, S. (2019). Using National Student Survey (NSS) qualitative data and social identity theory to explore students' experiences of assessment and feedback . *Higher Education Pedagogies*, 4 (1): 315–330.

Mastnak, T., Elyachar, J. and Boellstorff, T. (2014). Botanical decolonisation: Rethinking native plants. *Environment and Planning D: Society and Space*, 32 (2): 363–380.

Nixon, R. (2011). *Slow violence and the environmentalism of the poor*. Harvard University Press.

Roy, I. (2023). *Ordering hope: Reimagining the future of citizenship, IGDC Working Papers & Briefings - Working Paper No. 3*, Interdisciplinary Global Development Centre, University of York.

Siperstein, S., Hall, S. and LeMenager S. (2017). *Teaching climate change in the humanities.* Routledge.

Solnit, R. (2010). *Hope in the dark: The untold history of people power.* Canongate Books.

Solnit, R. (2016). 'Hope is an embrace of the unknown': Rebecca Solnit on living in dark times. *The Guardian,* 15 July2016: https://www.theguardian.com/books/2016/jul/15/rebecca-solnit-hope-in-the-dark-new-essay-embrace-unknown.

Tree , I. (2019). *Wilding.* Pan Macmillan.

Van Heertum, R. (2006). Marcuse, Bloch and Freire: Reinvigorating a pedagogy of hope. *Policy Futures in Education,* 4 (1): 45–51.

Wowra, L. (2023). Overcoming the Green Blur [Podcast]: https://on.soundcloud.com/i42XD.

Chapter 7

Enhancing learning outside the classroom with social media

Liam Taylor, Julie Peacock and Karen Bacon

Using social media-based activities to enhance undergraduate fieldwork has been a tried-and-tested pedagogical approach since the advent of such platforms (Chawinga, 2017; Clark et al., 2021; Evans, 2014). With social media, students can readily collect geotagged information to complement field diaries (Welsh et al., 2012), are more engaged in fieldwork (Davies et al., 2019), and improve their employability skills as they gain professional online presences (Peacock and Bacon, 2018). Indeed, in the social sciences, the blurred boundary of the 'field' in fieldwork allows for these platforms to become useful tools for data collection (Airoldi, 2018). Outdoor learning as a practice, and organisations which offer such experiences, can also benefit from the advertisement of this connection to nature (Bolliger et al., 2021), though the strength of this *connection* has been questioned when a smartphone is the lens through which nature is viewed (Leather and Gibson, 2019).

At first glance, the use of social media to enhance outdoor learning experiences may appear oxymoronic (Smith et al., 2016) and there are numerous debates in the academic literature about the pros and cons of such an approach (summarised by Hills and Thomas (2020)). However, as smartphones become increasingly important in conducting academic field research (e.g. Lee et al. 2018; Luetzenburg et al., 2021; Tavani et al., 2022) and social media becomes increasingly important as a tool for academic interaction and networking (Lacassin et al., 2020; Luc et al., 2021; Veletsianos, 2012), we believe that it is important to expose students to these tools during their undergraduate degrees in order to create resilient and well-prepared graduates. There is a consensus that this should not necessarily be in the form of assessment (Stathopoulou et al., 2019), but through reimagining 'traditional' outdoor learning and fieldwork pedagogies to take advantage of these tools.

While there are many examples of individual cases of using social media to enhance pedagogy (Tang and Hew, 2017), detailed long-term reflections on the potential of using social media to enhance outdoor learning are largely absent from the literature. Given the rapidly changing nature of social media, many academic reflections may represent only a snapshot in time of a particular platform that has limited wider temporal applicability. In this chapter, we reflect on our use

DOI: 10.4324/9781003436928-10

of social media in fieldwork learning over seven years and in institutions in both the UK and Ireland to offer our recommendations to educators looking to conduct similar activities. Our reflections are primarily based upon activities that have taken place in biology and geography undergraduate degrees on Twitter (now rebranded as 'X'), but we also discuss the wider directions in which the intersections between social media and pedagogy, and the tools available to educators, are heading from the mid-2020s.

The pedagogic benefits of social media

Learning outside of the classroom is often conducted for many of the same pedagogic reasons as using technology to enhance learning experiences – to improve learner engagement, provide professional expertise, and to deliver authentic and relevant experiences (Thomas and Munge, 2017). When using social media as part of a learning activity, students tend to agree with this assessment, noting in particular that social media platforms enhance critical self-awareness and personal literacy in outdoor learning (France et al., 2016). Furthermore, outdoor learning activities that are conducted on social media platforms improve collaboration, teamwork and cohort cohesion (Welsh et al., 2015) – a particular issue for undergraduate cohorts which can be hundreds of students. Social media also offers direct, real-time access between students and staff, breaking typical barriers to engagement by meeting students in a space and format with which they can be (but not always) more comfortable. This must be carefully performed in order to maintain professional standards in the online space (Purvis et al., 2020) but, by engaging with students through academic activities, we see an opportunity to role-model responsible online behaviour to large cohorts.

Digital profiles allow students to showcase their skills, experiences and achievements to potential employers and colleagues in a convenient and easily accessible manner. In addition, students can demonstrate their digital literacy, proficiency with technology, breadth of interest, and build their professional networks. To some, this professional online identity has been noted as a 'personal brand' (Johnson, 2017), which can yield lucrative opportunities in some instances. Where students have created digital profiles as part of academic work, the value of continuing to develop these profiles after the activity is realised – e.g. 87% of STEM students continued using LinkedIn two years after an activity run by Lexis et al. (2023). There remains, however, a dearth of literature examining the long-term outcomes of students who have participated in social media-based activities that are not based on LinkedIn – a platform built to curate professional identities. In addition to curating an identity for themselves, social media has a role in aiding students (and academics) in finding collaborations, opportunities and new networks. Students who are adept at using these platforms will have a potential professional advantage, leveraging social media to aid in career progression, which highlights their ability to look beyond resources and guidance provided by lecturers to prospective employers (Sutherland et al., 2020).

Social media in outdoor learning: #GEOG1000

At the University of Leeds, we have used Twitter from 2016 to 2023 to conduct campus-based field-trips for first-year Geography undergraduates to teach concepts around biodiversity and urban ecology. Following a short introduction, students use Twitter to post pictures of urban ecology around the University campus and offer commentary on the ecosystem services that they provide. A handout accompanies a set of learning criteria that offers question prompts for students to respond to. Students are encouraged to 'like' good examples and reply to create threads of discussion. Using the hashtag #GEOG1000 (also run as #GEOG1000Eco and #GEOG1045) allows discussion to take place in a quasi-private sphere within the platform and all tweets are returned to a single, browsable channel. This format runs similarly to Middleton and Spiers' (2019) concept of a 'Twalk' (Twitter walk), but with only one point of direction from the educator and more autonomy and co-creation of online space from student participants.

Throughout the 90-minute fieldwork session, most students are able to become more familiar with biodiversity on our campus. Our key learning objectives for students were to:

1   Understand the role that ecology plays in creating sustainable urban systems;
2   Explore ways in which the University of Leeds campus could become more biodiverse;
3   Create a professional online social media presence to begin your University career.

Responding to students in real-time allows the educator to stretch highly-engaged students with follow-up questions, while also supporting students who have mis-understood key concepts, echoing the experiences of Davies et al. (2019). We have also used this activity to teach concepts around campus air quality, but this resulted in noticeably lower attendance, likely due to it being timetabled towards the end of term when assessments began to run.

The benefits of such an activity are significant, particularly considering staff time and logistics. Unlike many other forms of fieldwork, preparation required by staff is minimal as students direct the fieldwork through community-based learning. Indeed, this activity has been successfully run with 250+ undergraduate students with just one member of staff for a number of years replying to tweets to encourage discussion (Figure 7.1) and selecting highlight examples to showcase in a follow-up lecture sequence (Figure 7.2). However, while only one member of staff is necessary to directly co-ordinate the activity, staff from across the University regularly join in to engage with students in this novel format. This, in turn, benefits students further by seeing positive examples of professional social media accounts use and has been found to improve student–staff collegiality (Chawinga, 2017). Students who could not participate in the activity, or who did not wish to create a Twitter account for personal reasons, could email the educator their reflections and these were shared on the educator's Twitter profile. A minority (~5%) of students engaged in this way.

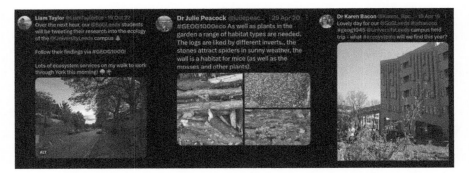

Figure 7.1 Example tweets from instructors leading this activity and engaging with students to create discussion topics.

Liam Taylor: Over the next hour, our #SoGLeeds students will be tweeting their research into the ecology of the #UniversityLeeds campus. Follow their findings via #GEOG1000! Lots of ecosystem services on my walk to work through York this morning!

Dr Julie Peacock: #GEOG1000eco As well as plants in the garden a range of habitat types are needed. The logs are liked by different inverts, the stones attract spiders in sunny weather, the wall is a habitat for mice (as well as the mosses and other plants).

Dr Karen Bacon: Lovely day for our #SoGLeeds #urbaneco #geog1045 #UniversityLeeds campus field trip - what #ecosystems will we find this year?

During the COVID-19 pandemic, fieldwork was considerably impacted, particularly early on (Bacon and Peacock, 2021), but the utility of this activity meant that it could be easily modified to allow students to showcase a more diverse range of urban ecologies in and around their homes and not to lose out on learning during lockdowns. Even students isolating at home could engage with the session with many choosing to talk about ecology in the home, from houseplants to spiders. In subsequent years, operating a hybrid approach (whereby some students completed the activity on-campus and some chose to stay-at-home) enhanced the accessibility of this activity by ensuring that all students could engage in real-time with their peers regardless of location. This provides an alternative approach to the 'virtual vs physical' fieldwork debate (Larsen et al., 2021), whereby all students can continue to engage with physical environments as traditional, but with the learning outcomes fulfilled virtually. Through the activity, students become more engaged with the employability benefits of a professional social media presence (discussed further in Peacock and Bacon, 2018) as well as enhancing their ecological skills and understanding.

Anecdotally, many of our students created Twitter profiles for this activity and maintained them to discuss academic work in the months following. While this activity has successfully engaged students for seven years, the challenges of working on a public social media platform only became evident in 2022/23. In this isolated instance, the hashtag became hijacked by external parties who posted highly inappropriate material that was a clear breach of University social media

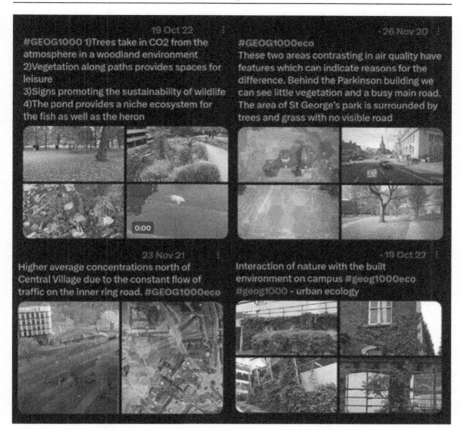

Figure 7.2 Anonymised tweets from students engaging with both the ecosystem services and air quality activities. Numbers in the top left tweet refer to prompt questions which students were encouraged to consider as they walked.

#GEOG1000 1) Trees take in CO2 from the atmosphere in a woodland environment. 2) Vegetation along paths provides spaces for leisure. 3) Signs promoting the sustainability of wildlife. 4) The pond provides a nice ecosystem for the fish as well as the heron.

#GEOG1000eco These two areas contrasting in air quality have features which can indicate reasons for the difference. Behind the Parkinson building we can see little vegetation and a busy main road. The area of St George's park is surrounded by trees and grass with no visible road. Higher average concentrations north of Central Village due to the constant flow of traffic on the inner ring road. #GEOG1000eco

Interaction of nature with the built environment on campus #geog1000co #geog1000 - urban ecology.

policies (which were themselves not necessarily fit for purpose for this activity). As a result, our students browsing the hashtag likely saw inappropriate and offensive material. The tweets were removed within an hour of the activity through Twitter's reporting function but, by this point, the activity had ended.

Overcoming the challenges of using social media in learning

The activity was trialled in 2019 in the University of Galway as an on-campus field session. Students were highly reluctant to engage with Twitter and declined the activity. The instructor offered it but did not insist on participation. Students stated that it was 'too embarrassing' to tweet about university work or plants and were clearly uncomfortable at the suggestion of the activity, so it was not pursued. Several also said that they were not on Twitter. Students being embarrassed by using social media for university work was not something that had come up in Leeds and had not been something that the instructors had considered. The University of Galway group was much smaller however (less than 15 students), and given that the number of participants in the University of Leeds sessions were not high despite larger class sizes (where approximately one-third of students posted on Twitter, though many chose to work in groups and post together), it is therefore understandable that the activity was unsuccessful with the much smaller group.

In the case study of #GEOG1000, when challenges regarding inappropriate activity occur, a large impact is felt by the lead educator who has a duty of care to keep their students safe. University social media policies at the time were limited to responsible use of personal social media accounts, with no discussion of keeping students safe in online activities. At the time of writing, we have not run #GEOG1000 in its previous format through Twitter as we cannot be confident that students will remain safe during this activity, particularly given changes to Twitter/X as a platform in 2023. In the 2023/24 academic year, this activity will take place on Instagram, using a dedicated account (@GEOG1000) to share Instagram stories that the account is tagged in. The account will then repost these stories for the cohort to see, thereby meaning that the same learning objectives will be fulfilled while the lead educator remains in control of what is shared to the cohort. Students can like and comment on highlighted posts (Figure 7.3) that are shared to the main feed by the lead educator to engage with the objectives, while also viewing all of the students' work via the account's story. The move from Twitter to Instagram is primarily due to the lack of available tools to assist educators in curating lists (Twitter Moments is only available for 'professional content creators'), but also moves the activity to a social media platform that students are vastly more likely to be already using (91% of UK 16–24 year olds use Instagram regularly, compared to 48% who use Twitter; Ofcom (2023)).

One challenge that we did not have to address while working on university campuses was data availability. The university campus has much to recommend it for local fieldwork (Bacon and Peacock, 2016) and this includes usually having Wi-Fi in all areas for social media-based activities. However, this may not be the case in more remote locations (Welsh and France, 2012), should this activity be run in a hybrid capacity in, for example, an alternate, off-

Figure 7.3 The permanent feed of the Instagram account allows students to engage with posts that directly ask questions related to the learning objectives, if they do not wish to create their own stories as part of the activity.
GEOG1000 - Planet Under Threat. Understanding the climate and biodiversity crisis on our 'Planet under Threat' module in the School of Geography, University of Leeds.
geog1000 This Weeping White Willow in St George's Cemetery sequesters around 47 kg of carbon each year! Which other species are significant contributors to the overall 18 tonnes of carbon that are sequestered each year on campus?

campus location. With over 96% of UK adults aged 16–24 owning a smartphone (Hiley, 2023), and students working in groups, access to devices was also not a challenge that we needed to overcome. Students are also willing to use their own devices for academic activities, though the ability for older devices to engage with the activity can create some student anxiety (Clark et al., 2021).

Future directions in this space

With the regularly changing nature of social media platforms, the quality of results from the activity will vary between platforms. The newfound focus on free speech by the new management of Twitter/X can affect safeguarding of participants within the platform (Scharlach et al., 2023) and academics have been rapidly leaving the platform in favour of competitors or leaving social media altogether (Vidal Valero, 2023). With changes on the visibility of posts from users who do not pay a subscription fee, the benefits of Twitter as a platform to build an audience to network with are rapidly diminishing.

Mastodon, which occupies a similar niche through bite-sized content creation, experienced significant academic interest as Twitter declined, but has its own problems with hate speech and lack of moderation such that it too is not a straightforward 'replacement' of Twitter for pedagogic activities (Braun, 2023). Our upcoming move to Instagram represents a turn into unchartered territory as there are few case studies of using Instagram in a higher education context (Manca, 2020), but we believe that this represents an area of growing academic interest. Indeed, given the creation of Threads to rival Twitter's text-based content and Reels to rival TikTok's short-form videos, this offers a more diverse range of opportunities for students to engage, thereby increasing the likelihood of students contributing (Neier and Zayer, 2015).

It is also notable that different platforms mean different things to students. To some, Twitter is a space for professionalism and to broaden their network, akin to LinkedIn. For others, the same platform offers a unique anonymity to engage with niche circles (Peddinti et al., 2014). This perception is different at different times too. At its release, Instagram was an informal platform for sharing photos and daily snapshots of life through its 'Stories' function. Now, it is not uncommon to see academics or research projects with their own Instagram pages (Carpenter et al., 2020), and some educators use this platform to conduct learning activities (Davies et al., 2019). TikTok also has a distinctly academic subsection and there may be significant pedagogical benefits to this platform (Escamilla-Fajardo et al., 2021), however there are also some more toxic spheres (as well as easy-to-access harmless, but nevertheless distracting, content) which need to be considered by those using it as a tool for education.

While the #GEOG1000 activity was generally, if not universally, well-received by Leeds students, some aspects of using social media platforms can generate negative experiences. However, other platforms are being considered for use in outdoor learning and we would hope to incorporate Twitter and other social media platforms in future outdoor learning sessions in a revised format. Students find these highly engaging and we consider them to be a good means of facilitating learning through fun and use of platforms that many students are already engaged with.

Conclusions

Seven years on from our first venture into using social media to enhance outdoor learning, we have refined an exciting and valuable activity which uniquely delivers many pedagogical benefits for first-year students. In synergy with other studies, we find that our students gain a greater sense of professionalism, collaboration and digital literacy by using social media to complement their fieldwork. We also break down traditional concepts of fieldwork – being in the same place at the same time – as students can achieve the same learning objectives from wherever they are joining while also collaborating with their peers in real-time. Academic staff also gain from this activity, by developing closer partnerships with students, and by gaining more time back as a result of the efficiencies that social media brings. Different cohorts bring unique challenges, but we urge perseverance when using social media to find solutions to the barriers that can unexpectedly arise. While we have run this activity exclusively on Twitter, we believe that there are now other platforms (such as Instagram) that should be explored in order to make these challenges easier for the educator to overcome.

References

Airoldi, M. (2018). Ethnography and the digital fields of social media. *International Journal of Social Research Methodology*, 21(6), 661–673. https://doi.org/10.1080/13645579.2018.1465622.

Bacon, K. L., & Peacock, J. (2016). Making the most of the University campus for teaching ecology. *New Directions in the Teaching of Natural Sciences*, 11, Article 11. https://doi.org/10.29311/ndtps.v0i11.585.

Bacon, K. L., & Peacock, J. (2021). Sudden challenges in teaching ecology and aligned disciplines during a global pandemic: Reflections on the rapid move online and perspectives on moving forward. *Ecology and Evolution*, 11(8), 3551–3558. https://doi.org/10.1002/ece3.7090.

Bolliger, D. U., McCoy, D., Kilty, T., & Shepherd, C. E. (2021). Smartphone use in outdoor education: A question of activity progression and place. *Journal of Adventure Education and Outdoor Learning*, 21(1), 53–66. https://doi.org/10.1080/14729679.2020.1730204.

Braun, J. (2023). Journalism, media research, and Mastodon: Notes on the future. *Digital Journalism*, 1–8. https://doi.org/10.1080/21670811.2023.2208619.

Carpenter, J. P., Morrison, S. A., Craft, M., & Lee, M. (2020). How and why are educators using Instagram? *Teaching and Teacher Education*, 96, 103149. https://doi.org/10.1016/j.tate.2020.103149.

Chawinga, W. D. (2017). Taking social media to a university classroom: Teaching and learning using Twitter and blogs. *International Journal of Educational Technology in Higher Education*, 14(1), 3. https://doi.org/10.1186/s41239-017-0041-6.

Clark, K. A., Welsh, K. E., Mauchline, A. L., France, D., Whalley, W. B., & Park, J. (2021). Do educators realise the value of Bring Your Own Device (BYOD) in fieldwork learning? *Journal of Geography in Higher Education*, 45(2), 255–278. https://doi.org/10.1080/03098265.2020.1808880.

Davies, T., Lorne, C., & Sealey-Huggins, L. (2019). Instagram photography and the geography field course: Snapshots from Berlin. *Journal of Geography in Higher Education*, 43(3), 362–383. https://doi.org/10.1080/03098265.2019.1608428.

Escamilla-Fajardo, P., Alguacil, M., & López-Carril, S. (2021). Incorporating TikTok in higher education: Pedagogical perspectives from a corporal expression sport sciences course. *Journal of Hospitality, Leisure, Sport & Tourism Education*, 28, 100302. https://doi.org/10.1016/j.jhlste.2021.100302.

Evans, C. (2014). Twitter for teaching: Can social media be used to enhance the process of learning? *British Journal of Educational Technology*, 45(5), 902–915. https://doi.org/10.1111/bjet.12099.

France, D., Powell, V., Mauchline, A. L., Welsh, K., Park, J., Whalley, W. B., & Rewhorn, S. (2016). Ability of students to recognize the relationship between using mobile apps for learning during fieldwork and the development of graduate attributes. *Journal of Geography in Higher Education*, 40(2), 182–192. https://doi.org/10.1080/03098265.2016.1154931.

Hiley, C. (2023). *UK mobile phone statistics 2023—Mobiles facts and stats report*. Uswitch. https://www.uswitch.com/mobiles/studies/mobile-statistics/.

Hills, D., & Thomas, G. (2020). Digital technology and outdoor experiential learning. *Journal of Adventure Education and Outdoor Learning*, 20(2), 155–169. https://doi.org/10.1080/14729679.2019.1604244.

Johnson, K. (2017). The importance of personal branding in social media: Educating students to create and manage their personal brand. *International Journal of Education and Social Science*, 4(1), 21–27.

Lacassin, R., Devès, M., Hicks, S. P., Ampuero, J.-P., Bossu, R., Bruhat, L., Daryono, Wibisono, D. F., Fallou, L., Fielding, E. J., Gabriel, A.-A., Gurney, J., Krippner, J., Lomax, A., Sudibyo, M. M., Pamumpuni, A., Patton, J. R., Robinson, H., Tingay, M., & Valkaniotis, S. (2020). Rapid collaborative knowledge building via Twitter after significant geohazard events. *Geoscience Communication*, 3(1), 129–146. https://doi.org/10.5194/gc-3-129-2020.

Larsen, T., Tabor, L., & Smith, P. (2021). End of the field? Hacking online and hybrid environments for field-based learning in geography education. *Journal of Geography*, 120(1), 3–11. https://doi.org/10.1080/00221341.2020.1858325.

Leather, M., & Gibson, K. (2019). The consumption and hyperreality of nature: Greater affordances for outdoor learning. *Curriculum Perspectives*, 39(1), 79–83. https://doi.org/10.1007/s41297-019-00063-7.

Lee, S., Suh, J., & Choi, Y. (2018). Review of smartphone applications for geoscience: Current status, limitations, and future perspectives. *Earth Science Informatics*, 11(4), 463–486. https://doi.org/10.1007/s12145-018-0343-9.

Lexis, L., Weaver, D., & Julien, B. (2023). STEM students see the value of LinkedIn as a career development tool and continue to use it in the long-term post-assignment. *Journal of Teaching and Learning for Graduate Employability*, 14(1), Article 1. https://doi.org/10.21153/jtlge2023vol14no1art1510.

Luc, J. G. Y., Archer, M. A., Arora, R. C., Bender, E. M., Blitz, A., Cooke, D. T., Hlci, T. N., Kidane, B., Ouzounian, M., Varghese, T. K., & Antonoff, M. B. (2021). Does tweeting improve citations? One-year results from the TSSMN prospective randomized trial. *The Annals of Thoracic Surgery*, 111(1), 296–300. https://doi.org/10.1016/j.athoracsur.2020.04.065.

Luetzenburg, G., Kroon, A., & Bjørk, A. A. (2021). Evaluation of the Apple iPhone 12 Pro LiDAR for an application in geosciences. *Scientific Reports*, 11(1), Article 1. https://doi.org/10.1038/s41598-021-01763-9.

Manca, S. (2020). Snapping, pinning, liking or texting: Investigating social media in higher education beyond Facebook. *The Internet and Higher Education*, 44, 100707. https://doi.org/10.1016/j.iheduc.2019.100707.

Middleton, A., & Spiers, A. (2019). Learning to Twalk: An analysis of a new learning environment. In C. Rowell (Ed.), *Social media in higher education* (1st ed., pp. 223–236). Open Book Publishers. https://doi.org/10.11647/OBP.0162.20.

Neier, S., & Zayer, L. T. (2015). Students' perceptions and experiences of social media in higher education. *Journal of Marketing Education*, 37(3), 133–143. https://doi.org/10.1177/0273475315583748.

Ofcom. (2023). *Adults' media use and attitudes report 2023.* Ofcom. https://www.ofcom.org.uk/research-and-data/media-literacy-research/adults/adults-media-use-and-attitudes.

Peacock, J., & Bacon, K. L. (2018). Enhancing student employability through urban ecology fieldwork. *Higher Education Pedagogies*, 3(1), 440–450. https://doi.org/10.1080/23752696.2018.1462097.

Peddinti, S. T., Ross, K. W., & Cappos, J. (2014). 'On the internet, nobody knows you're a dog': A Twitter case study of anonymity in social networks. In *Proceedings of the Second ACM Conference on Online Social Networks* (pp. 83–94). https://doi.org/10.1145/2660460.2660467.

Purvis, A. J., Rodger, H. M., & Beckingham, S. (2020). Experiences and perspectives of social media in learning and teaching in higher education. *International Journal of Educational Research Open*, 1, 100018. https://doi.org/10.1016/j.ijedro.2020.100018.

Scharlach, R., Hallinan, B., & Shifman, L. (2023). Governing principles: Articulating values in social media platform policies. *New Media & Society*, 1–20. https://doi.org/10.1177/14614448231156580.

Smith, H. A., Dyment, J. E., Hill, A., & Downing, J. (2016). 'You want us to teach outdoor education where?' Reflections on teaching outdoor education online. *Journal of Adventure Education and Outdoor Learning*, 16(4), 303–317. https://doi.org/10.1080/14729679.2016.1147966.

Stathopoulou, A., Siamagka, N.-T., & Christodoulides, G. (2019). A multi-stakeholder view of social media as a supporting tool in higher education: An educator–student perspective. *European Management Journal*, 37(4), 421–431. https://doi.org/10.1016/j.emj.2019.01.008.

Sutherland, K., Freberg, K., Driver, C., & Khattab, U. (2020). Public relations and customer service: Employer perspectives of social media proficiency. *Public Relations Review*, 46(4), 101954. https://doi.org/10.1016/j.pubrev.2020.101954.

Tang, Y., & Hew, K. F. (2017). Using Twitter for education: Beneficial or simply a waste of time? *Computers & Education*, 106, 97–118. https://doi.org/10.1016/j.compedu.2016.12.004.

Tavani, S., Billi, A., Corradetti, A., Mercuri, M., Bosman, A., Cuffaro, M., Seers, T., & Carminati, E. (2022). Smartphone assisted fieldwork: Towards the digital transition of geoscience fieldwork using LiDAR-equipped iPhones. *Earth-Science Reviews*, 227, 103969. https://doi.org/10.1016/j.earscirev.2022.103969.

Thomas, G. J., & Munge, B. (2017). Innovative outdoor fieldwork pedagogies in the higher education sector: Optimising the use of technology. *Journal of Outdoor and Environmental Education*, 20(1), 7–13. https://doi.org/10.1007/BF03400998.

Veletsianos, G. (2012). Higher education scholars' participation and practices on Twitter. *Journal of Computer Assisted Learning*, 28(4), 336–349. https://doi.org/10.1111/j.1365-2729.2011.00449.x.

Vidal Valero, M. (2023). Thousands of scientists are cutting back on Twitter, seeding angst and uncertainty. *Nature*, 620(7974), 482–484. https://doi.org/10.1038/d41586-023-02554-0.

Welsh, K., & France, D. (2012). Smartphones and fieldwork. *Geography*, 97(1), 47–51. https://doi.org/10.1080/00167487.2012.12094337.

Welsh, K. E., France, D., Whalley, W. B., & Park, J. R. (2012). Geotagging photographs in student fieldwork. *Journal of Geography in Higher Education*, 36(3), 469–480. https://doi.org/10.1080/03098265.2011.647307.

Welsh, K. E., Mauchline, A. L., Powell, V., France, D., Park, J. R., & Whalley, W. B. (2015). Student perceptions of iPads as mobile learning devices for fieldwork. *Journal of Geography in Higher Education*, 39(3), 450–469. https://doi.org/10.1080/03098265.2015.1066315.

Chapter 8

Moving away from the desk

An introduction to Physically Active Learning (PAL)

Jamie Heywood

This chapter aims to provide an introduction into the background and context, including current theory, practice, and research, of Physically Active Learning (PAL) within higher education. Contemporary issues, themes, research, and areas will be explored, through three distinct sections, outlining the current landscape, synergies, and challenges. When possible, research which is specific to a higher education context has been prioritised, but it is acknowledged and recognised that research from a range of educational contexts can support the chapter, identifying connections, relationships, and areas for future considerations. The three distinct sections of this chapter focus on the *what*, the *how*, and the *why*, to provide a comprehensive picture of Physically Active Learning.

- Section 1: Desk-based and physically inactive higher education. This section focuses on physical inactivity and sedentary behaviour within higher education. This includes the extent of, and the effects of, physical inactivity and sedentary behaviour on learning and health outcomes.
- Section 2: Learning away from the desk: Physically Active Learning (PAL) pedagogies. This section focuses on introducing PAL pedagogies. These include methods which provide opportunities for learning whilst active and moving, such as walking, with consideration given to potential advantages and challenges of incorporation, and how individuals and institutions could be supported to introduce PAL.
- Section 3: Moving, learning and thriving: The impact of Physically Active Learning (PAL). This section focuses on the potential impact of introducing PAL principles and methods within higher education teaching practices and the wider curriculum, with a particular focus on the impact of learning, and the impact of wellbeing.

Section 1: Desk-based and physically inactive higher education

The wider context of physical inactivity and sedentary behaviour

The prevalence of physical inactivity is an increasing cause of concern amongst the UK population (Vitality, 2021), and is a considerable burden to the NHS (Heron

DOI: 10.4324/9781003436928-11

et al., 2019). Physical inactivity prevalence within the UK has also been shown to be higher compared to the global average, with 35.9% of adults being physically inactive, and has been increasing in high-income countries (Guthold et al., 2018). Suggested causes for this increase are multifactorial and include both political and social drivers, such as limited available space for physical activity, increased use of screens, including watching television and using a computer, and increased time spent sitting (also referred to as 'sedentary behaviour') within occupational contexts, including more office-based roles, and increased reliance of screen-use (Salman et al., 2019; Park et al., 2020). Sedentary behaviour within occupational settings is seen as an increasing concern due to these factors, with 77% of adults being inactive within their workspace (Mulchandani et al., 2019).

Physical inactivity has been linked to increasing risk of health conditions such as physical health issues including heart disease, stroke, types of cancer, diabetes, and being overweight, but also mental health issues such as increased risk of depression and anxiety, alongside higher stress levels (NHS, 2023a; NHS, 2023b; Silva et al., 2020). Sitting has been deemed the "smoking of our generation" due to these negative outcomes (Merchant, 2013).

NHS guidelines state that adults should do some type of physical activity each day, with specific recommendations around reducing the amount of time spent sitting and breaking up periods of inactivity (NHS, 2023a; NHS, 2023b). Physical activity has shown to have a plethora of benefits, including physical, mental, social, learning, environmental, and economical, leading a Public Health England report (2020) to state: "If physical activity were a drug, we would refer to it as a miracle cure, due to the great many illnesses it can prevent and help treat." Physical benefits included reducing the risk of long-term conditions, and maintaining a healthy weight, whilst mental benefits included self-esteem being enhanced, and happiness and enjoyment being found from engaging in physical activity. Improved learning, attainment, productivity, social interaction, and social skills have all been linked as wider benefits of physical activity (Public Health England, 2020).

Physical inactivity and sedentary behaviour within higher education

The prevalence of physical inactivity and sedentary behaviour has been researched across all life stages, including school-aged children, working aged adults, and older adults (Castro et al., 2018). This prevalence also extends to a higher education context, and is a significant issue, with some suggestions that university students are the most likely section of the population to adopt sedentary behaviours (Carballo-Fazanes et al., 2020). Research studies have highlighted the relationship between physical inactivity and university students, including significant proportions (typically between 44%-62%) of university students being inactive (Pengpid et al., 2015; Edelmann et al., 2022), however it is important to acknowledge that these levels can differ between countries. Discipline area is also shown to impact physical inactivity and sedentary behaviour with those studying natural sciences, mathematics, and informatics at higher risk (Edelmann et al., 2022).

Some evidence suggests that university students have an equal to, or even higher rate of physical inactivity to desk-based workers and in comparison to the general young adult population (Moulin & Irwin, 2017; Castro et al., 2020). This has been compounded by the Covid-19 pandemic due to the former restrictions and increase of online teaching methods which have resulted in more sedentary behaviour (Bertrand, et al., 2021; Rivera et al., 2021).

High levels of physical inactivity and sedentary behaviour within university students is challenging to attribute to a single reason. Transitioning between life stages, such as moving to university from school, typically means significant lifestyle changes and within that means individuals are more vulnerable to risk behaviours, including reduced physical activity (Ndupu et al., 2023). The prevailing dependence on technology and screen-use, used for studying, completing assessments, and recreational activities such as watching television, are all further contributing factors, as are characteristics of university life including sitting in lectures and classes, using the library, and travelling to university using a train, car, or bus (Rissel, Mulley & Ding, 2013; Deliens et al., 2015; Edelmann et al., 2022). Doherty & Forés Miravalles (2019) argue that: "the traditional lecture-style lesson relegates students to a passive and sedentary role, precluding physical movement." This emphasises the importance of how curriculum design, including modes and formats for teaching and learning, affects levels of physical inactivity. Moulin & Irwin (2017) supported this, detailing how sitting in class is one of the largest barriers for students to be able to engage with more physically active activities. Whilst wider university and Government initiatives and policies are required to support these issues, including highlighting the impact of physical inactivity and sedentary behaviour and providing opportunities to engage in physical activity such as sport programmes, travel initiatives, and consideration of campus space, it is perhaps most crucial to further explore how the experience within the university classroom and teaching practice can support this issue (Moulin & Irwin, 2017; von Sommoggy et al., 2020).

The impact of physical inactivity and sedentary behaviour within higher education on learning and health and wellbeing

With physical inactivity and sedentary behaviour being prevalent in higher education, it is important to consider the impact this has on the student, both in terms of learning and on health and wellbeing. Classroom sitting time has been associated with increased discomfort and sleepiness, even after just fifteen minutes of uninterrupted sitting which can further affect alertness and academic performance (Hosteng et al., 2019). Further to this, academic achievement has been seen to improve when sedentary behaviour is reduced (Felez-Nobrega et al., 2018). However, it is important to note that terms such as academic performance and academic achievement are challenging to measure objectively due to the multitude of extraneous variables, and current research is not always clear about how these measures are constructed and valid.

For health and wellbeing, sedentary behaviour has been shown to be associated with an increased risk of depression amongst university students (Tashiro et al., 2021). Increased stress and anxiety have also been seen to be positively correlated with increased sitting time (Lee & Kim, 2018) alongside a higher risk of more general mental disorders and feeling low (Sanchez-Villegas et al., 2008; Carballo-Fazanes et al., 2020). These factors can significantly impact academic performance, social relationships, and successful transitions to university life (Lee & Kim, 2018). Poor health and wellbeing has been reported to be the number one reason why UK students withdraw from their studies (Neves & Hewitt, 2021), so it is paramount that any factor that can significantly impact health and wellbeing is explored further with appropriate interventions introduced.

Further research data is available in school-based settings and could be comparable, with a large systematic review, comprising over 1,300,000 participants, identifying that active lessons, which reduce sedentary behaviour, can positively impact health and wellbeing (Kuzik et al., 2022).

Further research into the relationship between the impact of physical inactivity and sedentary behaviour on learning, health, and wellbeing within university students is required, with a specific focus on informing and exploring future inventions to suppress and manage these issues. Universities have a responsibility, as key institutions for education and health, to create safe and supportive learning environments, where students can engage with healthy lifestyles, and have the best chance to succeed with their studies (Lee & Kim, 2018).

Suggestions have been made including incorporation of active lessons and breaking up lectures with activities, such as discussions, games, and group-work, which could incorporate physical activity and movement, to support engagement, learning, health, and wellbeing (Hosteng et al., 2019; Kuzik et al., 2022).

Section 2: Learning away from the desk: Physically Active Learning (PAL) pedagogies

With the extent and impact of physical inactivity and sedentary behaviour observed, it appears that curriculum design and teaching practices are a source of these behaviours, primarily as existing structures enable these behaviours. This includes classroom time, such as being in lectures and seminars, and time spent studying, incorporating, and being reliant on sitting as a traditional convention. It is important to consider how Physically Active Learning (PAL) pedagogies can be incorporated and embedded within higher education teaching practices and the wider curriculum to enhance movement and reduce sedentary behaviour.

Physically Active Learning (PAL)

Physically Active Learning (PAL), also sometimes referred to as kinaesthetic pedagogy, can be described as integrating elements of physical activity and movement within academic content to stimulate learning (Chisholm & Spencer, 2017; Daly-Smith et al., 2021). It gives students the "opportunity to move out from behind their desks and interact with their surroundings" (Mobley & Fisher, 2014, p. 301).

PAL is inextricably linked with outdoor learning, with outdoor, open spaces providing opportunities to combine physical activity with educational content, enabling explorative, discovery-based learning to take place (Ayotte-Beaudet, 2021). Outdoor learning can also enable students to contextualise learning into authentic situations, which promotes better understanding, for example examining wildlife or living species (natural sciences), the infrastructure of buildings (engineering), and behaviours of communities (psychology), whilst moving and being active (Giamellaro, 2017; Ayotte-Beaudet et al., 2020).

PAL is also closely correlated with embodied learning, which emphasises the importance of body, feeling, and non-mental factors involved in the learning process (Burns & Paniagua, 2017). As PAL incorporates movement within learning, it can be seen to connect body and mind, and action and thinking, rejecting the notion of a dichotomy between them (Nguyen & Larson, 2015; Sanako, 2021). Embodied learning approaches are shown to have significant positive effects on cognitive abilities, academic performance, and improved learning (Kosmas et al., 2018; Zhang et al., 2021). Whilst embodied learning appears to generally be an unaccustomed pedagogical approach within higher education, Covid-19 has further hindered its growth due to the increased use of online teaching and learning, leading to educators needing to think of new and innovative ways to promote embodiment (Quinn & Maddox, 2022).

Physically Active Learning (PAL) methods

PAL methods can significantly vary and be adapted, based on the learning context, mode, and resources. Some educators may choose to introduce guidelines and norms with new cohorts, such as encouraging students to stand, move and stretch when desired (Dhillon, 2022), however this can be problematic depending on the learning space, for example a lecture hall which could result in distractions or views being blocked. Short breaks from sitting or stretches, which can be outdoors, and which incorporate movement are also suggested as an effective method. This can be coupled with discussion tasks, or personal reflections, to stimulate learning and thinking (Braybrook, 2022).

There are a multitude of activities which support PAL which can be incorporated or used to adapt existing activities. Scavenger hunts, where students search for information, resources, or even experiences can be used to stimulate movement, whilst providing opportunities to engage in active, collaborative, and explorative learning. This could include finding information around the campus, such as types of building in an engineering course, or to find parts of the campus (during inductions). This can be incorporated into outdoor contexts by utilising the wider campus or nearby outdoor spaces (Jones et al., 2017). Gallery walks, also referred to as stations activities, or the carousel method can be utilised, where groups move in rotations to different areas of the learning environment. Each area can have questions, prompts, or instructions, supporting students to collaborate and engage with varied learning tasks, whilst moving between stations or exploring new areas. Whilst this can take place in an indoor classroom context, this can work particularly effectively in an outdoor learning space, where students could be given a map or guidance around different areas to visit, with a task to complete in each one (Chisholm & Spencer, 2017; Hrach, 2021; Magkoufopoulou, 2022). Extending from this is place-based learning, which connects learning to a physical space and emphasises learning through exploring the environment (Yemini et al., 2023). Placed-based learning can utilise different environments such as museums, local communities, or campus buildings/green spaces. This could be collecting data and photographs of historic events or environmental issues, or through completing work-placements (Gruenewald, 2003). For place-based learning to be effective, it has been identified that a focus should be on connecting places to the discipline area and own personal contexts alongside enabling other perspectives to be explored relative to that place (Zimmerman & Land, 2013).

Embedding opportunities for walking is one of the most advantageous, and feasible methods for PAL, meaning it appears to be one of the most utilised within a higher education context. Walking up to ten minutes per day can have health benefits (NHS, 2023c), and coupled with being outdoors and viewing pleasant rural or urban scenes can increase these effects, alongside enhancing self-esteem, mood, happiness, general sense of well-being (Pretty et al., 2005; Weight et al., 2018; Bälter et al., 2018), decreasing stress (Olafsdottir et al., 2018), and enhanced connectedness to nature (Zhang et al., 2014). Considerations should be made around route and location, as unpleasant scenes, such as pollution or environmental degradation, can negatively affect wellbeing, alongside weather, as students may be less engaged or willing to walk during cold or wet conditions (Pretty et al., 2005).

Walking and learning can be traced back to Aristotle, who is known to have founded the peripatetic school of learning, where students would walk in local areas and make connections to their learning, to develop curiosity, creativity, and inspiration whilst making a deep connection to their own humanity (Bälter et al., 2018; Vasileiou, 2021). This was also seen to introduce the notion that walking facilitates talking, and, presumably, thinking, through taking part in an embodied experience which heightens feelings and perceptions (Beyes & Steyaert, 2020). Combined with learning, walking can be used as a reflective activity, to enrich creative thinking or instigate ideas, or as part of a discussion and intellectual exchange with others, to talk through a problem and share opinions, and has been shown to have even better outcomes when outside in a natural environment (Oppezzo & Schwartz, 2014; Keinänen, 2015; Querol, 2019). Furthermore, walking whilst discussing, sometimes referred to as walking seminars, facilitates richer dialogue and discussion to take place due to students feeling more open and expressive with others, which can lead to higher quality seminars (Bälter et al., 2018), and aided by the absence of the sometimes perceived formality of a classroom, can lead to more free-flowing, creative conversations (McKay, 2022).

Walking activities within learning can also be enhanced through technology, including podcast-based learning, where students can flexibly engage with audio-based learning materials whilst engaging with physical activity, which has been seen to support retention of information, and allow for learning to continue in different contexts such as commuting (Biber & Heidorn, 2020). Twalks, where social media is utilised to capture ideas and discussion, can also enhance engagement by providing structure and supporting walking groups to stay connected (Spiers & Middleton, 2019). By embedding opportunities for walking, and other PAL methods, within current teaching practices and harnessing the variety of these methods, this can result in significant pedagogical as well as health and wellbeing benefits.

It is important to highlight that whilst research has shown advantages to these methods, both in terms of learning and wellbeing, there are potential challenges which should be considered. Students may feel anxious or concerned about leaving the classroom, and there are concerns around health and safety as movement and exploring unknown areas can increase risk of accidents (Boyle et al., 2007; Goodlad & Leonard, 2018). Recommendations also include providing flexibility and alternatives to engagement to enhance accessibility and inclusion (Oprandi, 2019).

It is important to distinguish the difference between physical activity being integrated with learning opportunities, for example walking seminars, and physical activity being encouraged during learning but without being linked to learning outcomes or the curriculum, for example a movement break. PAL should be purposeful, valuable, and aligned to learning outcomes and not superficial to achieve the best results, ensuring coherent constructive alignment (Biggs, 2003; Chisholm & Spencer, 2017; Ayotte-Beaudet, 2021), and consideration should be given to ensuring students are aware of the purpose, benefits, and expectations (Ayotte-Beaudet et al., 2020). PAL practices should be inclusive and adaptable, especially in reference to those with disabilities to ensure students are not disadvantaged (WHO, 2020; Clughen, 2022).

Supporting Physically Active Learning (PAL)

With any pedagogical approach, sufficient and considered support is required to enable educators to embed within their own teaching practices. Teacher confidence and competence, alongside resources and opportunities to collaborate and discuss with others have been identified as key priorities to support the implementation of PAL (Daly-Smith et al., 2020). Teacher confidence and competence with PAL can be supported through training and continued professional development, with a focus on the impact of the approach and the importance of maximising meaningfulness and engagement. Collaborative networks, also referred to as "Communities of Practice", are also recommended to provide space for teachers to share practice and experiences, and learn from each other within a supportive and encouraging environment. Resources, such as example lesson plans and schemes of works can also help to provide knowledge and skills, whilst access to open spaces can support opportunities to integrate PAL (Daly-Smith et al., 2020). However, it is important to note that research is limited within a higher education context. Institutional support is also required, such as inclusion of PAL within education strategy and approach, alongside a commitment to supporting and raising awareness of PAL (Deliens et al., 2015). Adopting trials of PAL have also been shown to reduce barriers to incorporation, as educators can experiment in their own contexts and discipline areas, becoming accustomed to methods and approaches and measuring the impact through their own reflections and student feedback (Howie et al., 2014).

Section 3: Moving, learning and thriving: The impact of Physically Active Learning (PAL)

Having explored PAL as a pedagogy, how to support it within practice, and the specific methods which could be incorporated, it is important to consider the potential impact of PAL on both learning and health and wellbeing.

Impact on learning

Physical activity has been shown to contribute to healthy brain functions and support cognition functioning within learning contexts (Doherty & Forés Miravalles, 2019). Blood flow increases the brain's function and performance, and can enable critical thinking, attention, and motivation for learning (Hillman et al., 2008; Nicksic et al., 2020), alongside increased focus, interaction, and enjoyment as a direct result of PAL opportunities (Ferrer & Laughlin, 2017). Due to this, retention has also been shown to increase (Prince, 2004), allowing students to engage with deeper, immersive learning experiences. Higher order thinking skills including creativity and the ability to design and produce have been linked to PAL (Rominger et al., 2022), alongside enthusiasm, engagement, and interest in the learning (Vazou et al., 2012; Ferrer & Laughlin, 2017), enabling a wide range of pedagogical benefits to be seen. This can have drastic benefits on student achievement and retention, whilst enhancing secondary benefits such as confidence and enthusiasm for learning. Movement has been recognised to engage more of the senses, and activating these senses can support higher cognition (Lengel & Kuzala, 2010). When all senses are engaged, this can foster memorable, immersive learning experiences to take place. When this occurs, there is a significant shift to student-led learning, enabling and empowering students to take active ownership and responsibility of their own learning, enabling intrinsic motivation and personal growth to be supported (Wright, 2011).

Conversely, academic outcomes were seen to not be affected when PAL and NAL (Non-Active Learning) were compared (Bacon & Lord, 2021), and this could imply that an individual's context and preferences are more likely to impact findings, suggesting the need for further research to be explored within a higher education context.

Impact on health and wellbeing

PAL has also been seen to impact student health and wellbeing, which affects the whole student experience and engagement with learning. As expected, even modest levels of PAL have been shown to directly increase physical activity levels (Bacon & Lord, 2021).

Increased physical activity in students was found to lead to higher mental and personal wellbeing, alongside feeling less lonely, and more socially included (British Universities College Sport, 2020). This can also benefit students post-university, by forming healthy lifestyle habits and behaviours. Satisfaction with life, leading to enhanced self-esteem and self-efficacy, has also been shown to increase when physical activity is engaged with (Maher, et al., 2014). Studies have tended to focus on the significance of physical activity, as opposed to physically active learning, and further research is required to examine the specific connection and impact of PAL within teaching practices and the wider curriculum.

The positive impacts of outdoor learning, which are frequently incorporated within PAL pedagogies, are also prominent within literature. Outdoor learning can foster positive mental health and mindfulness, through connection with the natural world and being in a novel environment, usually away from typical distractions and sometimes detached from technology (Mutz & Müller, 2016). Outdoor learning is also seen to benefit group-work and collaborative learning. Cooley et al. (2014) identified the positive attitudes and confidence that group-work engendered, as well as the social environment that developed, enhancing the success of collaborative tasks and projects. This could coincide with the notion that outdoor learning provides a safe space for dialogue and reflection (Breunig et al., 2015), possibly because it can be perceived as a more informal learning context, alongside having a separate focus which takes pressure off conversations and dialogue, allowing students to feel more comfortable expressing views and feelings. These can provide opportunities for further immersion and absorption within learning experiences, enhancing cognition further (Thorburn & Marshall, 2014). Communication and motivation of students were also seen to be strengthened, albeit with an emphasis being placed on the need to allow time to adjust to new learning environments (Fägerstam, 2014). Other individual benefits include moral and character development, personal growth, and leadership being developed through engaging with outdoor environments (Ewert & Garvey, 2007).

Whilst these benefits are comprehensive, and impact a multiple of areas, including enhancing physiological functioning to stimulate cognitive performance, development of higher order thinking skills such as creativity, engagement and enthusiasm for learning, positive mental health, group-work and collaborative learning, and personal growth, it must be considered that the range of literature incorporates samples from a diverse variety of educational settings, countries, and cultures, which makes it challenging to generalise and apply these benefits to all university students. It is recommended further research is conducted on the impact of PAL, which is contextual to higher education, to further explore and refine the potential advantages and implications of incorporating PAL within teaching practices and the wider curriculum.

Conclusion

This chapter has aimed to provide a comprehensive insight into PAL, including the *'what'* (the current situation and context), the *'how'* (the methods and approaches which could be used with a PAL pedagogy), and the *'why'* (the potential impact of incorporating PAL).

Section 1

Section 1 identified that physical inactivity and sedentary behaviour is prevalent across the worldwide population, and can be seen to be increasing due to the reliance of screen-use and dependence on sitting in occupational contexts. Recommendations have been made around physical activity to reduce negative health and wellbeing outcomes. These behaviours are also prevalent within higher education contexts, and it is identified that students are at a particular risk group, due to life stage, and the traditional conventions of education contributing to sedentary behaviour. This was seen to have significant negative outcomes, impacting academic performance and wellbeing, with recommendations to embed more opportunities for physical activity within teaching and learning practices.

Section 2

Section 2 introduced PAL as a pedagogical approach, utilising movement, embodiment, and outdoor spaces to improve learning and health outcomes. Outdoor learning, in partnership with PAL, was seen to have the most significant benefits, due to opportunities to connect with natural and authentic spaces. PAL methods are varied, and need to be contextualised depending on the learning outcomes and disciplines but can include group-work, movement breaks, and place-based learning, alongside walking, which was seen to be one of the most advantageous approaches due to its versatility and the benefits on discussion and thinking. Support is required to embed PAL within teaching practices and the wider curriculum through support to individuals, and adoption and encouragement by the wider institute, as well as ensuring that PAL is inclusive and accessible, so no students are disadvantaged, and that PAL is purposeful and constructively aligned to the wider module.

Section 3

Section 3 explored the impact of incorporating PAL, and identified a plethora of learning benefits, including enhanced cognition, motivation, and focus and retention, alongside other thinking skills such as creativity. It was also seen to provide more immersive and memorable experiences, enabling students to take more ownership and responsibility of their own learning. PAL was also seen to have health benefits, including self-esteem and belongingness. Outdoor learning was key to this, which further benefited collaboration, communication, and personal growth. It is recommended that further research around PAL within higher education is conducted to gain a clearer picture into the potential incorporation, impact and implications.

References

Ayotte-Beaudet, J., Beaudry, M., Bisaillon, V. & Dube, M. (2020, August). *Outdoor education in higher education during the context of Covid-19 in Canada: Pedagogical guide to support teachers*. Université de Sherbrooke. Retrieved 15 July 2023 from https://savoirs.usherbrooke.ca/bitstream/handle/11143/17311/Outdoor+classes+in+higher+education_pedagogical+guide_UdeS_August2020.pdf?sequence= 1.

Ayotte-Beaudet, J. (2021, January 3). Outdoor education at universities can be a positive legacy of COVID-19. *The Conversation*. https://theconversation.com/outdoor-education-at-universities-can-be-a-positive-legacy-of-covid-19-149308.

Bacon, P. & Lord, R.N. (2021). The impact of physically active learning during the school day on children's physical activity levels, time on task and learning behaviours and academic outcomes. *Health Education Research36(3)* 362–373. https://doi.org/10.1093/her/cyab020.

Bälter, O., Hedin, B., Tobiasson, H. & Toivanen, S. (2018). Walking outdoors during seminars improved perceived seminar quality and sense of well-being among participants. *International Journal of Environmental Research and Public Health*, 15(2), 303. https://doi.org/10.3390/ijerph15020303.

Bertrand, L., Shaw, K.A., Ko, J., Deprez, D., Chilibeck, P.D. & Zello, G.A. (2021). The impact of the coronavirus disease 2019 (COVID-19) pandemic on university students' dietary intake, physical activity, and sedentary behaviour. *Applied Physiology, Nutrition and Metabolism* [Physiologie appliquee, nutrition et metabolisme], 46(3), 265–272. https://doi.org/10.1139/apnm-2020–0990.

Beyes, T. & Steyaert, C. (2020). Unsettling bodies of knowledge: Walking as a pedagogy of affect. *Management Learning*, 52(2),224–242. https://doi.org/10.1177/1350507620979713.

Biber, D.D. & Heidorn, J. (2020). Tailoring the walking classroom to promote college student engagement. *College Teaching*, 69(3),169–172. https://doi.org/10.1080/87567555.2020.1833177.

Biggs, J. (2003). *Teaching for quality learning at university* (2nd ed). Open University Press/Society for Research into Higher Education.

Boyle, A., Maguire, S., Martin, A., Milsom, C., Nash, R., Rawlinson, S., Turner, A., Wurthmann, S. & Conchie, S. (2007). Fieldwork is good: The student perception and the affective domain. *Journal of Geography in Higher Education*, 31(2), 299–317. https://doi.org/10.1080/03098260601063628.

Braybrook, S. (2022, March, 22). Why and how to bring physical movement into the classroom. *THE Campus*. https://www.timeshighereducation.com/campus/why-and-how-bring-physical-movement-classroom.

Breunig, M., Murtell, J. & Russell, C. (2015). Students' experiences with/in integrated environmental studies programs in Ontario. *Journal of Adventure Education and Outdoor Learning*, *15*(*4*), 267–283. https://doi.org/10.1080/14729679.2014.955354.

British Universities College Sport (2020). *British active students survey: Higher education 2019/2020 report*. https://www.ukactive.com/wp-content/uploads/2020/06/BASS-201920-HE.pdf.

Burns, T. & Paniagua, A. (2017). *Innovative pedagogies for powerful learning progress report*. Directorate For Education And Skills Centre For Educational Research And Innovation (CERI) Governing Board. https://one.oecd.org/document/EDU/CERI/CD(2017)16/en/pdf.

Carballo-Fazanes, A., Rico-Díaz, J., Barcala-Furelos, R., Rey, E., Rodríguez-Fernández, J. E., Varela-Casal, C. & Abelairas-Gómez, C. (2020). Physical activity habits and determinants, sedentary behaviour and lifestyle in university students. *International Journal of Environmental Research and Public Health*, *17*(*9*), 3272. https://doi.org/10.3390/ijerph17093272.

Castro, O., Bennie, J., Vergeer, I., Bosselut, G. & Biddle, S.J.H. (2018). Correlates of sedentary behaviour in university students: A systematic review. *Preventive Medicine*, *116*, 194–202. https://doi.org/10.1016/j.ypmed.2018.09.016.

Castro, O., Bennie, J., Vergeer, I., Bosselut, G. & Biddle, S.J. (2020). How sedentary are university students? A systematic review and meta-analysis. *Prevention Science*, *21*(*3*), 332–343. https://doi.org/10.1007/s11121-020–01093-8.

Chisholm, A. & Spencer, B. 2017 Let's get moving!: Eight ways to teach information literacy using kinesthetic activities. *Pennsylvania Libraries: Research & Practice*, *5*(*1*), 26–34. https://doi.org/10.5195/palrap.2017.141.

Clughen, L. (2022). *A guide to embedding movement into higher education*. Trent Institute for Learning & Teaching. https://www.ntu.ac.uk/__data/assets/pdf_file/0019/1734211/A-Guide-to-Embedding-Movement-in-HE-Classrooms.pdf.

Cooley, S.J., Burns, V.E. & Cumming, J. (2014). The role of outdoor adventure education in facilitating groupwork in higher education. *Higher Education*, *69*(*4*), 567–582. https://doi.org/10.1007/s10734-014–9791-4.

Daly-Smith, A., Quarmby, T., Archbold, V.S.J., Routen, A.C., Morris, J.L., Gammon, C., Bartholomew, J.B., Resaland, G.K., Llewellyn, B., Allman, R. & Dorling, H. 2020 Implementing physically active learning: Future directions for research, policy, and practice. *Journal of Sport and Health Science*, *9*(*1*), 41–49. https://doi.org/10.1016/j.jshs.2019.05.007.

Daly-Smith, A., Morris, J.L., Norris, E., Williams, T.L., Archbold, V., Kallio, J., Tammelin, T.H., Singh, A., Mota, J., von Seelen, J., Pesce, C., Salmon, J., McKay, H., Bartholomew, J. & Resaland, G.K. (2021). Behaviours that prompt primary school teachers to adopt and implement physically active learning: A meta synthesis of qualitative evidence. *International Journal of Behavioral Nutrition and Physical Activity*, *18*(*1*), 151. https://doi.org/10.1186/s12966-021–01221-9.

Deliens, T., Deforche, B., De Bourdeaudhuij, I. & Clarys, P. (2015). Determinants of physical activity and sedentary behaviour in university students: A qualitative study using focus group discussions. *BMC Public Health*, *15*, 201. https://doi.org/10.1186/s12889-015–1553-4.

Department of Health (2005). *Choosing activity: A physical active action plan*. https://www.physicalactivityplan.org/resources/UK.pdf.

Dhillon, S. (2022, June 22). Our desk-based higher education is not good for our health and our diversity. *WonkeHE Blogs*. https://wonkhe.com/blogs/our-desk-based-higher-education-is-not-good-for-our-health-and-our-diversity.

Doherty, A. & Forés Miravalles, A. (2019). Physical activity and cognition: Inseparable in the classroom. *Frontiers in Education*, *4*, 105.   https://doi.org/10.3389/feduc.2019.00105.

Edelmann, D., Pfirrmann, D., Heller, S., Dietz, P., Reichel, J.L., Werner, A.M., Schäfer, M., Tibubos, A.N., Deci, N., Letzel, S., Simon, P., & Kalo, K. (2022). Physical activity and sedentary behavior in university students–the role of gender, age, field of study, targeted degree, and study semester. *Frontiers in Public Health*, *10*, 821703. https://doi.org/10.3389/fpubh.2022.821703.

Ewert, A. & Garvey, D. (2007). Philosophy and theory of adventure education. In D. Prouty, J. Panicucci & R. Collinson Eds *Adventure education: Theory and applications* pp. 19–32 Human Kinetics.   https://doi.org/10.5040/9781492596189.ch-0002.

Fägerstam, E. (2014).   High school teachers' experience of the educational potential of outdoor teaching and learning. *Journal of Adventure Education and Outdoor Learning*, *14*(*1*), 56–81. https://doi.org/10.1080/14729679.2013.769887.

Felez-Nobrega, M., Hillman, C.H., Dowd, K.P., Cirera, E. & Puig-Ribera, A. (2018). ActivPALTM determined sedentary behaviour, physical activity and academic achievement in college students. *Journal of Sports Sciences*, *36*(*20*), 2311–2316. https://doi.org/10.1080/02640414.2018.1451212.

Ferrer, M.E. & Laughlin, D.D. (2017).   Increasing college students' engagement and physical activity with classroom brain breaks. *Journal of Physical Education, Recreation & Dance*, *88*(*3*), 53–56. https://doi.org/10.1080/07303084.2017.1260945.

Giamellaro, M. (2017). Dewey's yardstick. *SAGE Open*, *7*(*1*), 1–11.   https://doi.org/10.1177/2158244017700463.

Goodlad, K. & Leonard, A. (2018). Place-based learning across the disciplines: A living laboratory approach to pedagogy. *InSight: A Journal of Scholarly Teaching*, *13*, 150–164. https://doi.org/10.46504/14201808GO.

Gruenewald, D.A. (2003). The best of both worlds: A critical pedagogy of place. *Educational Researcher*, *32*(*4*), 3–12. https://doi.org/10.3102/0013189X032004003.

Guthold, R., Stevens, G.A., Riley, L.M. & Bull, F.C. (2018). Worldwide trends in insufficient physical activity from 2001 to 2016: A pooled analysis of 358 population-based surveys with 1.9 million participants. *The Lancet Global Health*, *6*(*10*), e1077-e1086. https://doi.org/10.1016/S2214-109X(18)30357–30357.

Heron, L., O'Neill, C., McAneney, H., Kee, F. & Tully, M.A. (2019). Direct healthcare costs of sedentary behaviour in the UK. *Journal of Epidemiology and Community Health*, *73*(*7*), 625–629. https://doi.org/10.1136/jech-2018–211758.

Hillman, C.H., Erickson, K.I. & Kramer, A.F. (2008). Be smart, exercise your heart: Exercise effects on brain and cognition. *Nature Reviews Neuroscience*, *9*(*1*), 58–65. https://doi.org/10.1038/nrn2298.

Hosteng, K.R., Reichter, A.P., Simmering, J.E. & Carr, L.J. (2019). Uninterrupted classroom sitting is associated with increased discomfort and sleepiness among college students. *International Journal of Environmental Research and Public Health*, *16*(*14*), 2498. https://doi.org/10.3390/ijerph16142498.

Howie, E.K., Beets, M.W. & Pate, R.R. (2014). Acute classroom exercise breaks improve on-task behavior in 4th and 5th grade students: A dose–response . *Mental Health and Physical Activity*, *7*(*2*), 65–71. https://doi.org/10.1016/j.mhpa.2014.05.002.

Hrach, S. (2021, November 26). Embodied learning: how to bring movement into the classroom, and why it matters. *THE Campus*. https://www.timeshighereducation.com/campus/embodied-learning-how-bring-movement-classroom-and-why-it-matters.

Jones, J.A., Smith, S. & Royster, M. (2017). The scavenger hunt as an active learning technique. *NACTA Journal 61 1*, 94–95.

Keinänen, M. (2015). Taking your mind for a walk: A qualitative investigation of walking and thinking among nine Norwegian academics. *Higher Education, 71(4)*, 593–605. https://doi.org/10.1007/s10734-015-9926-2.

Kosmas, P., Ioannou, A. & Zaphiris, P. (2018). Implementing embodied learning in the classroom: Effects on children's memory and language skills . *Educational Media International, 56(1)*, 59–74. https://doi.org/10.1080/09523987.2018.1547948.

Kuzik, N., da Costa, B.G., Hwang, Y., Verswijveren, S.J., Rollo, S., Tremblay, M.S., Bélanger, S., Carson, V., Davis, M., Hornby, S., Huang, W.Y., Law, B., Salmon, J., Tomasone, J.R., Wachira, L.-J., Wijndaele, K. & Saunders, T.J. (2022). School-related sedentary behaviours and indicators of health and well-being among children and youth: A systematic review. *International Journal of Behavioral Nutrition and Physical Activity, 19(1)*, 40. https://doi.org/10.1186/s12966-022-01258-4.

Lee, E. & Kim, Y. (2018). Effect of university students' sedentary behavior on stress, anxiety, and depression. *Perspectives in Psychiatric Care, 55(2)*, 164–169. HYPERLINK " https://doi.org/10.1111/ppc.12296" https://doi.org/10.1111/ppc.12296.

Lengel, T., & Kuczala, M. (Eds.) (2010). *The kinesthetic classroom: Teaching and learning through movement*. Corwin Press.

Magkoufopoulou, C. (2022). Introducing contemporary controversial subjects through a carousel. In T. Betts & P. Oprandi (Eds.), *100 ideas for active learning* (pp. 559–565). University of Sussex Library. https://doi.org/10.20919/OPXR1032/68.

Maher, J.P., Doerksen, S.E., Elavsky, S. & Conroy, D.E. (2014). Daily satisfaction with life is regulated by both physical activity and sedentary behavior. *Journal of Sport and Exercise Psychology, 36(2)*, 166–178. https://doi.org/10.1123/jsep.2013-0185.

McKay, A. (2022). Interdisciplinary walks: Investigating the benefits of walking for research. *LIAS Working Paper Series, 9(1)*. https://doi.org/10.29311/lwps.202294112.

Merchant, N. (2013, February). Got a meeting? Take a walk *[Video]*. TED Conferences. https://www.ted.com/talks/nilofer_merchant_got_a_meeting_take_a_walk?language=en.

Mobley, K. & Fisher, S. (2014). Ditching the desks: Kinesthetic learning in college classrooms . *The Social Studies, 105(6)*, 301–309. https://doi.org/10.1080/00377996.2014.951471.

Moulin, M. & Irwin, J. (2017). An assessment of sedentary time among undergraduate students at a Canadian university. *International Journal of Exercise Science, 10(8)*, 1116–1129. https://ir.lib.uwo.ca/etd/ 3699.

Mulchandani, R., Chandrasekaran, A.M., Shivashankar, R., Kondal, D., Agrawal, A., Panniyammakal, J., Tandon, N., Prabhakaran, D., Sharma, M. & Goenka, S. (2019). Effect of workplace physical activity interventions on the cardio-metabolic health of working adults: Systematic review and meta-analysis. *International Journal of Behavioral Nutrition and Physical Activity, 16(1)*, 134. https://doi.org/10.1186/s12966-019-0896-0.

Mutz, M. & Müller, J. 2016 Mental health benefits of outdoor adventures: Results from two pilot studies. *Journal of Adolescence, 49(1)*, 105–114. https://doi.org/10.1016/j.adolescence.2016.03.009.

Ndupu, L.B., Faghy, M., Staples, V., Lipka, S. & Bussell, C. (2023). Exploring the predictors of physical inactivity in a university setting. *BMC Public Health*, 23(59). https://doi.org/10.1186/s12889-022-14953-5.

Neves, J., & Hewitt, R. 2021 *Student Academic Experience Survey 2021.* Advance HE and HEPI. https://www.hepi.ac.uk/wp-content/uploads/2021/06/SAES_2021_FINAL.pdf.

Nguyen, D.J. & Larson, J.B. (2015). Don't forget about the body: Exploring the curricular possibilities of embodied pedagogy. *Innovative Higher Education*, 40(4), 331–344. https://doi.org/10.1007/S10755-015-9319-6.

NHS 2023a *Physical activity guidelines for adults aged 19 to 64.* https://www.nhs.uk/live-well/exercise/exercise-guidelines/physical-activity-guidelines-for-adults-aged-19-t o–64.

NHS (2023b). *Why we should sit less.* https://www.nhs.uk/live-well/exercise/exercise-guidelines/why-sitting-too-much-is-bad-for-us.

NHS (2023c). *Walking for health.* https://www.nhs.uk/live-well/exercise/running-and-aerobic-exercises/walking-for-health.

Nicksic, H., Lindt, S. & Miller, S. (2020). Move, think, learn: Incorporating physical activity into the college classroom. *International Journal of Teaching and Learning in Higher Education*, 32(3), 528–535. https://files.eric.ed.gov/fulltext/EJ1299970.pdf.

Olafsdottir, G., Cloke, P., Schulz, A., van Dyck, Z., Eysteinsson, T., Thorleifsdottir, B. & Vögele, C. (2018). Health benefits of walking in nature: A randomized controlled study under conditions of real-life stress. *Environment and Behavior*, 52(3), 248–274. https://doi.org/10.1177/0013916518800798.

Oppezzo, M. & Schwartz, D.L. (2014). Give your ideas some legs: The positive effect of walking on creative thinking. *Journal of Experimental Psychology: Learning, Memory, and Cognition*, 40(4), 1142–1152. https://doi.org/10.1037/a0036577.

Oprandi, P. (2019, October 15). Outdoor learning: Introducing the Twalk, Twitter in the wild. *University of Sussex Educational Enhancement.* https://blogs.sussex.ac.uk/tel/2019/10/15/outdoor-learning-introducing-the-twalk-twitter-in-the.wild.

Park, J.H., Moon, J.H., Kim, H.J., Kong, M.H. & Oh, Y.H. (2020). Sedentary lifestyle: Overview of updated evidence of potential health risks. *Korean Journal of Family Medicine*, 41(6), 365–373. https://doi.org/10.4082%2Fkjfm.20.0165.

Pengpid, S., Peltzer, K., Kassean, H.K., Tsala Tsala, J.P., Sychareun, V. & Müller-Riemenschneider, F. (2015). Physical inactivity and associated factors among university students in 23 low-, middle- and high-income countries. *International Journal of Public Health*, 60(5), 539–549. https://doi.org/10.1007/s00038-015–0680-0.

Pretty, J., Peacock, J., Sellens, M. & Griffin, M. (2005). The mental and physical health outcomes of Green Exercise. *International Journal of Environmental Health Research*, 15(5), 319–337. https://doi.org/10.1080/09603120500155963.

Prince, M. (2004). Does active learning work? A review of the research. *Journal of Engineering Education*, 93(3), 223–231. http://dx.doi.org/10.1002/j.2168–9830.2004.tb00809.x.

Public Health England (2020). *Health matters: Physical activity – prevention and management of long-term conditions.* https://www.gov.uk/government/publications/health-matters-physical-activity/health-matters-physical-activity-prevention-and-management-of-long-term-conditions.

Querol, N. (2019). The art of walking. Fostering experiential learning through observation and creative practice. *Creative Pedagogies Imprint*, 1(2). 21–26. https://www.open-a ccess.bcu.ac.uk/id/eprint/6991.

Quinn, B. & Maddox, C. (2022). The body doesn't lie: Yoga and embodiment in the higher education classroom. *Teaching in Higher Education*, 1–17. https://doi.org/10.1080/13562517.2022.2066467.

Rissel, C., Mulley, C. & Ding, D. (2013). Travel mode and physical activity at Sydney University. *International Journal of Environmental Research and Public Health*, 10(8), 3563–3577. https://doi.org/10.3390/ijerph10083563.

Rivera, P.A., Nys, B.L. & Fiestas, F. (2021). Impact of covid-19 induced lockdown on physical activity and sedentary behavior among university students: A systematic review . *Medwave*, 21(8), e8456. https://doi.org/10.5867/medwave.2021.08.8456.

Rominger, C., Schneider, M., Fink, A., Tran, U.S., Perchtold-Stefan, C.M. & Schwerdtfeger, A.R. (2022). Acute and chronic physical activity increases Creative Ideation Performance: A systematic review and multilevel meta-analysis. *Sports Medicine − Open*, 8(1), 62. https://doi.org/10.1186/s40798-022-00444-9.

Salman, D., Farooqi, M., McGregor, A. & Majeed, A. (2019) Time spent being sedentary: An emerging risk factor for poor health. *British Journal of General Practice*, 69(683), 278–279. https://doi.org/10.3399/bjgp19X703781.

Sanako (2021). *An introduction to embodied learning techniques*. https://sanako.com/an-introduction-to-embodied-learning-techniques#:~:text=This%20learning%20model%20is%20called%20embodied%20learning.

Sanchez-Villegas, A., Ara, I., Guillén-Grima, F., Bes-Rastrollo, M., Varo-Cenarruzabeitia, J. J. & Martínez-González, M.A. (2008). Physical activity, sedentary index, and mental disorders in the SUN cohort study. *Medicine and Science in Sports and Exercise*, 40(5), 827–834. https://doi.org/10.1249/MSS.0b013e31816348b9.

Silva, L.R., Seguro, C.S., de Oliveira, C.G., Santos, P.O., de Oliveira, J.C., de Souza Filho, L.F., de Paula Júnior, C.A., Gentil, P. & Rebelo, A.C. (2020). Physical inactivity is associated with increased levels of anxiety, depression, and stress in Brazilians during the COVID-19 pandemic: A cross-sectional study. *Frontiers in Psychiatry*, 11, 565291. https://doi.org/10.3389/fpsyt.2020.565291.

Spiers, A. & Middleton, A. (2019). Learning to Twalk: An analysis of a new learning environment. In C. Rowell Ed *Socialmedia in higher education: Case studies, reflections and analysis* (pp. 223–236). Open Book Publishers. https://doi.org/10.11647/OBP.0162.

Tashiro, T., Maeda, N., Tsutsumi, S., Komiya, M., Arima, S., Mizuta, R., Fukui, K., Nishikawa, Y. & Urabe, Y. (2021). Relationship between sedentary behavior and depression among Japanese medical students during the COVID-19 pandemic: A cross-sectional online survey. *BMC Psychiatry*, 22(1), 348. https://doi.org/10.1186/s12888-022-03997-x.

Thorburn, M. & Marshall, A. (2014). Cultivating lived-body consciousness: Enhancing cognition and emotion through outdoor learning. *Journal of Pedagogy*, 5(1), 115–132. https://doi.org/10.2478/jped-2014-0006.

Vasileiou, F. (2021, October 4). Royal Geographical Society and 'peripatetic learning'. University of Sunderland. https://london.sunderland.ac.uk/about/news-home/lecturers-staff/peripatetic-learning.

Vazou, S., Gavrilou, P., Mamalaki, E., Papanastasiou, A., & Sioumala, N. (2012). Does integrating physical activity in the elementary school classroom influence academic motivation? *International Journal of Sport and Exercise Psychology*, 10(4), 251–263. https://doi.org/10.1080/1612197X.2012.682368.

Vitality (2021). *The prevalence of physical inactivity in the UK and why this needs to change.* https://adviser.vitality.co.uk/insights/prevalence-of-physical-inactivity-uk.

von Sommoggy, J., Rueter, J., Curbach, J., Helten, J., Tittlbach, S. & Loss, J. (2020). How does the campus environment influence everyday physical activity? A Photovoice study among students of two German universities. *Frontiers in Public Health, 8,* 561175. https://doi.org/10.3389/fpubh.2020.561175.

Weight, E., Harry, M., Lewis, M., Jensen, J., Popp, N. & Osborne, B. (2018). *The walking classroom: Oak Foundation classroom testing study 2018.* The University of North Carolina at Chapel Hill. https://www.thewalkingclassroom.org/wp-content/uploads/2018/09/TWC-Final-Report-Classroom-Testing-Project.pdf.

World Health Organisation (2020). *WHO guidelines on physical activity and sedentary behaviour.* https://www.who.int/publications/i/item/9789240015128.

Wright, G. (2011). Student-centered learning in higher education. *International Journal of Teaching and Learning in Higher Education, 23(3),* 92–97. https://eric.ed.gov/?id=EJ938583.

Yemini, M., Engel, L. & Ben Simon, A. (2023). Place-based education: A systematic review of literature. *Educational Review,* 1–21. https://doi.org/10.1080/00131911.2023.2177260.

Zhang, J.W., Howell, R.T. & Iyer, R. (2014). Engagement with natural beauty moderates the positive relation between connectedness with nature and psychological well-being. *Journal of Environmental Psychology, 38,* 55–63. https://doi.org/10.1016/j.jenvp.2013.12.013.

Zhang, W., Chen, Z. & Zhao, R. (2021). A review of Embodied Learning Research and its implications for information teaching practice. In *2021 IEEE 3rd International Conference on Computer Science and Educational Informatization (CSEI)* (pp. 27–34). https://doi.org/10.1109/CSEI51395.2021.9477754.

Zimmerman, H.T. & Land, S.M. (2013). Facilitating place-based learning in outdoor informal environments with mobile computers. *TechTrends, 58(1),* 77–83. http://dx.doi.org/10.1007/s11528-013-0724-3.

Zimmerman, H.T. & Land, S.M. (2013). Facilitating place-based learning in outdoor informal environments with mobile computers. *TechTrends, 58(1),* 77–83. http://dx.doi.org/10.1007/s11528-013-0724-3.

Chapter 9

Harnessing outdoor spaces in an urban university to promote student wellbeing

Jo Peat, Carrie Winstanley and Sabiha Iqbal

The challenges of engaging students

Higher education in the UK has diversified exponentially in the last decade. According to a report published by the Office for Students (2022) the proportion of UK-domiciled undergraduate students who identify as white has fallen 8.3 percentage points, from 78.7% in 2010–11 to 70.4% in 2020–21. Meanwhile, the proportion of students from each minority ethnic group has risen. 13.2% of undergraduate entrants in 2020–21 were from an Asian background, 9.3% identified as Black, and 7.2% were from mixed ethnic backgrounds or other minority ethnic groups. Equally, in 2020–21, 21.8% of English undergraduate students were from the most deprived areas, as measured by Index of Multiple Deprivations (IMD), more than any other IMD quintile. This has risen 4.8 percentage points in the last decade, from 17.0% in 2010–11 (Office for Students, 2022). Roehampton ranks among the top institutions for social inclusion in *The Times*' higher education rankings (Institute for Fiscal Studies, 2021, as evidenced by demographic data) and the student population at Roehampton reflects these national changes. 50% of our students are from minority ethnic groups and 80% of new entrants belong to at least one underrepresented group. In 2022, 18% of our students came from the most deprived quintile. Most of our students now commute from across London and beyond with only around one-fifth of our undergraduate students being resident on campus.

While our outdoor projects benefit all students, this paper focuses on students from diverse cultural backgrounds and those affected by economic deprivation within our university. However, our student cohort is primarily female and these students often juggle significant caring responsibilities with their studies. We also have a higher number of care leavers than the sector average, resulting in a notable proportion of vulnerable students.

A significant number of our students report a feeling of imposter syndrome, not believing that they merit their place in higher education. This gives them a tenuous grip on their status as students and means that a significant element of our work is around student wellbeing, helping them develop a sense of belonging, develop their identity as a student, raise their aspirations and recognise that they

DOI: 10.4324/9781003436928-15

have a right to access opportunities both at university and beyond. Integral to the University's mission is the belief that the experience of university changes lives for the better.

Froebelian ideas and ideals

Roehampton is made up of four colleges, which connect the university to its values of social justice and inclusion, and to wider national and international networks. Students feel a real connection to their colleges and not just to the university itself: the colleges offer a sense of community, which is particularly important for those who have no previous links to – or experience of – what it means to be a student in higher education.

One college is Froebel College, founded on the ideas of the German educationalist, Friedrich Froebel (1782–1852). Froebel proposed that learning about our place in the world is easier when we are given the opportunity to make direct connections with nature. He conceptualised the notion of the kindergarten ('children's garden') through his studies of the natural world and founded the first one in 1837, in Blankenburg, Germany. In outdoor settings Froebel provided children with spaces for gardening and nurturing plants and animals; places for contemplation and reflection; open spaces for play; and the wider environment for larger scale investigation, discovery and exploration (see Liebschner, 1992 for details). Although Froebel's work was focused on children, the broader ideas and the influence of his work continue to be evident in the university, specifically and unsurprisingly in Froebel College. As one of our emeritus professors noted:

> At times, the Froebelian tradition was like a collective conscience which pervaded the College, placing in people's minds the question: Is this in-keeping with the values and beliefs of the Froebelian community?
>
> (Best, 2016)

This influence is marked in programmes across the School of Education, located in Froebel College, where tutors take advantage of the campus and local outdoor areas to help students understand the value of engaging with the environment. One of the aims is to enrich the student experience and enhance student well-being; the other is linked to programmes of study where students learn how to manage outdoor activities with children and young people as part of their career development. By moving sessions or activities outdoors, it is possible to put Froebelian ideas and ideals into practice in ways that chime with contemporary learning. Such principles include sensory engagement: focusing on the sights, sounds, smells and textures of nature can be stimulating and mindful, and can help to foster respect and understanding of ecological systems and the interdependence of all living things. Some modules teach directly about observing and exploring ecosystems, but even where this is not core to the programme, simply being outside brings with it insights into the complexity of habitats and natural processes, leading in turn to an appreciation of our roles and responsibilities within these interconnected systems.

In the early 19th century it was innovative of Froebel to suggest that learning should not be compartmentalised into discrete areas, but should be integrated, emphasising links and synergies. As we equip our students for their careers and lives in the 21st century, this emphasis on interconnectedness remains, and nature can provide a unifying context for interdisciplinary learning and making connections across subject areas. Some subjects lend themselves obviously to the outdoors, such as adventure activities, environmental stewardship projects, art, geography and orienteering, and activities designed for leadership, teamwork and organisational management. These could include psychology, business management, environmental studies and outdoor recreation, along with field-based research incorporating multiple disciplines. Outdoor settings can also serve as a real-world context for cross-disciplinary work and problem-solving exercises, with students cooperating to address complex challenges and wicked problems related to sustainability, urban planning, conservation or community development. Less obviously, interdisciplinary outdoor classes can showcase the intersection of nature, society, faith and culture, with discussions and activities involving literature, philosophy, history, theology and cultural studies examining the social, ethical and aesthetic elements of the human relationship with the natural world. It is possible to include activities as part of taught modules that require students to engage with the outdoors regardless of subject area, as a reflective task, encouraging individuals to consider the impact of space and place on their learning in general (Winstanley, 2018).

Although Froebel College is non-religious, Froebel himself was deeply spiritual. Scholars continue to argue over the details of his religious life, but all agree that it brought him into conflict with contemporaneous Christian understandings (Liebschner, 1992). He is most often described as a pantheist (holding that the entire universe is divine; God is everywhere and everything) or believer in panentheism (acknowledging a distinction between the divine and the natural world, but recognising their interconnections; God is in everything but also beyond it). For example, Froebel considered trees to be 'a mirror, or rather a symbol of human life in its highest spiritual relations', and claimed: 'No more perfect representation of organic life and the mutual relation of its parts can be found in nature than a tree' (Von Marenholtz-Bülow, 1892, p. 31).

These ideas continue to inform our work with students, now using the language of mindfulness and wellbeing. Fundamentally though, we are still building on Froebelian understandings of the natural world to provide a space for reflection and contemplation, allowing us all to slow down, to notice surroundings and to contemplate. Offering a respite from the fast-paced modern world, the opportunity to forge direct connections through being immersed in nature can evoke powerful emotions and be a tool for self-reflection.

Importantly, Froebel was not alone in focusing on the impact of the outdoors on learning. Maria Montessori (1870–1952), for example, encouraged children to move freely between indoor and outdoor learning spaces. Her emphasis was on learning useful and practical skills to develop independence and tackle problem-solving and decision-making. At a similar time, Rudolf Steiner (1861–1925) made use of the natural world to help children learn about respect for themselves, others and the environment. For Steiner, movement and activity were integral to learning and time should be devoted to outdoor education, in order to develop sensory and motor stimulation and also because of the harmony and beauty of nature which he believed were in accord with a child's imagination. All three of these educators felt the role of the teacher was to facilitate and enable, guiding and supporting rather than directing or teaching. Higher education is not what they had in mind; nevertheless, their ideas are still helpful in considering how we encourage learning and interconnectedness. In part because of our uniquely Froebelian history, we are particularly well-placed to reflect on what we can take from these educators to support our adult learners, because that has been our tradition.

Harnessing nature supports the university community: Our campus

Research has shown that academic success is largely predicated on developing a sense of belonging at a university (Tinto, 1993; Kuh et al., 2006; Meehan & Howells, 2019; Peddler et al., 2022). Jackson (2022) identifies four foundational areas of belonging: connection, inclusion, support and autonomy. Here we consider primarily the areas of connection and inclusion, extending these beyond academic belonging to focus on both academic and social integration, i. e. academic and social connection and inclusion (Tinto, 1993). Universities have a duty to foster social inclusion and, at Roehampton, we achieve this via student communities and networks, both within the university itself and with our local community as well as opening our students to opportunities they may otherwise not have.

To achieve this, complementing the academic offer, there are extra- and co-curricular activities. Many of these focus on the wellbeing of students and staff and link closely to sustainability. The physical location and structure of the university enable local and campus-based initiatives, which link students and staff to the outdoors, the natural world and their local community. Examples include the creation of growing spaces across the site and opening wildlife corridors across the campus. The flowers and crops benefit insects, as do the bug hotels made by students and the five beehives on the roof of the Students' Union building. The chickens (cared for by students) provide eggs that are sold in the student-run organic Hive Café together with campus-grown salads, jams and cordials. The Hive Café has become a community hub and meeting place for people from the local area, all of whom are welcomed by the university in line with its open-campus ethos.

Many universities have interesting green campus settings, but for our students, the juxtaposition of these spaces with the urban university setting is what makes it stand out. The Roehampton campus is remarkable: its 54-acre parkland campus is enhanced by two lakes, a wisteria arch and numerous trees, several of which are protected under the Tree Preservation Order (Wandsworth Borough Council, 2018).

Set in the grounds of the university is Froebel's Orchard, originally planted in 1922 when Froebel College first began training teachers. There are twenty remaining apple trees from the original orchard, which are now veteran trees. There are also young pear trees recently planted in the old orchard, and a younger orchard integrated onsite. Students have access to a Vatican Garden situated in the Catholic Digby Stuart College, an area of calm, open to all, where students can sit, work, contemplate and relax. The college is home to petting rabbits, and across the university, geese, swans and ducks populate the campus.

Another small garden houses a statue by renowned local sculptor, Nathan David. These examples serve to illustrate the importance that the University of Roehampton places on the outdoors as a resource to complement the academic element of university life and to add a dimension of wellbeing.

Figure 9.1 Wisteria flowers in front of university building.

Figure 9.2 Goose and two goslings on grass in front of university building.

The campus adjoins Richmond Park, a National Nature Reserve with rich biodiversity and Red and Fallow deer, herds of which have been roaming here since the 1600s. Recently, local school children and Roehampton students met with Sir David Attenborough to plant 70 new young broadleaved trees as part of the Queen's Green Canopy initiative. Whitelands College, a neo-classical Palladian villa and former home of Gerard Manley Hopkins also overlooking the park, sits within the Alton Estate, a site of architectural significance. Its urban modernism was 'considered to be the crowning glory of post-World War II social housing' (Twentieth Century Buildings, 2023), whose 'beauty lies in the fusion of a variety of modern housing types with pre-existing landscaping, public sculpture and social facilities' (Stjernstedt, n.d.). Grade II listed buildings are found amongst the Corbusian 11-storey slab blocks, and whilst less obviously appealing than the green spaces on campus, the estate has a stark beauty of its own. Its architectural heritage and interesting landscaping provide a contrasting space where students are encouraged by tutors to sketch, walk, think and discuss.

Unlike much of London and other major UK cities, Roehampton is surrounded by green spaces. The university bus provides free access to the campus along semi-rural routes, exposing our students to wide natural spaces within the urban environment. An endpoint of one of the university bus routes is the

Figure 9.3 Buildings on a university campus.

Wildfowl and Wetland Trust (WWT) London Wetland Centre (LWC). WWT Barnes is built on four old Victorian reservoirs. In the 1990s plans were drawn up to develop the area into buildings. Thanks to Sir Peter Scott, the founder of WWT, the reservoirs became a protected space for nature and, as Sir David Attenborough explains, an extra lung for Londoners (WWT, 2021). Sir Peter Scott was the son of the Antarctic explorer, Captain Scott, who wrote to Peter's mother in his dying letter that she should 'make the boy interested in natural history' (WWT, 2021). In 1946 Sir Peter Scott set up the first WWT (Slimbridge) as a centre for science and conservation and, unusually for the time, it was opened to the public so that people could enjoy nature. In May 2022 Roehampton University and LWC entered into a partnership with the aim to lower barriers for the students and local community to access nature.[1] A year later, the relationship is firmly in place and of significant benefit to our university community, offering, amongst others, blue therapy through Blue Prescribing[2], cross-organisation volunteering and internships, knowledge-exchange particularly about freshwater life, as well as tapping into cross-benefit activity such as scavenger hunts and bat walks.

Realities and practicalities

Whilst these ideas are embraced by many staff and students, making use of the campus and other spaces is not without difficulties. In an age driven by technology, persuading students to work in a space where technology takes a back seat can be challenging. We are also at the vagaries of the weather and so best-laid plans have to be abandoned at the last minute. Often, the value of being outdoors and even the type of work being undertaken constitutes learning that cannot be easily measured and quantified (Hawxwell et al., 2019). This can make it hard to justify, if metrics are predominantly driving university quality assurance processes.

Access to green spaces, such as forests, parks, grasslands and recreational areas, and blue spaces, such as rivers, oceans, seas and lakes, improves health and wellbeing (Ebi and Bowen, 2023). The benefits of blue and green spaces are, however, understood variously by different communities of people and nature appeals to different people in different ways (Krymkowski et al., 2014). Many of our students experience barriers to engagement with the outdoors, feeling that these spaces are not their domain. At Roehampton we have an increasing number of Muslim and Hindu students: 31% of our students are Muslim in contrast to 27% Christian. This is pertinent, as research suggests that for students of colour:

> barriers [to nature include] a lack of inclusive imagery, insufficient facilities for social gathering, prior instances of discrimination, the perceived whiteness of protected areas, and unfamiliarity with these spaces.
>
> (Edwards et al., 2023, p. 1)

The exposure of our students to opportunities to interact with nature, through nature and in nature during their time at Roehampton cannot, therefore, be underestimated.

Potentially the most significant barrier to some students is their feeling of marginalisation. Research has repeatedly shown that people who are generally marginalised in education are often also marginalised in terms of outdoor leisure (non-sporting) activities (Humphrey, 2020; Waite et al., 2021). Given the mixed demographic of our students, there can be very different responses to suggestions for outdoor activities, some of which mirror the difficulties highlighted in the research. BIPOC[3] students' engagement in outdoor activities is much less than for other groups of people and there are complex reasons for this. Staddon Foster (2021), for example, points to the deep anxiety towards the countryside, harboured by many Black individuals in Britain due to its historical lack of diversity and associated racist cultures:

Black communities have become culturally disenfranchised from the outdoors, with just 26.2 percent of Black people spending time in the countryside compared to 44.2 percent of white people.

This is echoed in the US, where:

close to 70 percent of people who visit national forests, national wildlife refuges, and national parks are White, while Black people remain the most dramatically underrepresented group in these spaces.

(Humphrey, 2020)

In researching the views of young people, Waite et al. (2021, p. 67) uncovered a prevailing view that:

nature engagement is seen as controlled principally by white middle-class able-bodied males, excluding those lacking social capital in terms of class, ethnicity and physical ability.

This is clearly a significant concern, but there are ways to address the problems.

Academic and co-curricular strategies to address barriers

Role models are key, and it has been vital to use them to inspire our students and to show them that they have a legitimate place in this learning environment. Particular examples include Zahrah Mahmood, also known as 'The Hillwalking Hijabi' (Parveen, 2020), and Pammy Johal, who established 'Backbone' to encourage and celebrate diversity through adventure (Bailey, 2021). In an Evidence Briefing from Natural England (2022), among various recommendations, two stand out as being manageable and relevant for higher education practitioners: accepting diverse perceptions and enjoyments of what is 'nature'; building confidence in using different greenspace, including focusing on safety.

Although outdoor spaces can be beautiful, relaxing and calming, safety can be a real concern for some students who find dense wooded areas intimidating or threatening. Others are anxious about dirt and the lack of hygiene in touching natural materials. Some of these fears stem from childhood (Milligan and Bingley, 2007) and tutors need to be aware of these worries. One of the ways the university community is gently invited into the outdoors is through Growhampton, a sustainability initiative with a focus on food growing. Growhampton was established in September 2013 (initially funded by the NUS Student Green Fund) and is delivered by Roehampton Students' Union in partnership with the university. Growhampton has established an edible campus that promotes biodiversity and helps the university community to engage with sustainability initiatives.

The multi-faith chaplaincy (with Hindu, Muslim, Christian and Jewish representation) presents holistic and co-curricular opportunities to engage in community, discovering personal identity with support to flourish in faith and friendship. Faith is portrayed in the day-to-day experiences of the student community, who are invited to spend time in worship and reflection by use of prayer rooms and chapels on the university campus. Prayer rooms are designed with access to windows and views to help disconnect from the hustle and bustle of student life and connect with spirituality, reflection and nature. Furthermore, chaplaincy activities invite the student and staff community to immerse themselves in nature to dig, weed and sow in the Peace Garden, paint in the Bible Garden or plant flowers and make bird feeders in the quiet of the Vatican Garden. Over the pandemic, the Chaplaincy extended a self-guided faith walk through the campus grounds, which enabled a spiritual connection using the exercise of prayer, meditation and offering of gratitude for the environment that is lived, worked and studied in. With many commons and Richmond Park in the vicinity, walks ('URban Rambling') are organised to encourage the university community to spend time learning about culture, heritage and the natural world in London's green spaces. Emphasis is on facilitating these excursions, recognising how perceived and experienced socio-cultural and socio-economic factors have determined marginality for individuals and groups from outdoor spaces, whether they are common (public) or protected. Recognising the need to balance the responsibility to God and God's creation, particularly through the lens of Islam, the Muslim Chaplain proactively engaged in setting up the partnership with the London Wetland Centre, which has lowered barriers to access therapeutic blue spaces by modelling good practise. Secular opportunities are also encouraged and offered, particularly through the Growhampton community.

Issues highlighted by research (i.e. reluctance, exclusion, nervousness, disengagement, fear, etc,) make it imperative that tutors prepare students sensitively for learning outdoors. Increasingly, the field of educational development is becoming involved in this outdoor pedagogy, working with tutors to help them support adults in less common forms of higher education learning. Amongst the roles adopted by guiding adults is a spectrum of options ranging from significantly directing or joining in with activities through more hands-off, laissez-faire approaches, to situations where the students take full control of their learning.[4]

Conclusion

Although the importance of learning outdoors has been discussed at length for children, this has not been the case for students and adult learners. The COVID-19 pandemic changed this by throwing into sharp relief the need to forge connections with and between our students and spaces. 72% of our students commute to Roehampton and they can struggle to feel fully 'at home' when they are at university. It may seem counter-intuitive to take them out of the classroom and away from campus. However, when trying to remove barriers to access university life, and to cultivate a sense of identity, visits and trips to local green spaces and the use of the outside areas of the campus help to bridge the gap between the university community and nature-connectedness.

Across academic, support and community roles, we strive to make good use of our campus and the local area. We take time to get to know our students, allowing us to see how they react to the suggestion of activities in nature, and adapting our roles to support them appropriately, adjusting the intensity of staff direction and involvement. Our green campus is seen as a relatively safe space in which to begin the exploration of learning in and through nature, which helps to induct students into activities that may initially seem alien. It is consequently a relatively simple matter to encourage students to step outside and engage with nature as part of their time on campus.

Our final words go to a Year Two undergraduate student reflecting on activities designed to increase independence through tutor-led and facilitated outdoor activities linked to a taught module:

> I began suffering from crippling anxiety and detrimental homesickness; subsequently I found myself confined to the four walls of a bleach-smelling office in an uncomfortable reading chair being prescribed [a] medication. At first it worked wonders, but it began to wear off. [...] Around the same time, I had begun the Learning Beyond the Classroom module which to my surprise provided me with effective tools and resources to better my mental health through the outdoor setting. [...] After a few weeks of making well-being walks a priority in my lifestyle I began to feel remarkably better and my symptoms of anxiety began to reduce. [The walks] have significantly decreased my anxiety symptoms.

Notes

1 Previous relationships for work placements, volunteer programmes and visits have been arranged since the centre opened in 2000. These have waxed and waned depending on staff capacity, funding and student need.
2 https://www.wwt.org.uk/our-work/projects/blue-prescribing/what-is-blue-p rescribing/
3 The acronym BIPOC refers to Black, indigenous, and other people of colour.
4 See Winstanley (2015) for pedagogical ideas. See also Waite et al. (2021, pp. 61–2) for a breakdown of different pedagogies: 'supervised, facilitated, self-led, young people as decision makers'.

References

Bailey, D. (2021). Meet the Activists Helping to Diversify the Outdoors: Pammy Johal. Accessed June 24, 2023. Available at: https://www.ukclimbing.com/articles/fea tures/meet_the_activists_helping_to_diversify_the_outdoors_pammy_johal-12841.
Best, R. (2016). *Exploring the Spiritual in the Pedagogy of Friedrich Froebel.* Paper presented at the 15th International Conference on Children's Spirituality – Spirituality and the Whole Child: Interdisciplinary Approaches, Bishop Grosseteste University, Lincoln, UK,July 26–29, 2016.

Ebi, L. K., and Bowen, K. (2023). Green and Blue Spaces: Crucial for Health, Sustainable, Urban Futures. *The Lancet*, 401, (10376): 529–530. https://doi.org/10.1016/S0140-6736(23)00096-X.

Edwards, R. C., Larson, B. M., and Burdsey, D. (2023). What Limits Muslim Communities' Access to Nature? Barriers and Opportunities in the United Kingdom. *Environment and Planning E: Nature and Space*, 6, (2): 880–900. https://doi.org/10.1177/25148486221116737.

Hawxwell, L., O'Shaughnessy, M. A., Russell, C. T., and Shortt, D. (2019). Do You Need a Kayak to Learn Outside?: A Literature Review into Learning Outside the Classroom. *Education 3–13*: 322–332. https://doi.org/10.1080/03004279.2018.1444074.

Humphrey, N. (2020). Breaking Down the Lack of Diversity in Outdoor Spaces. Accessed May 29, 2023. https://nationalhealthfoundation.org/breaking-down-lack-diversity-outdoor-spaces/.

Institute for Fiscal Studies (2021). English Universities Ranked on Their Contributions to Social Mobility – and the Least Selective Post-1992 Universities Come Out on Top. Accessed May 29, 2023. Available at: https://ifs.org.uk/news/english-universities-ranked-their-contributions-social-mobility-and-least-selective-post-1992.

Jackson, A. (2022). The four foundations of belonging at university. https://wonkhe.com/blogs/the-four-foundations-of-belonging-at-university/.

Krymkowski, D. H., Manning, R. E., and Valliere, W. A. (2014). Race, Ethnicity, and Visitation to National Parks in the United States: Tests of the Marginality, Discrimination, and Subculture Hypotheses with National-Level Survey Data. *Journal of Outdoor Recreation and Tourism*, 7, (8): 35–43.

Kuh, G. D., Kinzie, J., Buckley, J. A., Bridges, B. K., and Hayek, J. C. (2006). What Matters to Student Success: A Review of the Literature. Retrieved from: http://nces.ed.gov/npec/pdf/kuh_team_report.pdf.

Liebschner, J. A. (1992). *Child's Work: Freedom and Play in Froebel's Educational Theory and Practice*. The Lutterworth Press.

Meehan, C. and Howells, K. (2019). In Search of the Feeling of 'Belonging' in Higher Education: Undergraduate Students' Transition into Higher Education. *Journal of Further and Higher Education*, 43 (10): 1376–1390. doi:10.1080/0309877X.2018.1490702.

Milligan, C., and Bingley, A. (2007). Restorative Places or Scary Spaces? The Impact of Woodland on the Mental Well-being of Young Adults. *Health and Place*, 13 (4): 799–811.

Natural England (2022). *Included Outside: Engaging People from Ethnic Minority Backgrounds in Nature*. Retrieved April 10, 2023, from https://publications.naturalengland.org.uk.

Office for Students (2022). Students at English Higher Education Providers between 2010–11 and 2020–21. Retrieved September 6, 2023, from https://www.officeforstudents.org.uk/media/79a7bb57-83cf-4c50-a358-6bcfe80f165c/ofs2022_29.pdf.

Parveen, N. (2020). The BAME Women Making the Outdoors More Inclusive. *The Guardian*. https://www.theguardian.com/travel/2020/dec/02/the-bame-women-making-the-british-outdoors-more-inclusive.

Pedler, Megan Louise, Willis, Royce, and Nieuwoudt, Johanna Elizabeth (2022). A Sense of Belonging at University: Student Retention, Motivation, and Enjoyment. *Journal of Further and Higher Education*, 46 (3): 397–408. doi:10.1080/0309877X.2021.1955844.

Staddon Foster, L. (2021). "We Outside" but Do We Belong? – Discovering Sports, Leisure, and the Outdoors While Black. *Race Ed.* University of Edinburgh. Retrieved May

2, 2023, from https://www.race.ed.ac.uk/we-outside-but-do-we-belong-discovering-sp orts-leisure-and-the-outdoors-while-black/.

Stjernstedt, R. (n.d.). Alton Estate London, United Kingdom. *Architectuul.* Retrieved April 10, 2023, from https://architectuul.com/architecture/alton-estate.

Tinto, Vincent (1993). *Leaving College: Rethinking the Causes and Cures of Student Attrition.* Chicago: University of Chicago Press.

Twentieth Century Buildings (2023). Campaigning for Outstanding Buildings: Buildings at Risk Alton Estate, Roehampton. Retrieved April 10, 2023, from https://c20society.org.uk.

Von Marenholtz-Bülow, B. M. F. (1892). *Reminiscences of Friedrich Froebel.* (Translated by Mann, H.). Boston: Lee and Shepard.

Waite, S., Husain, F. T., Scandone, B., Forsyth, E., and Piggott, H. (2021). "It's Not for People Like (Them)": Structural and Cultural Barriers to Children and Young People Engaging with Nature Outside Schooling. *Journal of Adventure Education and Outdoor Learning,* 23 (1): 54–73. https://doi.org/10.1080/14729679.2021.1935286.

Wandsworth Borough Council (2018). List of Properties Where Trees are Covered by Tree Preservation Orders. Available at: https://www.wandsworth.gov.uk/media/3765/ tree_preservation_orders_december_2018.pdf.

Winstanley, C. (2015). Spaced Out: Impact of Museum Spaces on Teaching and Learning. *Education Sciences and Society, Arte e Musei, Educazione e Formazione,* 5 (2): 65–82.

Winstanley, C. (2018). Learning Experiences in Museums: Harnessing Dewey's Ideas on Continuity and Interaction. *Education 3–13,* 46 (4): 424–432. https://doi.org/10. 1080/03004279.2018.1445476.

Wildfowl and Wetland Trust (2021). Ten Fascinating Facts about WWT Founder Sir Peter Scott. Available at: https://www.wwt.org.uk/news-and-stories/blog/ten-fascinating-fa cts-about-sir-peter-scott/.

Part 3

Tools and techniques

Chapter 10

Twalks

Walking, talking and tweeting

Andrew Middleton

The twalk model

Definition

A twalk was originally conceived as a learning walk augmented by a Twitter-based tweetchat and used to explore, co-create, capture and share key ideas amongst connected, dispersed or co-located walking groups. The specific role of Twitter as a platform has become problematic since its acquisition by Elon Musk in 2022. Nevertheless, and significantly, the rationale for the pedagogic approach demonstrates the value of designing technology-enhanced conversation-based learning activities that build upon social media behaviours. As such, it is generalisable to other technologies, platforms and behaviours as will be explored here. The concept makes connections for the integrated use of social media, personal smart technologies and atypical peripatetic learning spaces. The ideas intersect to produce an engaging form of student-centred and experiential learning (Middleton & Spiers, 2019).

In a twalk the learning cohort follows a route designed by a twalk leader. Leaders are often the teacher but can be students or others seeking to guide a group through a set of ideas, tasks or situated problems. The idea emerged from my concurrent use of learning walks and tweetchats. The following sections introduce both methods and their rationales, and note the similarities that led to this converged model.

Learning walks and learning spaces

A learning walk is an event in which people walk together in conversation in pursuit of a common goal. As a co-operative social constructivist pedagogy, learning walks mix social purpose and individual agency by accommodating learning through conversation. It is a method I have used frequently to engage co-walkers in learning about the affordance of spaces in learning space design. I learnt that ambling in conversation with others is an enjoyable, humanising experience and an effective way of designing inclusive learning. Walking reflects ideas of ill-structured problem-based learning (Kapur & Kinzer, 2007) and helps us to become friendly co-operators, even when our motivations are different (Middleton, 2018).

DOI: 10.4324/9781003436928-17

An important outcome of using walks to aid learning came from scheduling Learning Spaces walks during the 'twilight zone'. Positioning co-operative learning in the threshold space at the end of the working day helped to heighten a sense of agency and convivial home space (Oldenburg, 1989). The regular Learning Spaces walk I organised had a reputation and presence that steadily grew due to the people we picked up along the way. Its 'public' visibility raised interest and understanding amongst people who had diverse perspectives and responsibilities for learning spaces. Over several weeks, the regular group of otherwise unrelated walkers steadily began to coalesce and appreciate the different ways of looking at the subject of space. The takeaway from this was that being outside may simply mean being outside one's norm. A learning walk is an example of non-formal learning (Eraut, 2000), an idea that intrinsic learning occurs in many situations with some light structuring.

To replicate the learning walk approach, I recommend:

- Establish a regular pattern of events.
- Assign a theme, topic or inquiry for each walk and ensure it is open-ended.
- Frame the walk by using a series of ill-structured 10-minute discussions.
- Publish the route and timings online so people can join along the way if necessary.
- Encourage walkers to change partners and cross-pollinate the outcomes of their micro discussions.
- Ensure space is available for end-of-walk wrap-ups.
- Aim to hand-over leadership of future walks to regular members of the group.

From walks to tweetchats

Tweetchats are chat sessions that happen on Twitter (now X) at a scheduled time, typically for an hour. Like learning walks, they are semi-structured events using a pre-planned series of five or six questions, with one posted every 10 minutes. Engagement is facilitated using a hashtag which acts as a meeting space for synchronous scheduled meetings.

The tweetchat leader typically has little to do other than devise the questions beforehand and post them on time during the session. Participants can follow the structure as laid out and respond to the questions as they appear or they can backtrack according to the exchanges they have. Behaviours such as liking, retweeting, copying others into tweets, linking to related web-based resources, double-hashtagging and so forth indicate how the dynamic of a tweetchat is networked rather than hierarchical.

Learning from social media

How does social media play a role in this experience?

- **Multilogues** – Depending on the number of participants (which is often hard to gauge), a tweetchat can be a frenetic 'multilogue' (Megele, 2014) with multiple micro-conversations flowing back and forth as determined by participants. Like learning walks, tweetchats scaffold synchronous conversations in which there is a high degree of participant autonomy.
- **Hashtags** – The hashtag is an example of a functional symbol which, when examined more closely, reveals alternative meanings and possibilities. This indicates how the tweetchat, when incorporated in the twalk concept, may serve a variety of purposes that can complement in-person activities.
- **Devices** – A device is needed to connect social media postings so they can be aggregated, filtered or sorted, assigned by the individual as a way to associate their thinking or experience with others.

However, hashtags can be understood spatially too (Middleton, 2023b), and can have more nuanced meanings and purposes, such as:

- A beacon – signalling ideas, opportunities or a call to action.
- A hub – a gathering place, a place of association, a place to collect ideas and thinking.
- A badge – a sign of affiliation, e.g. a learning group or team, a professional network.
- A connector – a method for making connections, e.g. between unrelated post or through 'double hashtagging' conversations or groups that address similar interests in non-related contexts.
- A catalyst – a place to ignite or inspire each other.
- A record – source of data, and a record of action and research.

Media-enhanced learning – Being out and about or in the field should be a visually stimulating experience; one worth capturing. Ideas and experience can be reinforced by using photographs, video, audio and memes. Doing so helps to establish learner agency as reflected in the idea of 'learner gatherer' (Middleton, 2011). It reflects the practice of photovoice as a form of enquiry-based learning in which participants are activated by producing visual artefacts to enhance discussion, both during the event and when reflecting upon it later (O'Malley & Munsell, 2020). Twalks allow videos and voice notes to be made along the way. Typically, a twalk will involve specific photographic challenges (e.g. 'Find an object to represent this idea' or 'Record this process' or 'Make a memory note', etc.). Media captured on a walk can be assembled into an annotated slide deck to support later class-based discussion.

Polycontextual boundary crossing – Social media use is situated in multiple contexts, both simultaneously and over time. In a postdigital context (Fawns, 2019), the spaces we use for learning need to develop spatial fluency; a critical appreciation of how many contexts intersect and need to be negotiated and navigated. Having spatial fluency promotes, for example, digital agency, agility, inclusion and welfare.

Pedagogically, polycontexuality describes being:

> engaged not only in multiple simultaneous tasks and task-specific participation frameworks within one and the same activity, [actants] are also increasingly involved in multiple communities of practice.
>
> (Engeström et al., 1995, p. 320)

Engagement in multiple contexts concurrently affords boundary crossing opportunities or liminal transgressions. Potentially, the moving between the digital and the physical, and their respective participants, can create an unusual stimulus in which participants interact differently.

Twalks: merging walks and tweetchats to create connected multimodal experiences

A twalk, fundamentally, is no more than a learning walk. However, connecting walking to tweeting by assigning a hashtag to the walk, and optionally using social media to connect to other walking groups, together with the incorporation of user-generated and found media, means that the vibrancy and associated possibilities of the learning walk multiply exponentially. This is explored in the following deconstruction in which facets of the twalk as a space for learning are considered.

Deconstruction of a twalk

Walkers, twalkers or participants

A twalk is a collaborative activity. Participants come together in person to explore an idea or problem together. They have a high degree of autonomy: wandering, wavering and deviating from the prescribed plan at their discretion. As an associative group, individuals coalesce as walking groups. This becomes clear when observing walking groups. While some people walk shoulder-to-shoulder, others will slip-and-slide between conversations as they catch sight of acquaintances or overhear remarks. This may be decisive splintering, or perhaps more nuanced connecting behaviours such as in-person or digital 'liking' or cross-pollinating ideas from earlier group discussions and connecting and multiplying thinking. Some partners will even pause for a moment to consider a point before resuming pace and catching up with the main body of the walking group. Individuals may wave to signal to others they are OK and still in touch, or beckon when they're not. Others will loiter and lurk, seeming to feed off overheard conversations. Such behaviours are observable in walks, tweetchats and twalks. Whether in-person or digitally, these natural behaviours demonstrate spatial fluency – a sense of ease in moving between the digital and physical experience. More than that, being together creates a motivational force that enables individuals to find their footing on their own terms.

Following a route

A twalk follows a route. Here, the term 'route' is used in both a geographic and metaphorical sense, being a plan to guide participants. The route is populated by landmarks or viewpoints (buildings, ideas, questions, etc.) that offer a structure to encourage walkers to pause, think and act in response to a series of provocations every 10 minutes or so. Once the next question is posted, twalkers start walking to their next viewpoint, discussing the question or undertaking the activity as they go.

The route is presented as a type of map. While the map graphically represents the walk to be taken (e.g. through a part of the campus, across town, etc.), it can be annotated with the hashtag that has been constructed for the twalk and posting its questions. Instructions on how to format the tweets that participants will post along the way can also be provided on the route map. If a twalk needs to engage walkers on several sites, a map can be produced for each site. Alternatively, the 'map' can be generalised with the viewpoints described in text, such as prompts like, 'Head for a shop selling stationary' or 'Find a PC Lab for the next challenge'. The actual places and instructions should reflect the topic as far as possible.

Photographs can be incorporated as part of the map too if this helps. For example, I have done Art Deco architecture twalks, public art twalks and twalks for Tourism students involving specific sites like hotels and museums. Using photographs on the maps can give participants something to look for and reassure them that they have found the right place.

It is useful to include intended timings so that walkers don't forget to move on to the next destination and to ensure they stay in sync with walkers in other places. Multi-site global twalks can be organised to compare intercultural perceptions and practices, so it is important to think about how timings are presented to keep everyone together.

Timings can have other uses. Firstly, tweet questions can be prepared beforehand and automated so they are posted to a schedule. This can be helpful when the twalk is being led by a single person who needs to focus on what is happening rather than on setting up the next tweet. If not automating the posting, I recommend preparing a Notes file with all the tweet posts set up in advance so they can be easily copied and pasted into the social app while walking.

Secondly, making the posting schedule explicit helps to ensure people send their responses to the question posts at the same time and this aids interaction amongst the various walkers. Maps can be produced as web pages or PDF documents. Be aware that smartphone connections can drop out and not everyone will want to use their mobile data. You can advise people to print out the maps or to download them to their mobile devices. Alternatively, consider printing and laminating some copies for your twalkers. This can help when it is pouring with rain and or when the blinding sun makes screens hard to read. Planning in shelter pauses for reviewing the social media feed can be useful and can help to ensure there is engagement with the ideas being generated by walkers. While many people are used to walking around towns and cities with eyes focused on their phones, it is recommended, especially where twalks are in public spaces, that twalkers are instructed to stop walking before interacting with their phones and guided to look after each other for safety reasons.

Twalks can be a useful way of connecting people from different courses in interdisciplinary or interprofessional learning, or other situations where common interests can be explored. I have organised twalks that involved two universities located in the same city as a co-development event. The context for this was a collaboration on learning space development between Sheffield Hallam University and the University of Sheffield. We started on one campus by examining a new development, sauntered across the city discussing the student experience of the city, before arriving at the second campus to look at developments there. I have also organised twalks for universities with large campuses. At the University of Leeds, for example, colleagues from different Departments enjoyed touring each other's classrooms and social facilities. I have also organised twalks within conferences which can provide a good networking opportunity while allowing the conference to reach out and connect with people who are not attending in person.

The twalk model can work to support most teaching contexts. Taking students out of the usual classroom environment can help them to think differently. Because of the conversational nature of twalks and the need to make posts, twalks can make great reflective interludes in the same way that some course inductions use treasure hunts (DML, 2017).

Incorporating a theoretical framework as a basis for a twalk design can help to develop students' awareness of reflection on learning. The Doing, Being, Belonging, Becoming & Connecting framework (Middleton et al., 2023), for example, provided just enough structure for a global twalk involving educators interested in active learning. Each keyword seeded questions: Q1 What do people like us do? Q2 What makes us distinctive? Q3 What do we value in each other? Q4 What are our aspirations? Q5 Who should we follow? While such a conversation requires some preliminary contextual introduction, a twalk can be a suitably ill-structured excursion in which to contemplate such questions. Equally, a field trip can direct more specific questions related to its focus.

A connection may be made between the actual location and the shift in conversation: arrival at the campus library, for example, may involve a task aimed at framing the next 10 minutes of conversation, such as 'discuss a paper you have read recently and a question it raised for you'. The location may provide a photo opportunity or the task itself may invite walkers to find an object and photograph it to help explain the twalk's topic or underlying theory metaphorically.

The use of social media differentiates a twalk from the simpler description of a learning walk above: it allows a connection to be made to other groups following the 'same' route, whether co-located or walking in another geographical location. Secondly, by using a social media hashtag and codes for each landmark question (e.g. #20thcenturypainters Q1), all participants have a common digitally connected space in which they can share their responses to the sequenced questions posed periodically by the twalk leader. The act of posting responses to a shared space is a form of social constructive learning through the co-creation of a feed and the formation of a collective record of the activity as it progresses. The contributions made by walkers along the way are typically text-based but may include links to websites and online media, photographs produced by the walkers, or audio summaries, for example.

A learning ecology

A twalk is ill-structured. While it is typically carefully planned, the significance of being ill-structured is that it is student-centred: the route and the topic are fundamentally navigated and negotiated by each participant as they meander through it with others. Meandering, rather than following or leading, represents the autonomous nature of walking and its intrinsic agency. This is best articulated by understanding the concept of learning ecologies (Barnett & Jackson, 2020, p. 2) which is integral to the idea of the twalk:

> The very idea of ecology links people and their ways of thinking, being, and doing in a fundamental way to the environment in which they are learning. By 'environment', we are not only talking about the physical environment that we can sense and perceive; we are talking also about the rich, fertile environments we can create in our minds. Fundamentally, a learning ecology is a place where learning and the environment are indivisible.

Environment, therefore, is defined not only by its physicality and its geographic boundaries, but by its social, spatial and psychological settings. The concept of learning ecologies recognises the agency of the individual within a social setting. This is an important principle in both tweetchats and learning walks, and multiplied therefore in the twalk concept.

Interaction: Recommendations on talking and posting in twalks

1   Be clear about how much tweeting and how much talking you expect. Before setting out, explain how twalkers should add their thoughts to the discussion to ensure they do more than simply 'like' postings. A dress rehearsal tweetchat in class may help students to learn how to formulate useful responses.
2   Advise each group to post one or two responses to each question and to reply to at least one other group.
3   Advise groups that they are co-creating by making a record of their experience. Beyond the twalk, explain how this record will be used to inform other learning activities.

4   Advise groups to post summaries of in-person conversations by drawing out and agreeing on the best ideas. Including photographs or memes can help twalkers to remember conversations and experiences later.

5   Respond to each other's posts along the way. Twalkers can do this by answering questions raised, posing further questions, liking and retweeting comments they find useful, taking photographs along the way, and sharing memes (animated gifs that capture reactions).

6   Consider allocating the role of Tweet Agent to one person in each group of three or four. This ensures that the group stays on task and that it formulates and posts a succinct response to each question. The Tweet Agent can report on what other groups are posting and co-ordinate one or more responses. Others in the group can choose to engage with the Twitter feed too, but it is recommended that groups have a person assigned to managing the social media feed and, thereby, making a living record of the activity.

7   Consider framing the twalk differently where multiple sites or stakeholders are involved (e.g. UK campus collaborations, international course collaborations, professional networks, multisite staff development, etc.). This could involve a pre-event discussion in which partners agree on what they want from the experience.

Being outside, on the move, and attached

The significance of 'outdoors' seems to be that it is 'not indoors as usual', but it is much more than this. The value of situated learning is multiplied by the mobility and dispersal of participants, as in the case of a twalk. As investigators, learners are on the front foot, being actants responding to the world around them, influenced by the spatial affordances that make up the physical or digital space which invites new and specific behaviours. Both Assemblage Theory (DeLanda, 2016) and Actor–Network Theory (Latour, 2005) are concerned with appreciating the relationship between space and agency as an outcome of human and non-humans in association (Müller, 2015). This helps to frame our interest in outdoors: the environment is an actant.

The concept of inviting affordances (Withagen et al., 2017) also provides insight on the value that can be gained by considering the spatial qualities of the twalk and outdoor learning more generally. More than simply going outside, the environment solicits actions by inviting the agent to feel drawn to act in a certain way. While 'having a change of scene' or 'getting a bit of fresh air' may be drivers for taking learning outside, the benefits of the twalk method can be heightened by examining its spatial affordances.

Being outside and in a situation designed to scaffold a formative conversation shows the twalk to be a novel learning space. However, novelty is problematic in spatial design. It is mostly an ephemeral benefit. Psychophysiology, however, shows how having a sense of novelty can activate the dopamine system, directly enhancing mood and creating a positive outlook in a continual mind-body feedback loop (Daugherty, 2022). At the same time, novelty is coupled with familiarity in the twalk design through the intrinsic conviviality in acts of walking and talking in groups.

Place attachment, the emotional bond between person and place (Lewicka, 2011), informs the following questions and may help in designing twalks and other forms of outdoor learning:

- How does the place reinforce or develop academic or professional identity?
- What associations (memories, experiences, perceptions, aspirations) already exist for participants with a particular place, community or technology? How can they be developed?
- What can we do here, specifically, that will be meaningful and memorable?
- How does the environment promote positive feelings for our topic, subject or discipline, and how can we foster such feelings in our activity?
- How can participants interact with the environment (as actant) to cultivate a sense of being, i.e. embodied and authentic learning? And can participants leave a legacy mark or trace evidence of their engagement?

Several of these questions suggest that participants need to attach themselves, not merely as visitors, but as legitimate actants within the chosen environment. Social media's facility to invite others to connect to the twalk event, for example, suggests possibilities such as inviting professionals to observe, interact or feedback on conversations, media, or actions. In physical space, meaning may be found through histories, technologies, occupation, and environmental conditions.

A public performance: Performance and public thinking

Beichner (2014) observes the dynamic of public thinking as a principle of active learning. The use of both social media and open spaces can situate learning in sight of others. There are ethical considerations to this but learning in 'public' acquires a frisson when actants are asked to take a stage and perform. Learning finds a new drive, a focus, and a thrill when enacted in the presence of strangers.

- How can acts of walking, talking, tweeting and twalking be made acts of performance and commitment?

Estrangement: Breaking through orthodoxy

Re-siting learning from the conventions of familiar learning spaces, and their associated expectations and assumptions, creates a challenge of estrangement that requires students to reorient themselves within that foreign space.

- How can moving learning outside invigorate the learner and remove them from their orthodoxy?
- How can shifting orthodoxies instil new vigour and habits that affect engagement in other learning environments, including non-formal spaces supporting self-directed and self-determined learning?

In a study of non-formal learning in pubs (Middleton, 2018a) and a study of geographic field trips (Middleton, 2018b), the role of the teacher and their relationship with their students had to be renegotiated because the respective environments did not support the pre-existing teacher–student power relationships. Similarly, wandering beyond the confines of the conventional classroom is an act of disruption – a 'de-territorialisation/re-territorialisation: the disassembling of phenomena we tend to take for granted' (Müller, 2015, p. 32).

This comes with implications for future relationships that should be considered – 'what happens here stays here' is probably an unrealistic strategy!

Conclusion: Learning outdoors and outside

This introduction to, and deconstruction of, the twalk method, and its relation to learning walks and tweetchats, has surfaced some principles that highlight the disruptive value of outdoor learning. What may be articulated simply as 'a walk using social media' becomes a highly sophisticated learning environment which opens possibilities for adapting the model to other situations.

Moving learning into an outdoor situation mediated by technology can:

- Make the experience troublesome and invigorating; the very situation can heighten the significance of the topic or problem while enjoying the liminal and communal learning experiences of encountering knowledge in strange places.
- Challenge the learner to engage with ideas in ways that are informed by unnoticed or unaccustomed spatial affordances.
- Accommodate high degrees of agency, self-determination, co-operation, and boundary crossing.
- Foster creative 'outsider' identities by disrupting the norms of the learning context.
- Reposition technology as an augmented space for learning rather than one perceived to be a determinant of what happens.
- Introduce media as a way to promote and provoke active engagement and agency.
- Promote the value of authentic *in situ* learning as a stimulus for changing the learning environment in general.
- Inspire and disrupt behaviours and habits, and influence expectations and learning in other situations.

References

Barnett, R., & Jackson, N. (2020). *Ecologies for learning and practice: Emerging ideas, sightings and possibilities and political paradoxes.* Routledge/Taylor & Francis Group.

Beichner, R. J. (2014). History and evolution of active learning spaces. *New Directions for Teaching and Learning,* (137): 9–16. https://doi.org/10.1002/tl.20081.

Daugherty, A. K. (2022, 21 January). The science of novelty: How new solutions to old problems can improve your mental health. *Psychology Today*. Online at: https://www.psychologytoday.com.

DeLanda, M. (2016). *Assemblage theory*. Edinburgh: University of Edinburgh Press.

DML (2017, 26 February). *Teaching through treasure hunts*. Online at: https://dmll.org.uk/teaching-through-treasure-hunts/.

Engeström, Y., Engeström, R., & Kärkkäinen, M. (1995). Polycontextuality and boundary crossing in expert cognition: Learning and problem solving in complex work activities. *Learning and Instruction*, 5(4): 319–336.

Eraut, M. (2000). Non-formal learning and tacit knowledge in professional work. *British Journal of Educational Psychology*, 70: 113–136.

Fawns, T. (2019). Postdigital education in design and practice. *Postdigit Sci Educ* (1): 132–145. https://doi.org/10.1007/s42438-018-0021-8.

Kapur, M., & Kinzer, C. K. (2007). Examining the effect of problem type in a synchronous Computer-Supported Collaborative Learning (CSCL) environment. *Educational Technology Research and Development*, 55(5): 439–459. https://doi.org/10.1007/s11423-007-9045-6.

Latour, B. (2005). *Reassembling the social: An introduction to actor-network theory*. Oxford University Press.

Lewicka, M. (2011). Place attachment: How far have we come in the last 40 years? *Journal of Environmental Psychology*, 31(3): 207–230. https://doi.org/10.1016/j.jenvp.2010.10.001.

Megele, C. (2014). Theorizing Twitter Chat. *Journal of Perspectives in Applied Academic Practice*, 2(2). https://doi.org/10.14297/jpaap.v2i2.106.

Middleton, A. (2011). Audio active: Discovering mobile learner-gatherers from across the formal-informal continuum. *International Journal of Mobile and Blended Learning*, 3 (2): 31–42. https://doi.org/10.4018/jmbl.2011040103.

Middleton, A. (2018). *Reimagining spaces for learning in higher education*. Palgrave Macmillan.

Middleton, A. (2018a). Case Study 12: Pol Nugent: The pub as learning space. In A. Middleton, *Reimagining spaces for learning in higher education*. Palgrave Macmillan.

Middleton, A. (2018b). Case Study 18: Derek France: Teaching and learning in the field. In A. Middleton, *Reimagining spaces for learning in higher education*. Palgrave Macmillan.

Middleton, A. (2023a). *Spatial fluencies: More than spaces, more than literacies*. Learning Landscapes Symposia: Flexibilities, 14 June 2023, SRHE.

Middleton, A. (2023b). *Spatial fluency: What we can learn about teaching and learning from social media*. British Academy Social Media for Learning Symposium, University of Birmingham, 12 June 2023.

Middleton, A., Mogridge, Z., & Foley, S. (2023). Becoming my future self: Student engagement with curriculum live brief assignments to scaffold employability outcomes. In D. Willison and E. Henderson (eds), *Perspectives on enhancing student transition into higher education and beyond*. IGI Global. doi:10.4018/978-1-6684-8198-1.

Middleton, A., & Spiers, A. (2019). Learning to twalk: An analysis of a new learning environment. In C. Rowell (ed.), *Social media in higher education: Case studies, reflections and analysis* (pp. 223–235). https://doi.org/10.11647/OBP.0162.20.

Müller, M. (2015). Assemblages and actor-networks: Rethinking socio-material power, politics and space. *Geography Compass*, 9(1): 27–41. https://doi.org/10.1111/gec3.12192.

Oldenburg R. (1989). *The great good place: Cafes, coffee shops, community centers, beauty parlors, general stores, bars, hangouts and how they get you through the day* (1st ed.). Paragon House.

O'Malley, L. J., & Munsell, S. E. (2020). PhotoVoice: an innovative qualitative method in research and classroom teaching. *Educational Research: Theory and Practice*, 31(1): 26–32.

O'Rourke, V., & Baldwin, C. (2016). Student engagement in placemaking at an Australian university campus. *Australian Planner*, 53: 103–116.

Withagen, R., Araújo, D., & de Poel, H. J. (2017). Inviting affordances and agency. *New Ideas in Psychology*, 45: 11–18.

Chapter 11

Tricks, practicalities and ethics of teaching outdoor walking research, including interviews and group tours

Aled Singleton

Walking pedagogy within higher education

Outdoor walking has grown in popularity as a tool for social research and within other aspects of higher education. Methods-focused papers explain how space triggers conversation between people (Moles, 2008), the art of 'go-along' conversations (Carpiano, 2009) and the advantages of participatory walking interviews (Evans & Jones, 2011). Such work has led to walking methodology textbooks, including: accounts of interdisciplinary social research (Bates & Rhys-Taylor, 2017); more-than-human approaches, including affect and movement (Springgay & Truman, 2018); and a focus on ethnography and participation (O'Neill & Roberts, 2020). However, there is smaller literature focused on walking pedagogy. Existing writing considers teaching physical sciences such as biology, chemistry and physics (Beavington, 2021), furthering the study of affect (Beyes & Steyaert, 2021), critical criminology (O'Neill et al., 2021), and embodied methods for business students (Hindley et al., 2019). There seem to be few textbooks which help teachers to guide students with methods and how to progress.

My biography is important to how I developed the techniques presented in this chapter. For over a decade I have worked on place-based initiatives, working with architects, engineers and urban designers on landscaping schemes, cycle routes and other built environment projects. To broaden my methodological range, I took an MSc in Social Research Methods. I was introduced to walking through a two-day 'critical urban ethnography' course run by the National Centre for Research Methods in 2016. Teaching in this case involved ethnographic methods, such as paying attention to the sounds, smells and visuals set within the context of an urban setting – read more about such methods in *Walking through social research* (Bates & Rhys-Taylor, 2017). Virtually all learning happened outside and on foot, save for the final group presentation. Later in this chapter I explore the balance of outdoor walks and indoor reflection.

Walking now appears on the agenda of conferences and there is a wide range of workshop sessions for walking methods. For example, the fundamental principles are covered in a blog aimed at university teachers (BERA, 2020). The teaching presented here is from the perspective of working in Geography. Though the

DOI: 10.4324/9781003436928-18

Geography Benchmark Statement is not explicit about walking, it hints at accessibility and ethics in guidance for fieldwork (QAA, 2022, pp. 12–14). Such factors influence the examples which are now outlined. The first case is an introductory technique aimed at undergraduates.

Technique 1: Setting and assessing an independent walking task

This approach is designed as a first step to walking practice. A classroom lecture or seminar of approximately 1 hour prepares students to take an independent 30-minute-long walk.

The taught element is framed within ethnography; a broad approach which includes participant observation and interviewing techniques adapted to specific contexts (Pink, 2009). The researcher aims to take a holistic approach by going to different settings to understand 'the significance of the meanings people give to objects, including them-selves, in the course of their activities, in other words culture' (Hammersley, 2018, p. 4). Walking is a vantage point from which to observe others. However, walking through a place means that students can get involved in the phenomena that they are observing.

> To observe means to watch what is going on around and about, and of course to listen and feel as well. To participate means to do so from within the current of activity in which you carry on a life alongside and together with the persons and things that capture your attention.
>
> (Ingold, 2014, p. 387)

Here Ingold, an anthropologist, helps to equate observation with being outside the phenomena and participation to being inside. There are degrees of 'insideness' (Seamon & Sowers, 2008) and walking a line allows the individual to explore the intersections between positions as they move from one space to another. Partly so that the teacher does not have to organise specific risk assessments, and partly to encourage learning, students are free to choose where they go.

The teacher provides a brief as a framework for feedback and development. The main task is for an individual to walk for 30 minutes. As they walk students are advised to take photos, record notes, and to track the route by GPS if they desire. This results in a 500-word digital submission, including five pieces of visual media. A key part of the submission is to be reflective, such as describing the setting and how they feel. Additionally, the brief requires them to address four broad elements:

1   Place (built form, trees, water, parkland, uses, etc.).
2   People (what they are doing, ages, relationships between people, etc.).
3   Signs and directions (visual notices, warnings, sounds, etc.).
4   Atmospheres (weather, events, moods, light, etc.).

The teacher gives an example of what could be found from a short walk. In the case of Swansea University Singleton Campus, there are different forms of built and natural environments within 1km. For example, there is a beach, residential areas, sporting facilities, and a busy hospital. The complexities of being around the hospital will become apparent later.

I have set the same task and marked nearly 70 assignments across two different academic years. Altogether there is clear evidence of students paying attention to place and the natural environment (Beavington (2021). To a lesser degree there is attention to signage and using photographs to back up visual stimuli. Students embrace the freedom of ethnography by walking in unfamiliar places or challenging atmospheres, such as being tourists, being caught up in events, walking when other people are on a night out, or venturing out early in the morning. The students bring the earlier definitions of observation and participation (Ingold, 2014) to life as they engage with their feelings, including fear, pleasure, boredom and more. Some students think about how to make public spaces more accessible. The highest grades are given to submissions which reference published literature – such as connecting their experience of weather, tourism, nature and other subjects to essays from the *Routledge handbook of place* (Edensor et al., 2020). Such a task could contribute 15% of the work for a 10-credit module.

Some submissions have challenged the notion of being physically located in a specific place. There have been cases seemingly composed from online maps and structured as walks. Whilst this misses the opportunities and multiple dimensions of being outside, this reveals opportunities for digital media to complement outdoor walks. Teachers are considering ethnographies of the internet (BERA, 2022). There are also some precedents of assignments which combine digital images, mobile tracking devices and online maps (Bell et al., 2019). In the following description there are examples of students using digital technologies as they walk (and work) together on group projects.

Technique 2: Psychogeography for group work and field trips

Group walks complement the individual tasks. By working (and walking) together they can broaden their understanding of ethnography, namely 'relationships rather than numbers, quality rather than quantity' (Mills & Morton, 2013, p. 186). The following case study offers a framework where students can explore positionality and gain feedback from their experimentation.

This example reflects on a human geography field trip to Berlin, a city to which very few students had a prior connection. I introduce the broad discipline of psychogeography to extend prior learning on observation and participation. Psychogeographical tactics are playful, such as the walking method called the dérive – or drift. This approach typically comprises a set of instructions which the walker must follow. The aim is to pursue Guy Debord's 1955 definition of psychogeography: 'The study of the precise laws and specific effects of the geographical environment, consciously organised or not, on the emotions and behaviour of individuals' (Coverley, 2018, p. 116).

A potential psychogeographical dérive could explore how a place has changed over time and through ongoing use by millions of people. I explored Berlin's history and composed four walking routes. The *Pink Route* (excerpt in Box 11.1) explores how the Berlin Wall once split the city and how Berlin has reinvented itself since its removal. The *Red Route* is a different section of the Berlin Wall. The *Green Route* follows the final stages of the Berlin Marathon, and the *Blue Route* follows a gay rights protest march. The walks are plotted as coordinates which can be accessed through Google Earth.

Box 11.1 Pink Route

The Berlin Wall was constructed in phases and was designed to prevent people escaping from the east to the west. Broadly, the wall on the western side was a big flat slab of concrete. There was a space of approximately 100m between the western side and the eastern inner wall. This 'death strip' gave people no cover and made it easier for East German border soldiers to shoot people trying to escape.

You will be exploring the space between that inner wall and the outer wall. Most of these spaces have since been built-over, in which case find the nearest road or footpath. The purpose of following the old line is to sense the juxtapositions between the old(er) and the new(er) architecture of the city. Does any evidence remain of the wall or any memorials?

We walked as a collective of 20 students and 2 teachers to the location where the 4 routes started. The students split into four smaller groups (of between three and six members) and stayed in these groups throughout the field trip. Backed up by a printed handout, I explained that each route is designed to explore the society and history of the place. For this reason, these lines on the ground are often not the most direct route from Point A to Point B. As such, this dérive could provoke emotional responses such as frustration, delight or indifference. I advised students to embrace this feeling as it could open their senses to what they discover (Ingold, 2014). They are asked to chart these spaces in a reflexive and experiential sense, considering the following factors:

- Built form and use of space. Looking out for prominent buildings, tourism businesses, monuments, forms of transport and other features in the environment which connect to the past and present uses.
- Position. Difference between walking alone and being in a group of two or more people. What happens when you swap between walking alone and walking as a group?
- Recording. Taking photos, notes, recording voice notes on mobile devices and interviewing each other.

We briefed each group in turn and gave students 3 hours to follow their mission. Though not immediately known to the teachers, three groups chose the Pink Route, and another one mixed the Green Route with elements of the Pink Route.

Post-walk feedback sessions

We held an early-evening collective debrief to follow the dérive. The students reported how the Pink Route linked open-air interpretation and memorials to the Berlin Wall, and so stimulated conversations (BERA, 2020; Beavington, 2021). One group explained how the Pink Route also revealed newer architecture, such as banks and universities, built in the former 'kill zone' between the outer and inner walls. Another group recognised that the route took them away from the sign-posted route. As a result, they appreciated their position as tourists and reflected more deeply on wayfinding and how transport systems are explained or not.

Across the three days it was noticeable that students gained confidence from each other to try different methods – such as recording experiences as voice notes or interviewing each other. However, the accessibility of outdoor teaching was tested when one student got injured and could no longer walk. An over-reliance on being able-bodied has been noted in writing about field trips (Rose, 2023). Connected to the opening for digital materials noted in Technique 1, one student stated that he would edit some videos from their walks and link them within their group assignment. This same Berlin walk could be modified and used by sociologists, historians, political scientists, architects, economists and others. It is important to stress that this dérive is designed to encourage (independent) group work. Overall, the students showed evidence of learning through their assignments submitted after the field trip.

In contrast to the previous two cases, the third technique involves a teacher being present throughout. I reflect on what is achievable with postgraduate students who may be less familiar with walking pedagogy but do have a degree of research experience and knowledge of the ethical considerations.

Technique 3: Developing social research methods

This account centres on a 2-hour outdoor session on a qualitative research methods module. Again, the case study is Singleton Campus at Swansea University, Wales. Some weeks in advance students received background reading – such as those referenced in this chapter. Starting from a classroom, students were briefed that the session would focus on interactions between people and place, incorporating a degree of observational ethnography. The first practical exercise explores the 'go-along' (Carpiano, 2009) through peer-to-peer conversations.

Go-along walking interviews

This 20-minute walk takes students from the campus, through a park and over to a nearby residential neighbourhood. The group are briefed to walk side-by-side in groups of up to three. They are invited to let the conversations be 'framed by place' (Evans & Jones, 2011, p. 849) and be stimulated by specific buildings or being in the park. Students were asked to notice what happens as the spaces change, such as stopping to go through a gate or when the way is blocked. In a safe space away from other people, I invited them to gather in a circle and to reflect on their experience. The following responses demonstrate the broad findings.

- The walk helps to develop empathy between people who may not know each other.
- People get into detailed conversations fairly quickly.
- Memories are triggered by being in certain spaces (Moles, 2008). One person recalled being chased by a dog some years ago in one location. She laughed and explained that the story helped to build a rapport with the other person.
- There is much less eye contact than in a normal conversation (BERA, 2020). One attendee expressed that this allowed 'attention to be used on the walk itself'. They suggest that this could be good technique for people with autism.

This feedback stresses the opportunities and qualities of the peer interview. Of note, all students have some connection to spaces near to Swansea University, which differs from the Berlin Fieldtrip (Technique 2). The next stage of the exercise takes the students away from the park and into busier urban spaces.

Ethnography in urban space

Having learned the basics of interviewing others on foot, this 30-minute exercise sets out to be more observational in busier spaces. We return to the psychogeographer's repertoire and use a tool called 'other points of view' (Overall, 2021, p. 18). Facing a given street, half of the group walk via the back lane or alleyway and half walk via the main road. Students are briefed to consider certain factors: animals, including humans; text in the street or on houses; and atmospheres. Like the peer-interviewing we will regroup at the end of the street. The following account combines responses of two different groups who followed this exercise.

Reflections from the first street represented two different versions of the same set of houses. For example, alleyway walkers encountered more animals *in* the alleyway, compared to the front, and saw signs such as 'beware of the dog'. Those who walked the street front witnessed more text, such as street signs and road markings, and evidence of people taking care of front gardens. We then proceeded to another street where the groups swapped over. Those who had walked the alleyway went to the front and vice versa. After regrouping students considered how the time when children go to school or when people return from work would change what they observe. Moreover, some students started to consider ethical issues: Is it right to be looking into houses and gardens? These issues of 'confidentiality, anonymity and intrusion' figure in the psychogeographical teaching of

Hindley et al. (2019, p. 4). A different form of ethics is clear when students considered whether researchers can be vulnerable (Batterham & Singleton, 2023). In this case students asked whether the alleyway is a safe place to walk.

This learning helped students to sense that informed consent and issues of anonymity also extend to naming certain streets or places. In the final case I present the outdoor spaces adjacent to a hospital. This is a sensitive research site with different challenges.

Ethics in sensitive places

Students spent approximately 15 minutes walking in a group to the hospital. They were briefed to consider signage, atmospheres, and whether they are causing a hazard themselves. I took another tool from psychogeography and briefed them to 'walk in character' (Overall, 2021, p. 47). The aim of being in character is to imagine emotional and affective responses to spaces. They would be open to feelings of boredom or frustration as well as heightened emotions such as being in urgent need of care or witnessing births and deaths.

For one group of students there was a visceral response when they reached the hospital canteen. There was a clear smell of hot cooked food, a sensation magnified by it being cold outside. Students observed that patients and visitors could see them. In response they had an almost visceral emotional response. They verbalised that it is inappropriate to be near the canteen and we immediately moved 15m away. This was a real-life example of how walking allows us to experience affect (Beyes & Steyaert, 2021). Though no formal research had taken place, this demonstrated the ethics of a group gathering in a sensitive space (Giddy & Hoogendoorn, 2018). In written feedback one student noted that this experience allowed them to integrate both 'bodily and intellectual knowledge', meaning that the physical act of walking and reflecting outside combined to aid their learning.

Though the hospital example is powerful, a similar response did not happen when the walk was repeated a year later. On the second occasion it was mid-afternoon rather than late-morning. Lunch had finished and there were no smells of food. This time the students were slightly younger. Perhaps they had more emotional distance from a time of heightened health awareness during the COVID-19 pandemic or other crises (Springgay & Truman, 2022). This last case completes my account of incremental techniques. To conclude and summarise this chapter, I outline four main points pertinent for the future development of this discipline.

Suggestions for future work

Levels of prior experience and engagement from students will change from year to year. Moreover, advances in digital technology are certain to influence how walks are recorded, mediated, interpreted and presented. For example, I have not detailed the potential of geographical information systems. All teaching therefore needs to be adaptable and responsive.

Outdoor teaching can be hard to organise. As a prerequisite I completed a two-day outdoor first aid course. Swansea University Occupational Health Team asked students to complete a pre-workshop fitness assessment. Institutions will have to plan and be creative if the momentum behind walking researchers is to transfer into teaching. As teachers plan, deliver and gain feedback, papers and books will emerge. In time we can develop entire modules and courses.

Choice of site is significant. The teacher having experience of one place gives students more independence to practise techniques. Moreover, the teacher can respond to feedback and amend future walks. The wider city offers a wider range of stimulation – such as the Berlin example (Box 11.1). However, travel is expensive, logistics can be more complicated, and indoor teaching space can be harder to find.

Seeking feedback and sharing practice is critical. I presented to teaching peers at the Swansea Academy of Learning and Teaching Conference (Singleton, 2022). One attendee from the Medical School proposed walking as a student supervision technique and another considered using it to debrief paramedic students. However, four respondents to a post-talk survey were unsure whether their students would be comfortable going outside. Therefore, a stronger evidence base will help make these approaches more inclusive for the future.

References

Bates, C., & Rhys-Taylor, A. (2017). *Walking through social research*. London: Routledge. doi:10.4324/9781315561547.

Batterham, M., & Singleton, A. (2023). Framing transdisciplinary research as an assemblage: A case study from a mental health setting. In B. C. Clift, I. C. Batlle, S. Bekker, & K. Chudzikowski, *Qualitative researcher vulnerability: Negotiating, experiencing and embracing* (pp. 206–221). London: Routledge. doi:10.4324/9781003349266–15.

Beavington, L. (2021). Walking pedagogy for science education and more-than-human connection. *Journal of the Canadian Association for Curriculum Studies*, 163–178. doi:10.25071/1916-4467.40626.

Bell, A., Taylor, K. H., Riesland, E., & Hays, M. (2019). Learning to see the familiar: Technological assemblages in a higher education (non) classroom setting. *British Journal of Educational Technology*, 50(4), 1573–1588. doi:10.1111/bjet.12800.

BERA. (2020, January 30). Walking and talking as and for methodological development. Retrieved from BERA: https://www.bera.ac.uk/blog/walking-and-talking-as-and-form ethodological-development.

BERA. (2022, June 14). Ethnography – Embodiment and the digital world. Retrieved from BERA: https://www.bera.ac.uk/event/ethnography-embodiment-and-the-digita l-world.

Beyes, T., & Steyaert, C. (2021). Unsettling bodies of knowledge: Walking as a pedagogy of affect. *Management Learning*, 52(2), 224–242. doi:10.1177/1350507620979713.

Carpiano, R. (2009). Come take a walk with me: The "go-along" interview as a novel method for studying the implications of place for health and well-being. *Health & Place*, 15(1), 263–272. doi:10.1016/j.healthplace.2008.05.003.

Coverley, M. (2018). *Psychogeography*. Harpenden: Oldcastle.

Edensor, T., Kalandides, A., & Kothari, U. (2020). *The Routledge handbook of place*. Abingdon: Routledge. doi:10.4324/9780429453267.

Evans, J., & Jones, P. (2011). The walking interview: Methodology, mobility and place. *Applied Geography*, 31, 849–858. doi:10.1016/j.apgeog.2010.09.005.

Giddy, J. K., & Hoogendoorn, G. (2018). Ethical concerns around inner city walking tours. *Urban Geography*, 39(9), 1293–1299. doi:10.1080/02723638.2018.1446884.

Hammersley, M. (2018). What is ethnography? Can it survive? Should it? *Ethnography and Education*, 13(1), 1–17. https://doi.org/10.1080/17457823.2017.1298458.

Hindley, C., Knowles, D., & Ruth, D. (2019). Teaching research methods: Introducing a psychogeographical approach. *Journal of Management & Organization*, 28(6), 13211333. doi:10.1017/jmo.2019.15.

Ingold, T. (2014). That's enough about ethnography! *HAU: Journal of Ethnographic Theory*, 4(1), 383–395. doi:10.14318/hau4.1.021.

Mills, D., & Morton, M. (2013). *Ethnography in education*. London: Sage. doi:10.4135/9781446251201.

Moles, K. (2008). A walk in thirdspace: Place, methods and walking. *Sociological Research Online*, 13(4), 1–9. doi:10.5153/sro.1745.

O'Neill, M., Penfold-Mounce, R., Honeywell, D., Coward-Gibbs, M., Crowder, H., & Hill, I. (2021). Creative methodologies for a mobile criminology: Walking as critical pedagogy. *Sociological Research Online*, 26(2), 247–268. doi:10.1177/1360780420922250.

O'Neill, M., & Roberts, B. (2020). *Walking methods: Research on the move*. London: Routledge. doi:10.4324/9781315646442.

Overall, S. (2021). *Walk write (repeat)*. Axbridge: Triarchy Press.

Pink, S. (2009). *Doing sensory ethnography*. London: Sage. doi:10.4135/9781446249383.

QAA. (2022). *Subject benchmark statement: Geography*. Gloucester: QAA. Retrieved August 09, 2023, from https://www.qaa.ac.uk/quality-code/subject-benchmarkstatements/geography.

Rose, M. (2023). Stuck in the mud? Finding the glee in all fieldworking bodies. *Area*, 54 (4), 536–540. doi:10.1111/area.12840.

Seamon, D., & Sowers, J. (2008). *Place and placelessness (1976): Edward Relph*. London: SAGE Publications. doi:10.4135/9781446213742.

Singleton, A. (2022, July 13). *Learning by walking: Outdoor workshops + online experiments*. Retrieved from Padlet: https://padlet.com/amsingleton1/dwqyrjhyqv5liybm.

Springgay, S., & Truman, S. E. (2018). *Walking methodologies in a more-than-human world: Walklab*. London: Routledge. doi:10.4324/9781315231914.

Springgay, S., & Truman, S. E. (2022). Critical walking methodologies and oblique agitations of place. *Qualitative Inquiry*28(2), 171–176. doi:10.1177/10778004211042355.

Chapter 12

Location-based learning

Case studies on technology-enhanced learning outdoors

Beth Hammond and Oliver Haslam

What is location-based learning?

Before presenting the case studies, it will be helpful to define some relevant concepts.

Place-based learning refers to learning that takes place in a specific location where the location gives context to the learning, usually to help learners connect with the natural or built environment or the community. This may prompt curiosity or provoke an emotional reaction. It is an educational philosophy developed by David Sobel and the Orion Society. Stickney (2020) gives a useful history of place-based learning and examples of how it is used today. A related concept is *sense of place*, defined in Grenni et al. (2020, p. 412) as "the collection of meanings assigned to a place, and place values, or the underlying feelings of importance connected to certain features of place".

Location-based learning is defined by Asakle and Barack (2022) as "place-based education conducted online with the use of geographic information systems and mobile devices". Other definitions of location-based learning also emphasise the use of mobile technology, which parallels definitions of location-based services (such as navigation systems and location-targeted advertisements) and location-based games (where game progress is connected with a player's location, such as Pokémon GO), which make use of mobile phones and GPS.

A definition of **mobile learning** can be found in Crompton (2013) as "learning across multiple contexts, through social and content interactions, using personal electronic devices". Again, this definition is tied to the use of digital technology; however, unlike location-based learning, mobile learning allows for learning not being dependent on place at all, such as a learner being able to access their course materials while at home or commuting on a train.

Location-based learning could perhaps be seen as the intersection between place-based and mobile learning, with pedagogical characteristics of both; the flexibility and learner-centred nature of mobile learning, and the situational context and connection to place given by place-based learning. It is worth noting, however, that place and location are not identical concepts. Compared with Grenni's understanding of place as a complex cultural concept (Grenni et al.,

DOI: 10.4324/9781003436928-19

2020), "location" is a more neutral concept of physical position which can be determined with precise coordinates. Location-based learning may make use of either concept, depending on the intended outcome of the learning. For example, a treasure hunt activity might identify specific locations for students to attend, but is not necessarily about experiencing the place, and the location itself is not necessarily a meaningful element of the learning. Whereas, other location-based learning activities may ask students to identify with and draw meaning from the location itself, such as site planning where the immediate neighbourhood is a relevant factor.

We also consider the use of mobile technologies for virtual experiences of locations. While physical presence may be preferable, engaging a sense of place through all the senses, there are times when physical access is not possible. Our use of location-based learning apps at the University of the West of England (UWE) has included modelling of spaces not available to students, and virtual field trips during the pandemic. This approach can help students relate to a context or environment that would otherwise be too distant, dangerous or otherwise unavailable, and allows learners with individual mobility restrictions to be included in the learning experience.

Something old, or something new?

While place-based learning clearly has a long history (Stickney, 2020), location-based learning has really only been possible with the advent of mobile technology. One could argue that the use of technology in place-based learning is not particularly new; taking measurements and recording data while in the field has always been a necessity for advancement of knowledge, whether the technology in question was ground penetrating radar, a camera, or pencil and paper. In subjects such as surveying, archaeology, environmental science and documentary filmmaking, practical elements have always benefited from learning that takes place at a specific location, using appropriate technology. Is location-based learning simply carrying on this tradition with more complex technologies?

There are a number of reasons why the particular affordances of modern mobile technologies allow for location-based learning to go beyond this paradigm.

First, there is typically some interaction between the location of the learner and the learning activities that are presented. Whether this location is supplied by the learner (such as clicking on a point on a map image), determined through GPS or recognised by some other method (such as QR codes placed at key points in the environment), learning can be scaffolded so that the tasks or information supplied refer to that specific location. While this can be done to some extent with an instructor as a physical guide, automation of this allows it to be done at scale, and in a more learner-centred way; i.e. control of the content and pace of the activity giving them more ownership and agency in their learning experience.

A second reason is that modern mobile technology enables communication – both with instructors and with peers. In social constructivist pedagogies, this interaction is a vital part of learning (Laurillard, 2009). Instructors can more easily give feedback and support to physically dispersed groups of students, making it more practical to take activities that might previously have been contained in a classroom out into the real world. Students can share in real time their experiences in different locations, and record their findings in collaborative spaces to work on with their peers after the event.

Finally, the range of different tools that can be made available from a single hand-held device means there are endless possibilities for place-based learning that did not previously exist. Higher levels of learning require application of knowledge and an understanding of its context in the world. While this may be done in authentic practical tasks on vocational courses such as the ones mentioned above, they have historically been limited to only the essential experiences, due to logistics, cost and the need for various types of equipment. It is now possible for such real-life application to be greatly expanded, as described in Asakle and Barack's study (2022), which shows that even the teaching of theoretical concepts can be enhanced through the use of location-based technologies. In this study, grade eight students from Israel, after instruction by the teacher on the topic of Newton's laws of motion, were given the task of demonstrating their understanding through writing multiple choice questions based on scenarios in their daily lives. They were encouraged to take pictures or videos and mark the location of the scenario on a digital map. This kind of task gives relevance to the topic which may not be felt in the classroom.

Case studies

Five members of academic staff from the School of Architecture and Environment at UWE were interviewed about their experiences with using digital learning tools in location-based activities with students. The digital tools were:

- Seppo (https://seppo.io/), a mobile-friendly tool that allows content and activities to be presented to students at a specific GPS location, and has an emphasis on gamifying learning.
- In The Zone, an in-house prototype that similarly uses GPS to present activities and content to students on a mobile device.
- Xerte (https://www.xerte.org.uk/), a tool for creating interactive online learning resources. While it does not use GPS, it was possible to set up a map image with clickable hotspots to guide students in the field.

Within the School of Architecture and Environment, field trips and site visits are an established practice. We were therefore able to explore not only the value of learning on location in general, but how the activities making use of digital tools compared to previous experiences. We asked questions about how students responded to the on-location activity, how location-based learning might be used in future, and how virtual field trips compared to the real thing.

The staff we spoke to had a range of examples to give, employing different activities and with different learning outcomes. The activities included:

- Site analysis.
- Sketching buildings in situ.
- Experiencing community spaces.
- Collecting photographs for an assignment.
- Teaching mathematics with real-world examples.
- A guided tour of an outdoor museum.
- Induction activities to help students get to know each other.

We will look at a few of these in more depth, and then discuss some of the themes drawn from all the case studies.

Architectural sketching

In this first year undergraduate course, students were expected to develop the core skill of observational drawing. Students made different types of sketches of buildings in situ. To do this, the group were taken to a particular location in Bristol offering a variety of architectural styles, and guided to draw specific buildings in prescribed ways (such as thumbnail, elevation, different types of perspective). It was important that students practise drawing from life rather than photographs, as it requires different observational skills and gives a situational context that is missing if students work from secondary sources.

The Seppo app was used to facilitate the activity. In Seppo, the tutor can use a digital map as a base to locate exercises. These can either be open to students at all times or only accessed when the student is in proximity to the location. The students accessed the app through their mobile phones.

When a student opened an exercise in Seppo, they were presented with all the information they would need for that activity; a description of the task, guidance on drawing and indicative photos or sketches. Students would make the sketch with pencil and paper, take a photograph of the completed drawing and upload it to the app. The final stage in each exercise was for students to reflect on their work, adding an audio or video clip through the app where they gave their thoughts on what they had done well and how they could improve.

There were numerous advantages to using Seppo. During the activity, each student could access the details of the task on their own device, at the time and place it was required. Previously, with a group of 20–40 students, it had been easy for some to miss verbal instructions. With the app, students could have much more confidence about what was required of them. It also gave them more autonomy and flexibility. They could return to the location and repeat the task on their own at a different time if desired. The app made it easy to track student engagement, as tutors could see who had completed which exercises, and identify anyone who seemed to need more support. It also meant the tutor had a copy of all the students' sketches, which could be looked at as a group after the event and used for feedback and discussion.

One of the issues noted was the up-front time cost in staff learning to use the technology and design the resources for it. Regardless of efficiency in the long term, they needed time in the short term to feel confident using the tool and adapt their previous lesson plans to make best use of it.

This case study shows a blended approach that makes the most of both digital and non-digital elements. The Seppo app complemented the use of hand-drawn sketches in a real environment, facilitating the learning without trying to replace the professional skills that were being developed.

Hidden river

In this activity, second year undergraduates on an Urban Planning module "Researching the City" followed the route of an underground river running through Bristol. They learned about key points on its route, made observations and took photographs. This helped students learn the practical skills needed for site visits, and was closely linked to the assessment. Notes and photographs taken as part of the activity were used in a publicity leaflet they would develop, using GIS data and presenting urban planning research to a target audience.

The activity was carried out initially with a prototype app, In The Zone, and later with Seppo. The app contained exercises located on a digital map which guided students along the route, and students could submit their photographs and notes at each location. As in the previous example, the app presented students with information, instructions and supplementary photos at appropriate points.

Part of the process was comparing pre-existing maps, photos and other sources with what was actually there, to gain an appreciation of the importance of visiting a site in person. The app meant that students could have this information at their fingertips while on location. It also allowed for historical comparisons, giving students a clear understanding of how the setting had changed over time.

The flexibility of a self-guided tour had particular benefit in this case as students could go back and get more information after the event for their final assessment, rather than being limited by what they had been able to take in on the day. It also helped students organise their findings – photographs were submitted against a particular location so it was easier for students to identify them afterwards.

One issue that had to be considered when selecting an appropriate technology for the activity was the initial investment for students in having to learn to use the system; if it was too complicated they would not engage with it. This can be mitigated with proper preparation, where students are introduced to the app in advance and shown how they will use it in the context of the activity.

Site analysis

This postgraduate module in Urban Planning used Seppo to build site analysis skills. Students walked around a site and undertook a SWOT analysis at different locations. This strengthened their professional observational skills, as well as helping them see how the realities of a site might inform their designs for development. Being on site meant they could experience the location in context, notice things that might not be evident from photographs, and make decisions based on all sensory inputs. The purpose of the exercise was to emphasise the importance of the analysis phase and how this type of recording was necessary in order to justify later design decisions.

In this activity, Seppo provided a good way for students to record their observations at a number of locations on the site. They could do this through text or audio, capturing their commentary in the Seppo app, as well as uploading photos. This proved much easier than recording notes on paper while on site. Students clearly found it a useful tool, as they subsequently requested it on other field trips.

This case study highlighted an interesting potential route for development with the app. Students at postgraduate level can benefit from having more freedom in their methods, as they are better equipped to make such choices. In this instance, students were restricted by having to do their SWOT analyses at predetermined locations, whereas a more student-led version might enable them to choose their own points of interest. In fact, one can imagine such tools developing along more professional lines, to allow graduates to take the skills they have learnt with these apps into the workplace.

Urban orienteering

This was another first year use case, across a set of programmes in the School of Architecture and Environment. It was an induction activity designed to help new students get to know the city and each other. The students, working in groups, visited famous sites across Bristol in a "treasure hunt" style challenge, answering questions based on the location, taking photos or doing an activity. The emphasis was on cohort building rather than gaining knowledge, but many of the locations and questions were relevant to students in this discipline. For example, visiting Banksy's "Girl with a Pearl Earring" exposed students to Bristol's street art culture and could potentially lead to discussions about the social context, tourism, art and the industrial urban environment. Another point on the route asked them to use features or clues in a building to guess at its historic use – an old granary, identifiable by the holes in the brickwork (training observation skills). Clifton Suspension Bridge and the SS *Great Britain* (famous Brunel landmarks) helped students identify with the history of their discipline. All these activities helped students connect with the city, their degree subject and each other.

In this instance, the gamification elements of Seppo helped to make an engaging activity, with points awarded for the exercises. It also showed the scalability of the app, with around 300 students taking part. The app included messaging facilities, so staff could receive and respond to queries from any of the groups at any part of the route, which ran over a mile and a half from the starting point, much further than could have been monitored by staff in person.

We received very positive feedback from students. Out of 46 groups we received 34 responses, answering "Agree" or "Strongly agree" with the following frequencies:

"I felt more engaged" – 97%.

"I felt more of a connection to Bristol" – 97%.

"I felt more connected to others on my course" – 85%.

"I learned something useful" – 79%.

There were no specific comments on the use of the app, which suggests it provided a fairly seamless experience.

Themes and analysis

Balancing the tech with the real

The strongest use of location-based learning apps seems to be when they are balanced appropriately with the non-digital skills that are the core of the activity. Technology can be a great tool for communication, for recording data and for making experiences accessible – but how to communicate with a particular audience, what data to record, and making meaning from the experiences is a very different matter. It is important that students are guided to engage with these aspects and not simply focus on the device in their hand. In the Architecture case study, students were asked to sketch with a pencil and paper. They would record their resulting sketch as a photograph in the app, but the manual process of sketching was not only a professional skill they needed to learn, but a way of engaging actively with the information in front of them – making decisions about what to include, informed by a wider context that came from all their senses and emotions. This learning process would have been bypassed by taking a photograph.

Inclusivity

There also seems to be a great advantage for inclusivity and accessibility. Students could do the walks at their own pace, and even return on a different date if they felt they needed more time. If uncomfortable in large groups, they could follow the route at a different time, on their own or with a few friends. Those who might struggle to hear in large outdoor groups can benefit from an app which provides the necessary information at the right time in a form the student can access. The ability to message the instructors directly also makes it more inclusive for those who are shy to ask questions in a larger group.

Engagement

While we may think of field trips as more engaging than being in a classroom, the reality seems to be that to get the most from an on-location experience, there needs to be a certain level of engagement to begin with. In order not to disadvantage certain groups of students, location-based experiences are frequently an optional extra; the downside of this is that less engaged students may simply choose not to attend, and those present may not engage fully. From the interviews we conducted, it was apparent that the students who got the most from the experience were the ones who did not see the work as a series of tasks to be completed, but were able to appreciate the experience as a whole – to have their curiosity invoked, explore and make connections. It may be that some students are also motivated by the independence from staff that comes with using an app; being able to take responsibility for their own learning rather than just follow along and do what they are told.

This suggests that positive engagement with location-based learning essentially comes down to good learning design. Students need to understand why they are doing the activities and what they will get from engaging with them. They may need to have been prepared for the kind of independent learning required, to understand the event in the context of the whole course, and to have familiarised themselves with the tools they will be using. This requires forethought and planning to create a successful experience.

Nevertheless, it may be that an event or one-off experience can in itself be a motivator, with the experiences that come of it being more memorable because of the contrast with usual classroom-based learning. It can also be motivating to form a personal connection to a place simply by knowing more about it – being able to share a piece of knowledge with friends or family, or just remembering an interesting fact every time you pass the place in question.

No substitute for being there

During the pandemic some courses experimented with virtual field trips, using video, 360-degree photos and interactive online learning tools. Such resources might help to create a sense of place and prompt more engagement from students. However, there was strong agreement from academic staff that there was no substitute for being in person at a location. Whether it was the ability to have informal conversation with peers, to experience the smells and textures and emotions a place provoked, to get a proper sense of whether a place feels safe or pleasant – virtual tours might be better than nothing but did not give a full picture. Virtual resources can also go out of date, an important lesson for those going into a career where field work and site visits are part of professional practice.

However, it was considered essential to offer an alternative, particularly where it was part of the assessment, as there are various reasons why students may not be able to attend. Ideally, a virtual tour could complement a real trip, being used to prepare for the visit and recap afterwards, with the virtual version being enhanced through drone footage, recorded interviews and the ability to see aspects that would not necessarily be accessible in person anyway.

Pros and cons of technology

Learning to use new technology can be time-consuming, and understandably, both students and staff are reluctant to put time into something unless it reaps other rewards. These rewards for staff could be efficiency in the long term, ease of monitoring engagement, better outcomes for students, and better student feedback. For students, they include ease of accessing information, communicating with others, being able to record and store data on location and revisit it after the fact. Whether the technology frees up students to be able to fully concentrate on the experience, or distracts them from it, will depend on a number of factors including how easy it is to use and how well prepared they were before the event.

Professional practice

For vocational courses such as these, particularly at postgraduate level, there is the potential for the experimental use of digital tools in these contexts to influence professional practice. A new generation of planners and designers going into the workplace will be more aware of what can be achieved with location-based apps.

Conclusion

The experience gained from these case studies indicates that, used well, location-based learning apps can enhance learning activities to make them more active, inclusive, relevant and engaging. They can give more autonomy to the student, while providing communication channels for support and social learning. There is the potential for such tools to provide a seamless and intuitive way to record data while in the field, and at the same time let the user fully understand and appreciate the real context and develop a sense of place.

To make the most of location-based learning apps, the following good practice has been identified:

- Design learning activities that will develop relevant skills – critical observation, reflection, recording data, team work, etc. – and use the technology to facilitate and enhance the activity.
- Consider the effect of the environment, and choose locations accordingly. Does the location provoke emotion, curiosity, a sense of belonging? Does it provide data? Is it an opportunity to gain field-based skills? What advantage does it give beyond a classroom environment?
- Prepare students in advance, both to use the technology and to understand the purpose of the tasks they will be undertaking. This will allow them to get the most out of their time on location, and be ready to engage with the experience as a whole.

Opportunities for future research

Despite the clear message that field trips give an unparalleled experience, staff reported that the difficulties of arranging them (transport, risk assessments, etc.) can lead to an overwhelming burden, and such experiences may disappear unless this effort is properly acknowledged and supported. Research into the value of in-person experiences may help to ensure their continuation. These experiences can be enhanced and supported by mobile technology, and there are many ways in which the design of location-based learning apps might be refined in line with modern pedagogies. This may include more emphasis on student-led functionality, improved peer-to-peer communication and collaboration features, apps which specifically prepare students for professional practice, and augmented reality. Studies of student engagement and outcomes where such features are present may influence future development of location-based learning technology.

Acknowledgements

Our thanks to the following members of staff who shared their experiences with us for the purposes of this chapter:

James Burch, Nick Croft, Danny Elvidge, Deepak Gopinath and Katie McClymont.

References

Asakle, S., & Barak, M. (2022). Location-based learning and its effect on students' understanding of Newton's laws of motion. *J Sci Educ Technol.*, 31, 403–413 DOI: doi:10.1007/s10956-022-09963-2.

Crompton, H. (2013). A historical overview of M-learning: Toward learner-centered education. In: Berge, Z.L. & Muilenburg, L.Y., (eds.), *Handbook of mobile learning*. Routledge. Retrieved from: https://learning-oreilly-com.ezproxy.uwe.ac.uk/library/view/handbook-of-mobile/9780415503693/09_Chapter-01.html#sec1_1.

Grenni, S., Soini, K., & Horlings, L.G. (2020). The inner dimension of sustainability transformation: how sense of place and values can support sustainable place-shaping. *Sustain Sci.* 15, 411–422. DOI: doi:10.1007/s11625-019-00743-3.

Laurillard, D. (2009). The pedagogical challenges to collaborative technologies. *International Journal of Computer-Supported Collaborative Learning*, 4 (1), 5–20. DOI: doi:10.1007/s11412-008-9056-2.

Stickney, J. (2020). Philosophical walks as place-based environmental education. *Journal of Philosophy of Education*, 54(4), 1071–1086. DOI: doi:10.1111/1467-9752.12469.

Part 4

Fieldwork

Fieldwork

Chapter 13

Research on the move

Walking as a research methodology and the importance of expeditioning

Suzie Dick

In this chapter the rationale and evidence base for expeditions overseas with higher education students is examined, looking at the benefits in relation to health and wellbeing, the opportunity for informal learning, and the potential impact for participants in doing so. According to the Britannica Dictionary (2023), an expedition can be defined as "a journey especially by a group of people for a specific purpose (such as to explore a distant place or to do research): organise/mount/launch a mountain-climbing *expedition or* a scientific *expedition* to Antarctica", and should be considered both a physical endeavour, and a social one, giving participants an opportunity to lead a flourishing life. This chapter will outline the role that a lived experience methodology, such as walking as a research methodology, can have in exploring those experiences and bringing the learning outcomes to the fore.

Why expedition? Beyond the formal

This is a question that is often asked, why should we use the time and expense of heading to an expedition either locally or in far-off lands? Is there truly a reason or a benefit to doing so? Expeditioning belongs to the realm of informal, rather than formal, learning (Neathery, 1998), and, as such, can be open to the charge of not being measurable, quantifiable, with the experiences being had as both group and individual, and not part of a tightly controlled structure (Johnson & Majewska, 2023). This is often the counter argument laid against those organising expeditions for students: Isn't it really you going off on holiday?

Research in this area focuses on understanding how individuals acquire knowledge, skills, and attitudes outside of formal educational settings, such as schools or structured training programmes (Eraut, 2004). Informal learning encompasses various activities and contexts, including everyday experiences, social interactions, self-directed learning, and participation in communities of practice, and in this case, being on expedition (Johnson & Majewska, 2023).

DOI: 10.4324/9781003436928-21

Understanding informal learning can be roughly split into these three areas (Berman, 2020):

- Learning Environments: Informal learning occurs in a wide range of environments and research explores how these environments shape learning opportunities, engagement, and outcomes.
- Learning Processes: The cognitive, social, and emotional processes involved in informal learning. These include examining how individuals actively seek out and engage with learning opportunities, make sense of new information, problem-solve, reflect on experiences, and develop expertise.
- Workplace Learning: Informal learning is prominent in the workplace, where employees acquire knowledge and skills through on-the-job experiences, interactions with colleagues, and self-directed learning.

When informal learning happens through expeditions, this can lead to a variety of experiences providing the opportunity for personal growth and development (Neathery, 1998). By participating in challenging and adventurous activities, people can have the opportunity to build self-confidence, resilience, and a sense of achievement in a new environment (Veletsianos et al., 2012). They can learn to step out of their comfort zones, overcome obstacles, and develop important life skills such as problem-solving, decision-making, teamwork, and leadership which can be applied to other life situations (Carreau et al., 2016), supporting what Martha Nussbaum (2000) refers to as having a "flourishing life".

Having a flourishing life

Martha Nussbaum is a prominent philosopher and ethicist known for her work on the concept of human flourishing. According to Nussbaum (2011), a flourishing life is one that is rich in capabilities and opportunities for individuals to develop and exercise their innate human capabilities. Elsewhere, she argues that human beings possess a set of fundamental capabilities that enable them to lead flourishing lives, regardless of their particular cultural or individual circumstances (2000). In her book *Creating capabilities: The human development approach* (2011), Nussbaum outlines a list of ten central capabilities that she argues are essential for a flourishing life:

1 Life
2 Bodily Health
3 Bodily Integrity
4 Senses, Imagination, and Thought
5 Emotions
6 Practical Reason
7 Affiliation

8 Other Species
9 Play
10 Control over One's Environment

According to Nussbaum, individuals should be able to live a full life with good health, being able to move freely and make choices about their own body. They should be able to use their senses, to experience a range of emotional states and be able to reason and reflect on their lives. Social relationships should be possible as should being able to participate in a community, and individuals should be able to interact freely with the natural world. Opportunities for leisure and play should be present and participation in political and legal decision should be enabled.

Nussbaum claims that these capabilities are not merely desirable but represent essential aspects of a life that is truly flourishing. She argues that societies should strive to create conditions that enable individuals to develop and exercise these capabilities, promoting social justice and enhancing the overall wellbeing of their citizens (Nussbaum, 2011). It can be argued that expeditions provide the opportunity for some of these capabilities to emerge, or be met, in that space and time.

Looking at the capabilities for health and for play, expeditions generally involve outdoor activities where engaging in these activities improves physical fitness, coordination, and overall health while also learning skills which can be valuable throughout their lives including, as previously mentioned, teamwork. Living and working together in challenging environments builds strong bonds and lifelong friendships (Veletsianos et al., 2012). Young people learn to communicate effectively, collaborate, and support each other, developing crucial social skills. They also gain an appreciation for the importance of teamwork and cooperation in achieving common goals.

Additionally, expeditions can provide an opportunity for self-reflection through being away from the distractions of everyday life (Links, 2018), and spending time in nature allows young people to disconnect from technology, connect with themselves, and gain a fresh perspective on their lives, values, and goals. This can lead to personal insights, self-discovery, and a better understanding of one's strengths and passions (Carreau et al., 2016). As such, this links to capabilities six and seven. Being able to participate in a community is reflected in another potential benefit when the expedition takes place overseas, where individuals have diverse cultures, traditions, and perspectives. This fosters a sense of global awareness, empathy, and understanding of different societies. By engaging with local communities and experiencing different ways of life, young people develop a broader worldview and gain a deeper appreciation for cultural diversity (Jackson, 2011).

Lastly, capability eight is being able to interact with and appreciate the natural world. Many youth expeditions focus on environmental education and conservation efforts with participants learning about ecosystems, sustainable practices, and the importance of protecting natural resources (Links, 2018). Through hands-on experiences like hiking, wildlife observation, or environmental projects, young people develop a greater understanding of environmental issues and become advocates for conservation.

It's important to note that the specific benefits experienced during expeditions can vary depending on individual factors, the nature of the expedition, and personal circumstances. This is where walking as a research methodology comes in to enable these individual factors to emerge, and the common themes to be created.

Walking as research methodology

Walking can be a valuable and powerful research methodology, particularly in fields such as anthropology, geography, urban studies, and environmental studies, for generating qualitative data, understanding context, and gaining an embodied experience of the research setting (O'Neill & Roberts, 2019). It allows researchers to immerse themselves in the research context and gain first-hand experiences and observations. Walking allows researchers to engage in participant observation, where they directly observe and interact with the environment and people being studied (Springgay & Truman, 2018). This method can provide rich qualitative data, capturing the nuances and details that may be missed through other research methods, and provide a greater contextual understanding around what participants are saying and how they are interacting with their environment (O'Neill & Roberts, 2019). Researchers can gain a deeper understanding of the social, cultural, and physical context, identify spatial patterns, and make connections between different elements of the environment. Additionally, walking can provide access to information and insights that may not be readily available through other means. Researchers can discover hidden or informal spaces, encounter unexpected encounters, and tap into local knowledge that may be overlooked in formal interviews or surveys (Springgay & Truman, 2018).

For the researcher, walking as a research methodology emphasises the embodied experience of the researcher (O'Neill & Roberts, 2019). By physically engaging with the environment, researchers can gain a more holistic understanding of the research context. They can feel the texture of the route they are walking, notice smells, sounds, and other sensory aspects that contribute to the overall understanding of what their participants are reflecting upon, while enabling researchers to engage in self-reflection and reflexivity throughout the research process (Springgay & Truman, 2018). By actively participating in the research setting, researchers can reflect on, and challenge, their own positionality – their biases, assumptions, and perceptions – thereby enhancing the quality of data collection and analysis.

Walking as a research methodology is considered a lived experience methodology and utilising it can provide valuable insights and perspectives that may be missed or overlooked by traditional approaches. A researcher may choose to use it for a number of reasons including, according to O'Neill and Roberts (2019):

- Authenticity and Empowerment: Where the voices and experiences of individuals who have direct personal knowledge of a particular phenomenon or issue are prioritised and are the true experts.

- Rich and Contextual Understanding: By engaging with individuals directly and allowing them to share their stories, researchers can gain insights into the complexity and diversity of human experiences that may not be captured by quantitative data alone.
- Humanising Research and Policy: By centring the experiences of real people, these methodologies help to humanise statistics, data, and abstract concepts. This can create more empathetic and compassionate approaches to addressing social issues and inform policy decisions that better reflect the needs and realities of those affected.
- Collaboration and Co-creation: This co-creation of knowledge fosters a sense of ownership and agency among participants and leads to more relevant and impactful outcomes.

As with every research methodology there are limitations. Researchers may have limited physical mobility, making it challenging to access certain areas, and equally it excludes participants with limited mobility making it a research method of the able-bodied, for the able-bodied (Bilsland & Siebert, 2023). Walking might not be suitable for all research contexts, due to the time-consuming nature of the interviews, and often small number of participants.

However, it is contended here, that being on expedition is an appropriate and highly relevant place in order to utilise this particular methodology; by talking while walking, it supports the researcher to understand the learning processes that are happening at the time, while the researcher is also living the experience themselves, alongside the participant (Springgay & Truman, 2018). It allows different insights to be pursued, multiple lines of enquiry to be taken during the interviews, and challenges the assumptions and positionality of the researcher and research participant, enabling deep learning to take place.

Expeditions in higher education

Moving from expeditions generally, to those involving higher education students and institutions, there is a strong rationale for their inclusion within courses, across various disciplines, with every course having the option to undertake an experience abroad, whether expedition, fieldwork, or other (Bonello, 2001).

While on expedition there is the opportunity for practical application of theoretical knowledge where students can apply the theoretical concepts they have learned in the classroom to real-world situations (Jackson, 2011). It provides an opportunity to bridge the gap between theory and practice by engaging in hands-on experiences. This practical application enhances their understanding of the subject matter and helps them develop critical thinking and problem-solving skills. It can also provide an opportunity to conduct research in an unfamiliar environment, including collecting data and analysing information (Little & Williams, 2010). Students learn valuable research skills, including how to adapt these skills to different cultures and institutions, for example designing surveys, interviewing subjects, using data collection tools, and analysing data. These skills are essential for academic research and are transferable to various professional settings as well. Students also gain first-hand experience and engage with the subject matter in a meaningful way by immersing themselves in real-world environments (Jackson, 2011).

This experiential learning approach can foster a deeper understanding, retention, and internalisation of knowledge compared to those undertaken in an environment they are familiar with, engaging greater cultural competence and appreciation of diversity and respect for different perspectives. This can also help address educational and social inequalities, particularly for marginalised populations and those looking at alternative learning pathways (Jackson, 2011; Neathery, 1998).

This cultural competence is increasingly important in our interconnected world. Through increasing interconnections, well-planned expeditions for higher education students provide opportunities for students to interact with professionals, experts, and practitioners in their field of study. They can build valuable connections and establish networks that may be beneficial for future career opportunities, internships, or research collaborations. These connections can also provide insights into industry trends, practical applications, and potential mentorship opportunities, leading onto enhanced employability (Bonello, 2001).

Career development

One of the purposes of higher education is to enable students to gain appropriate knowledge and skills to be able to contribute to the workforce. Additionally, one of the main concerns for students is the career or job they will be able to get at the end of their course (Velasco, 2012). By having an experience such as undertaking an expedition on a CV it can demonstrate to employers that students have practical skills, research experience, and the ability to apply knowledge in real-world settings. It can differentiate students from their peers and make them more marketable to future employers. The expedition (or fieldwork experience) showcases their ability to work independently, think critically, and solve problems, which are highly sought-after qualities in the job market. In addition, it gives students the opportunity to develop a wide range of skills that are essential for many careers. These may include critical thinking, problem-solving, data collection and analysis, communication, teamwork, adaptability, and decision-making skills. Having the opportunity to refine and strengthen these skills, makes them more marketable to potential employers but also enables the application of theoretical knowledge gained in the classroom to practical situations (Bonello, 2001). This practical experience is highly valued by employers (Byrne, 2022), as it demonstrates an ability to transfer academic knowledge into practical problem-solving skills.

Finally, by undertaking such an experience, it can demonstrate initiative, motivation, and independence as a professional (Carreau et al., 2016). It shows that one is willing to go beyond traditional learning environments and take the initiative to explore and gain practical experience, stepping outside a comfort zone and adapting to new environments. It also demonstrates your ability to handle unfamiliar situations and work effectively under various conditions, which are valuable qualities sought by employers (Byrne, 2022).

In summary, providing higher education students with invaluable opportunities to apply theory to practise, develop research skills, collaborate with peers, appreciate diversity, establish professional connections, and foster personal and professional growth. These benefits contribute to a well-rounded education and enhance students' readiness for future academic and professional endeavours.

Measuring impact

Measuring the impact of learning can be a complex task, as it depends on various factors such as the learning goals, the type of learning, and the context in which learning is taking place (Berman, 2020). Through the use of walking as a research methodology, the question of "when on expedition, how do you determine what success looks like, for whom, and is impact measurable?" can begin to be answered. By utilising this particular research methodology, one could argue that it gives an opportunity to hear and see first-hand what the learning impact of the expedition was and why, for each individual participant, at that point in time (Springgay & Truman, 2018). It gives insight into understanding their experiences, challenges, and the application of knowledge or skills gained.

This qualitative approach can provide deeper insights into the impact of learning beyond quantitative measures. By the collecting of numerous ethnographical accounts and observations, it enables the data to be cross-referenced, looking for common themes and ideas to emerge, leading to a conclusion of what the impact of a particular experience, such as expeditioning, may be during or shortly after the experience itself (O'Neill & Roberts, 2019).

Additionally, impact may be deciphered post-expedition when students return to their courses, as the assessment of their ability to retain and transfer the new knowledge or skills gained from the experience to another set of situations or contexts can be an indicator of learning impact. This can be done through follow-up assessments or performance evaluations conducted some time after the learning intervention. In higher education the impact may also be measured in terms of enhanced engagement, or performance in university assessments, compared to those who did not take part in the experience.

It's important to note that measuring the impact of learning is not limited to a single method or approach. Depending on the learning objectives, you may need to use a combination of these methods to obtain a comprehensive understanding of the learning impact; considering both quantitative and qualitative measures can provide a more holistic view of the outcomes. However, more importantly, impact may be unmeasurable, or it may take many years or decades for the full impact or influence an experience has had to become evident.

Conclusion

This chapter has sought to outline the importance of informal learning and how this can contribute towards what it means to having a flourishing life, including the benefits for physical and mental wellbeing, alongside supporting future career prospects. By utilising walking as a research methodology, this enables the highly individual benefits of the learning journey to be explored, and the collective benefits to emerge, providing support for informal education initiatives and alternative learning pathways.

References

Berman, N. (2020). A critical examination of informal learning spaces. *Higher Education Research & Development*, 39(1), 127–140.

Bilsland, K., & Siebert, S. (2023). Walking interviews in organizational research. *European Management Journal*.

Bonello, M. (2001). Fieldwork within the context of higher education: A literature review. *British Journal of Occupational Therapy*, 64(2), 93–99.

Britannica Dictionary (2023). Viewed June 2, 2023, at: https://www.britannica.com/dictionary/expedition#:~:text=%3A%20a%20journey%20especially%20by%20a,a%20scientific%20expedition%20to%20Antarctica.

Byrne, C. (2022). What determines perceived graduate employability? Exploring the effects of personal characteristics, academic achievements and graduate skills in a survey experiment. *Studies in Higher Education*, 47(1), 159–176.

Carreau, J., Bosselut, G., Ritchie, S., Heuzé, J., & Arppe, S. (2016). Emergence and evolution of informal roles during a canoe expedition. *Journal of Adventure Education and Outdoor Learning*, 16(3), 191–205.

Eraut, M. (2004). Informal learning in the workplace. *Studies in Continuing Education*, 26 (2), 247–273.

Jackson, J. (2011). Cultivating cosmopolitan, intercultural citizenship through critical reflection and international, experiential learning. *Language and Intercultural Communication*, 11(2), 80–96.

Johnson, M., & Majewska, D. (2023, May 15). *Formal, non-formal, and informal learning: What are they, and how can we research them?* Research report. Retrieved from Cambridge University Press and Assessment: https://www.cambridgeassessment.org.uk/Images/665425-formal-non-formal-and-informal-learning-what-are-they-and-how-can-we-research-them-.pdf.

Links, M. (2018). Nature, capabilities, and student well-being: An evaluation of an outdoor education approach. Retrieved from University of Manitoba: https://mspace.lib.umanitoba.ca/items/ef8c0946-45aa-41f3-baf6-e65eca0672e8.

Little, B., & Williams, R. (2010). Students' roles in maintaining quality and in enhancing learning: Is there a tension? *Quality in Higher Education*, 16(2), 115–127.

Neathery, M. F. (1998). Informal learning in experiential settings. *Journal of Elementary Science Education*, 10(2), 36–49.

Nussbaum, M. C. (2000). *Women and human development: The capabilities approach*. 3rd Edition. Cambridge: Cambridge University Press.

Nussbaum, M. C. (2011). *Creating capabilities: The human development approach*. Cambridge: Harvard University Press.

O'Neill, M., & Roberts, B. (2019). *Walking methods: Research on the move.* Routledge. Doi: https://doi.org/10.4324/9781315646442.

Springgay, S., & Truman, S. (2018). *Walking methodologies in a more-than-human world: WalkingLab.* Routledge. Doi: https://doi.org/10.4324/9781315231914.

Velasco, M. S. (2012). More than just good grades: Candidates' perceptions about the skills and attributes employers seek in new graduates. *Journal of Business Economics and Management,* 13(3), 499–517.

Veletsianos, G., Miller, B., Eitel, K. B., Eitel, J. U., & Hougham, R. J. (2012). Localizing adventure learning: Teachers and students as expedition leaders and members. In *Society for Information Technology & Teacher Education International Conference, Association for the Advancement of Computing in Education (AACE)* (pp. 2164–2169).

Chapter 14

Engaging undergraduate students in citizen science

Measuring air pollution as a pedagogical approach

Thomas E. L. Smith and Jonathan T. Schulte

Environmental change is central to the curricula of environmental programmes of study in both the physical sciences and social sciences. The BSc programme in Environment and Sustainable Development at the authors' university is heavily focused on environmental social science through the lens of human geography. Despite there being modules relating to issues of environmental degradation, pollution, and climate change, there were very few opportunities for students to engage in applied research in real-world, case-based learning environments. Teaching on these modules was restricted to theoretical learning, with no hands-on experience. Further, there were few links between the theoretical modules and the more practical, quantitative and qualitative methods modules, leading to a lack of integration at the programme level.

Citizen science, within the context of undergraduate education, offers a unique avenue for students to contribute meaningfully to scientific research. By actively participating in the process of data collection, students become citizen scientists, breaking down the traditional barriers between those active in undertaking research in their field of study (e.g. their lecturers) and the students and public. This approach not only promotes scientific literacy but also fosters a sense of empowerment and agency among students, instilling in them a deeper connection to their environment and potentially influencing their desire to make a positive impact and/or changes to their interaction with the environment (Haklay, 2017).

This chapter focuses on the use of low-cost air pollution sensors and a citizen science database on a module that explores environmental science, different methods of knowledge production, and the role that different knowledge production pathways play in environmental policy-making. By providing students with the means to measure their personal exposure to air pollution, the aim of the intervention was to provide a more constructivist learning environment, allowing students to reflect on both the physical science of air pollution, as well as social science approaches to understanding the public understanding of science and the role of citizen science in policy-making. By contributing to the citizen science project, students become "makers" rather than just "consumers" of their education (Alimisis & Zoulias, 2013). While the intervention was connected to just one of the environmental problems (air pollution) covered in the module, the activity was designed to address all of the module's intended learning outcomes (Table 14.1).

DOI: 10.4324/9781003436928-22

Low-cost sensor technology, citizen science, and opportunities for innovative education

Low-cost technology has long been seen as the key to "learner-shaped higher education technology" (Selwyn, 2007), facilitating a shift from centralised prescription of education technology towards decentralised technology that follows the interests of a particular department or individual academic. By allowing students to interact with the devices that are used to measure air pollution, this activity aims to crack open the "black box" of environmental monitoring and use the technology for their own purposes. This instrumentalism and pragmatism lies at the heart of John Dewey's constructivist theories of understanding as applied to learning (Koohang & Harman, 2005).

This form of education facilitates knowledge construction through a number of constructivist principles:

- Focus on knowledge construction, not reproduction.
- Present authentic tasks – contextualising rather than abstracting instruction.
- Provide real-world, case-based learning environments, rather than predetermined instructional sequences.
- Enable context- and content-dependent knowledge construction.

Perhaps most importantly, citizen science in education encourages ownership and voice in the learning process, one of the key goals in designing constructivist learning environments (Honebein, 1996).

To understand the pedagogical significance of using personal air pollution exposure devices in undergraduate education, it is important to explore the underlying theoretical framework and how this addresses the ILOs listed in

Table 14.1 Example of some adaptable intended learning outcomes that may be addressed by student-based citizen science activities in environmental education.

Intended Learning Outcomes (ILOs) for GY220 (Environment: Science & Society).
1   Identify and assess key conceptual approaches to the understanding of environmental science, environmental politics, and environmental risk.
2   Describe different forms of knowledge production and explain how knowledge producers are (dis)engaged with environmental policy-making.
3   Discuss and develop opinions on the relationships between science and environmentalism.
4   Understand key environmental processes relating to geohazards, environmental disasters, pollution, land-use change, climate change, and ozone depletion.
5   Evaluate the use and influence of scientific (as well as what may be considered non-scientific and unscientific) information in international, national, and regional environmental decision-making.

Table 14.1. First and foremost, hands-on, experiential learning has long been recognised as a powerful educational tool, enabling students to actively engage in their learning process and acquire practical skills. By immersing themselves in the collection and analysis of real-world data, students can develop critical thinking, problem-solving abilities, and a deeper understanding of environmental challenges. By participating in data collection and analysis, students experience first-hand the value and impact of their contributions, as well as some of the issues that arise concerning data integrity and the pitfalls of citizen science (Stevens et al., 2014). This involvement goes beyond traditional passive learning methods, as students become co-creators of knowledge, actively shaping the scientific process.

When specifically focusing on air pollution, personal air pollution exposure devices provide a tangible and accessible means of measuring and understanding this critical environmental issue. By equipping students with these devices, they can directly observe and analyse air pollution levels in their surroundings, leading to a more profound comprehension of the implications and consequences of pollution on human health and the environment (Tan & Smith, 2020; Snyder et al., 2013).

Beyond the specific ILOs of the module, participatory activities are often designed to have co-benefits to address broader programme aims that may involve lifelong skills and knowledge that can shape a student's career and trajectory long after completing their studies. Environmental citizen science projects may prompt students to reflect on their role as environmental stewards. Through direct exposure to the realities of air pollution, students can develop a personal connection to the issue and a heightened awareness of the importance of preserving and improving air quality. The act of collecting data and witnessing pollution levels can evoke a sense of responsibility among students. They may recognise the impact of human activities on the environment and the need for sustainable, less polluting practices. This reflection extends beyond the classroom, as students carry their newfound knowledge and commitment to environmental stewardship into their daily lives, influencing their choices and behaviours (Tan & Smith, 2020; Robinson et al., 2023). Students not only develop a sense of environmental responsibility but also become advocates for change. Through their engagement, they gain a deeper understanding of the consequences of air pollution on human health, ecosystems, and the broader community.

In the subsequent sections, we will delve into the design and implementation of the activity, highlighting some practical considerations, and an evaluation of the pedagogical benefits experienced by students engaging in this form of citizen science via a focus group with students who had completed the activity.

Activity design, implementation, and integration with module assessment

There are typically ~40 students taking the module each year. The topic of air pollution is introduced in the fifth week of the 19-week module that is taught over two terms. The lecture introduces students to the criteria air pollutants that are regulated in the UK, the EU, and other places worldwide (nitrogen dioxide, ozone, carbon monoxide, lead, particulate matter, and sulphur dioxide). The lecture includes a discussion of how air pollution is measured, with a focus on London's air quality network (londonair.org.uk). At the end of the lecture, low-cost particulate matter ($PM_{2.5}$) sensors are distributed to the students. Over the four years that this activity has been running, which have included the COVID-19 pandemic years, alternative arrangements for sensor distribution have included pick-up locations and posting/shipping.

The Xiaomi Mi $PM_{2.5}$ detector was selected for its price (~USD$25 per unit, with discounts for bulk buying), its clear LED display which shows a reading of the $PM_{2.5}$ concentration (in $\mu g\ m^{-3}$), and its sensor's accuracy according to comparisons with $PM_{2.5}$ monitoring equipment used by London's Air Quality Network (Chan et al., 2021). There are many alternatives currently on the market which use the same hardware (e.g. those manufactured by PurpleAir; purpleair.com). To instil confidence in the sensor, students are encouraged to unbox and turn on their sensors while still in the lecture theatre. A quick intercomparison will demonstrate that the sensors are responding coherently in this rudimentary cross-calibration exercise.

One of the pitfalls of low-cost sensors is usually their inability to log data. However, we use this to our advantage for this exercise. Instead of submitting large data files from automatic logging, students must submit each individual measurement using an online form. The online form is designed to be completed in less than 30 seconds, requiring only the measurement and some drop-down menus on the type of measurement relating to location, and an open comments box. The distribution of sensors takes place before 'Reading Week' (a week in the teaching term with a break from teaching). During the two weeks, students are encouraged to submit measurements to the database whenever they can and from environments that interest them. The exercise is purposefully unstructured to encourage curiosity and contribute to a diverse dataset that reflects that curiosity. The students are ultimately in control of their own sampling strategy (Stevens et al., 2014). The data from the online form submissions is collated automatically in a spreadsheet. Students have the option to include their names (a prize is awarded for the student who submits the most measurements), although the spreadsheet is anonymised before it is distributed to the module cohort.

After the two-week break, the following lecture on the module includes a reflective discussion including some presentation of results to the students (e.g. Figure 14.1), while the remainder of the lecture concludes the air pollution section of the module, including material on air pollution regulation policies. The students continue to submit measurements for the rest of term, with periodic encouragement via lectures

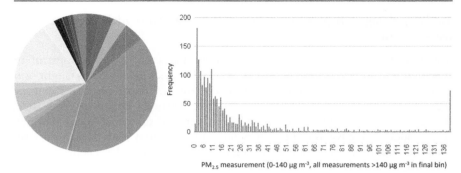

PM₂.₅ measurement (0-140 µg m⁻³, all measurements >140 µg m⁻³ in final bin)

Figure 14.1 (left) pie chart with each segment proportional to each individual student's contribution to the database (total number of students is 40); (right) histogram of data
collected over four years of the project.

and emailed online learning environment reminders. At the end of the term, the
anonymised database (including their measurements as well as those from previous
academic years) is made available to the students for use with an optional coursework
assessment which is due towards the beginning of the following term.

Module assessment includes one coursework component (40% of the final
mark), and an exam (60%). Both elements include questions relating to citizen
science and/or air pollution (Table 14.2).

Student engagement and activity evaluation

Over the four years that this activity has been part of the module curriculum
(2019/20–2022/23), students have contributed over 2,300 measurements to the

Table 14.2 Example of some assessment questions (coursework and exam) that are used to
allow students to reflect and make use of their experience of being air pollution
citizen scientists.

Assessment type	*Question*
Coursework (one question from a choice of three, 3,000 words)	In *The changing paradigm of air pollution monitoring*, Snyder et al. (2013) argued that advances in air pollution monitoring would provide new tools for individuals and communities to develop strategies to reduce pollution exposure and understand linkages to health indicators. To what extent has this been realised? (You may include primary or secondary datasets to illustrate your answer).
Exam (two questions from a choice of seven, 2 hours)	Using a case study, discuss the value and limits of citizen science.
Exam (two questions from a choice of seven, 2 hours)	What is "citizen science"? Examine its emergence and implications with particular reference to the concept of "scientisation".

citizen science database. Generally, all students who were given sensors submit data to the database. However, around ~30% of the students contribute ~90% of the submissions (Figure 14.1, left-hand side). From discussion with students, this does not mean that they are not using the sensors, but are choosing not to engage with the online form due to time constraints. There is also a significant drop-off in engagement with the online form (and therefore, the database) after the initial two weeks of deployment. This, in itself, can be used by students to critically evaluate the effectiveness and value of citizen science networks. The free comments box in the online form yields a diverse range of environments of interest to the students. Some examples include: "birthday candles", "smoking area", "university building rooftop", "underground platform, Temple station", "cooking with wok – stir fry", "frying eggs again", and "outside nightclub, lots of vapers".

To explore students' views and experiences of the project, we conducted a small focus group with students who had previously taken the module (n = 4). Three of the participants had completed the module in the academic year 2020/21 (three years ago at the time of writing) and one student had completed the module in academic year 2022/23 (the year of writing). Given the small sample size, we recognise that our findings are not representative of all participants' experience. Rather, we suggest treating the below as an initial exploration of key outcomes and enablers of learning from the participatory science project.

In our focus group, all participants described extensive usage of their air quality monitors across a wide range of environments and situations. This included taking ad hoc measurements in student accommodation and at home, in different rooms, during their commute, and even on holiday or in nightclubs. Some students also described more systematic approaches to measurement such as taking a measurement at the same time and in the same spaces repeatedly. Describing the "excitement" of using their monitors, and curiosity about personal exposure to air pollution and its variability, appeared as key motivations. Several students mentioned that they had considered air pollution a substantial issue, not least as their degrees had taught them about the problems of air pollution on an "academic" level. Yet, personal exposure to pollution had been essentially invisible to them. Now, the personal monitors gave air pollution a tangible quantity that allowed students to understand their exposure in a variety of everyday situations. As several of the students emphasised, this "making tangible" did bridge their "academic" and experiential knowledge of air pollution. Here, students also highlighted the devices' ease of use as an important enabler; being able to produce a measurement at the press of a button allowed exactly this embedded usage the project was hoping to encourage.

Beyond this "making tangible" of air pollution, the usage of the monitors also produced important pedagogic moments. As we argued above, the objectives of constructivist learning environments directly informed the design of the activity. Following Honebein's (1996) taxonomy, one goal for this was to provide realistic and relevant contexts for learning that are grounded in the "noise and complexity" that surrounds students outside the classroom. Here, the air monitor use did not just provide a context for learning that was directly relevant to the everyday lives of the students, but also a context in which to explore the limits of the measurement tools. As one student described it, they used the monitor to measure the air pollution above their morning cup of coffee. The surprisingly high measured concentration of $PM_{2.5}$ led them to a more critical examination of the measuring technology, and how in practice, the optical method of measurement used by their handheld devices can produce misleading estimates of $PM_{2.5}$ concentrations under certain conditions (Chan et al., 2021). Though not a member of the focus group, one former student further explored alternative complexities when it came to becoming knowledgeable of their personal exposure, writing about risk (e.g. less polluted streets might also be more hazardous to crime) and cultural (e.g. family members burning incense) trade-offs in a journal article published by the *Royal Geographical Society* (Tan & Smith, 2020).

Despite this consistent engagement with their air quality monitors, our focus group participants painted a more complicated picture for how the project had shaped their views on citizen science and behaviours. Here, we want to present two key themes: the role of assessment in facilitating learning from the project; and the role of engagement with others through citizen science.

Several students brought up the importance of the coursework and end of year exam on the citizen science topic (Table 14.2). As one student argued, it was only in the context of the more structured "academic reflection" of the assessment that they had drawn explicit links between their own and their classmates' use of the air quality monitor, and the broader role of citizen science in shaping the interface of "Science" and policy.

Another participant described how the question of how to conduct citizen science at scale and in areas such as water, air and soil pollution, only arose when thinking about their project during the assessment. It is particularly interesting to reflect on why some students may not have chosen the assessment on citizen science (the question in Table 14.2 was one option from a choice of three questions, and the exam requires students to answer two questions from a pool of seven). Asked about this, one student described struggling to describe data collection practices, concerns about the accuracy of data collected by others, or worries on how to cite the collective data source. These factors made the assessment feel less "safe" than the other available topics. It is hence interesting to note how citizen science's virtues of democratising knowledge and challenging established epistemic hierarchies (Kimura and Kinchy, 2016) can act as a source of uncertainty or even risk in a context where students are used to, and assessed on, traditional academic writing. Grading and pressure to achieve good degrees add to this. This highlights, again, the need to integrate the activity into the curriculum to encourage reflection spaces for all students, and to provide the scaffolding necessary for students to engage with their project on an academic level.

Asked about their views on citizen science, all participants agreed that throughout the project, they had come to view citizen science as an important tool to raise awareness of environmental issues and engage others with them, access local knowledges, and improve policy by building participatory structures – issues around scalability and reliability notwithstanding. Several participants also described how they viewed citizen science as an important part of 'Science' generally; however, they referred to lectures and the recent IPCC report (IPCC, 2023) as giving them a clear sense that citizen science was currently underrepresented in mainstream scientific practice. It is therefore interesting to note that none of the students mentioned participating in citizen science as *citizen scientists* outside the project. Rather, they described seeking more traditionally academic avenues to empower *others* to become citizen scientists. One student recounted how the experiences on GY220 had fed through into their bachelor thesis, and how they were now planning a PhD, seeking to empower young people to participate in the management of local environmental resources by using citizen sciences approaches. Another student described how they had taken up a multi-year research fellowship for a project using democratised data collection, citing GY220 and its emphasis on citizen science as a major factor for this. And yet another student drew on GY220 in their own teaching, using an air pollution monitor to make environmental pollution measurements in their classroom. As became clear throughout these discussions, this view on citizen science as a tool for engagement and knowledge building in others was grounded in the students' own extremely positive experience of using monitors as a tool to start conversations with flatmates, family, and friends about air pollution.

Of course, students changed their own behaviours too. Consistent with the impacts of air pollution monitoring described by Tan and Smith (2020), all students reported adopting small changes to routine behaviours after better understanding situational exposure, including changing commuting routes to avoid busy roads, opening windows when cooking, or lighting fewer candles. Similarly, the students referenced broader learnings from the project, describing how it had helped them better understand data collection practices, or "hands-on experience" with research.

However, the mostly indirect way by which students engaged with citizen science produces some tension to the objectives set out above. We were hoping for *students* to become agents in scientific research, encourage stewardship of environmental resources, and become more actively engaged in policy debates. Yet, the students we spoke to most commonly described a view of citizen science as engaging others, who might be less interested or aware of environmental issues than themselves. This raises an interesting conceptual point on the role of students in citizen science. Commonly, citizen science is defined as an "extramural" type of science conducted by individuals without affiliation to a research institution (Lave, 2015; Kimura & Kinchy, 2016). Students are affiliated with an institution, and many of the students we spoke to were actively pursuing paths deeper into academic institutions via post-graduate degrees, PhDs, and research fellowships. This, by definition, challenges their status as citizen scientists. Given this insider status in the academy, however, we effectively observe the case of students seeking to change academic practice from the inside, which presents an interesting virtue of citizen science as a student project that should be recognised as an important outcome of this work.

Although the available evidence from the focus group, as well as teaching evaluations, observational data on student engagement, and anecdotal feedback, make us confident that the project was engaging and beneficial to the vast majority of students, we must also highlight the variability of engagement across time and students. This likely reflects divergent preferences for learning styles within the cohort, with the activity appealing to students who prefer concrete experience, active experimentation, and reflective observation (kinaesthetic and visual learners), while being somewhat less appealing to those preferring abstract conceptualisation, including aural and read/write learners (Kolb, 2014; Fleming & Baume, 2006).

Conclusions

In conclusion, this chapter explores the potential of integrating citizen science projects into environmental education, particularly in the context of self-guided learning. By distributing low-cost air pollution exposure monitors to undergraduate students, we aimed to bridge the gap between theoretical classroom-based pedagogies and practical, real-world applications. Through active participation in data collection and analysis, students became citizen scientists, breaking down traditional barriers and fostering a sense of empowerment and agency. The project enabled students to explore concepts of knowledge production, civil society, and science and technology studies, while also emphasising the importance of data integrity, project management, and the role of different knowledge production pathways in environmental policymaking.

The integration of citizen science activities provided students with valuable constructivist learning experiences, allowing them to engage critically with the complexities of environmental issues. By making air pollution tangible and personal, students developed a deeper understanding of the implications of pollution on human health and the environment. Moreover, the project encouraged students to become environmental stewards, reflecting on their own role in advocating for change and shaping environmental policies.

However, challenges and variations in engagement were observed. While the majority of students actively participated in the project, some faced time constraints and chose not to engage fully with the online form for data submission. Assessment played a crucial role in facilitating deeper learning and reflection, providing structured opportunities for students to explore the role of citizen science in shaping scientific research and policy. It was evident that citizen science offered students an opportunity to engage others in environmental issues, but they themselves often did not see it as an activity to pursue outside of the course. As such, the project revealed how students perceived themselves as part of the academy, rather than as outsiders or amateurs, and how this influenced their aspirations and career choices. This demonstrates that citizen science can be a transformative tool for environmental education and personal development, not only by encouraging students to become agents of change in society, but also by enabling them to challenge and reshape academic practice from within.

The outcomes of this project suggest that citizen science can be an effective and enriching educational approach. Student participatory engagement with citizen science projects presents an authentic and contextual learning environment that links academic knowledge with practical real-world lived experiences. This aids the development of conceptual and evaluative skills, while also enabling students to become "change-makers" within academic institutions and beyond, long after completing the module. As we continue to refine and develop these initiatives, further research is needed to explore the long-term impacts of such interventions on students' attitudes, behaviours, and career trajectories, as well as their role in shaping environmental policies and driving positive change in society. Overall, citizen science holds significant promise as a catalyst for experiential environmental education and advocacy, empowering a new generation of environmentally-conscious citizens and professionals.

References

Alimisis, D., & Zoulias, E. (2013). Aligning technology with learning theories: A simulator-based training curriculum in surgical robotics. *Interactive Technology and Smart Education*, 10(3), 211–229.

Chan, K., Schillereff, D. N., Baas, A. C., Chadwick, M. A., Main, B., Mulligan, M., & Thompson, J. (2021). Low-cost electronic sensors for environmental research: Pitfalls and opportunities. *Progress in Physical Geography: Earth and Environment*, 45(3), 305–338.

Fleming, N., & Baume, D. (2006). Learning styles again: VARKing up the right tree! *Educational Developments*, 7(4), 4.

Haklay, M. (2017). Volunteered geographic information and citizen science. In R. Kitchen, T. P. Lauriault & M. W. Wilson (Eds.), *Understanding spatial media*. Sage Publications.

Honebein, P. C. (1996). Seven goals for the design of constructivist learning environments. *Constructivist Learning Environments: Case Studies in Instructional Design*, 11(12), 11.

IPCC (2023). *Climate change 2023: Synthesis report. Contribution of Working Groups I, II and III to the Sixth Assessment Report of the Intergovernmental Panel on Climate Change* [Core Writing Team, H. Lee and J. Romero (Eds.)]. IPCC, doi:10.59327/IPCC/AR6-9789291691647.

Kimura, A. H., & Kinchy, A. (2016). Citizen science: Probing the virtues and contexts of participatory research. *Engaging Science, Technology, and Society*, 2, 331–361.

Kolb, D. A. (2014). *Experiential learning: Experience as the source of learning and development*. FT Press.

Koohang, A., & Harman, K. (2005). Open source: A metaphor for e-learning. *Informing Science*, 8.

Lave, R. (2015). The future of environmental expertise. *Annals of the Association of American Geographers*, 105(2), 244–252.

Haklay, M. (2013). Citizen science and volunteered geographic information: Overview and typology of participation. In Sui, D., Elwood, S., Goodchild, M. (Eds), *Crowdsourcing Geographic Knowledge*. Springer. https://doi.org/10.1007/978-94-007-4587-2_7.

Robinson, J. A., Frantzidis, C., Sejdullahu, I., Persico, M. G., Kontić, D., Sarigiannis, D., & Kocman, D. (2023). Integrated assessment of personal monitor applications for evaluating exposure to urban stressors: A scoping review. *Environmental Research*, 115685.

Selwyn, N. (2007). The use of computer technology in university teaching and learning: A critical perspective. *Journal of Computer Assisted Learning*, 23(2), 83–94.

Snyder, E. G., Watkins, T. H., Solomon, P. A., Thoma, E. D., Williams, R. W., Hagler, G. S., & Preuss, P. W. (2013). The changing paradigm of air pollution monitoring. *Environmental Science & Technology*, 47(20), 11369–11377.

Stevens, M., (2014). M. Vitos, J. Altenbuchner, G. Conquest, J. Lewis and M. Haklay, "Taking Participatory Citizen Science to Extremes". *IEEE Pervasive Computing*, 13(2), 20–29, doi:10.1109/MPRV.2014.37.

Tan, S. H., & Smith, T. E. (2020). An optimal environment for our optimal selves? An autoethnographic account of self-tracking personal exposure to air pollution. *Area*, 53 (2), 353–361.

Robinson, J. A., Frantzidis, C., Sejdullahu, I., Persico, M. G., Kontić, D., Sarigiannis, D., & Kocman, D. (2023). Integrated assessment of personal monitor applications for evaluating exposure to urban stressors: A scoping review. *Environmental Research*, 115685.

Chapter 15

Embedding Education of Sustainable Development (ESD) and Universal Design for Learning (UDL) principles in a field trip to improve the student learning experience

Gustavo R. Espinoza-Ramos

The implementation of outdoor learning can be through different activities, including fieldwork and field trips. The difference between the two is that the former is implemented in long research projects (Spector, 2019) on which students apply theoretical concepts into practice and improve skills, such as observation, data collection and analysis (Pamulasari, 2017). Meanwhile, the latter are short-term study trips carried out by students that require observation of natural settings and where knowledge is developed through a personally relevant meaning to the experience (Behrendt & Franklin, 2014).

Research has demonstrated advantages of outdoor learning, including development of critical thinking, increased student engagement, and development of social and interpersonal skills (Pamulasari, 2017). Moreover, through self-reflection of their individual and collective roles in protecting the environment, outdoor learning improves the analysis of current issues in society, and promotes moral attitudes towards nature (Andersson & Öhman, 2015).

Despite outdoor learning constituting substantial potential advantages for learning, there have been some concerns as to whether this experience encourages passive learners and less engagement in the case of physics learning. Understanding the advantages and disadvantages of outdoor learning in higher education triggers some questions regarding its impact and implementation, including, "Can it improve student engagement on sustainability issues?" and "To what extent is it an inclusive practice that is aligned with students' learning preferences and abilities?"

Education for Sustainable Development (ESD)

The current socio-economic and environmental issues trigger the need for ways of raising awareness about these issues and developing competencies to find sustainable solutions. To address this, UNESCO developed Education for Sustainable Development (ESD) as a pedagogical response to the climate challenges the planet faces, seeking to empower people to develop a sustainable future (Afolabi, 2019). ESD is an interdisciplinary approach to learning that involves the improvement of the curricula

DOI: 10.4324/9781003436928-23

in higher education by applying a suitable pedagogy and learning activities, relevant to the discipline of study, that equip students with the knowledge and competencies for enhancing sustainable development (QAA & Advance HE, 2021).

UNESCO argues that the key competencies for sustainability are developed by the learners themselves during action, and on the basis of experience and reflection (UNESCO, 2017). Consequently, the learning outcomes will require applying these key competences so that students will have demonstrated the knowledge, skills and abilities about sustainability gained after completing the module. The key competencies for sustainability are divided into three main categories: Ways of thinking, ways of practising and ways of being, all of which can be seen in Table 15.1.

Table 15.1 UNESCO's key competencies for sustainability.

Category	Competency	A student who displays this competency can:
Ways of thinking	Systems thinking competency	• Recognise and understand relationships • Analyse complex systems • Consider how systems are embedded within different domains and scales • Deal with uncertainty
	Anticipatory competency (Future thinking)	• Understand and evaluate multiple outcomes • Create their own visions for the future • Apply the precautionary principle • Assess the consequences of actions • Deal with risks and changes
	Critical thinking competency	• Question norms, practices and opinions • Reflect on one's own values, perceptions and actions • Take a position in the sustainable development discourse
Ways of practising	Strategic competency	• Develop and implement innovative actions that further sustainable • Development at the local level and further afield
	Collaboration competency	• Learn from others (including peers, and others inside and outside of their institution) • Understand and respect the needs, perspectives and actions of others • Deal with conflicts in a group • Facilitate collaborative and participatory problem solving
	Integrated problem-solving competency	• Apply different problem-solving frameworks to complex sustainable development problems • Develop viable, inclusive and equitable solutions • Utilise appropriate competencies to solve problems

Category	Competency	A student who displays this competency can:
Ways of being	Self-awareness competency	• Reflect on their own values, perceptions and actions • Reflect on their own role in the local community and global society • Continually evaluate and further motivate their actions • Deal with their feelings and desires
	Normative competency	• Understand and reflect on the norms and values that underlie one's actions • Negotiate sustainable development values, principles, • Goals and targets, in a context of conflicts of interests and • Trade-offs, uncertain knowledge and contradictions

Source: QAA & Advance HE, 2021, p. 20.

After selecting and embedding some of the key competencies for sustainability in the learning outcomes, it is then necessary to select the learning activities and assessments suitable for them. To this end, creative learning activities that promote collaboration and enable students to learn about real-life social problems need to be developed. In this regard, Lozano et al. (2017) argue that educators should apply alternative methods of teaching, rather than traditional ones, to improve education for sustainable development. These alternative methods are not necessarily based in the class, for they can take place outside through such activities as field trips.

Field trips

Field trips are excursions or study tours that allow students to gain knowledge outside the classroom, permit the connection with and application of theoretical knowledge (Putz et al., 2018) and more importantly, promote the analysis of current real issues. The literature points to the wide range of advantages of field trips, including higher student interest, stronger motivation, the development of higher-order thinking skills (Paxton, 2015), improvement in the student learning experience, and enhancing students' social skills and networking opportunities (Malbrecht et al., 2016).

However, the planning and organisation of field trips raises three key inclusivity concerns related to mobility safety, financial restrictions and availability that have an impact on their implementation in higher education. The first concern pertains to the safety precautions for protecting students in outdoor surroundings (Tal & Morag, 2009), which represents an organisational challenge for educators.

Second, the lack of sufficient financial resources in organisations (Ho & Inoue, 2020) may discourage universities and students, as the organisation of field trips may require funding or paying some fees. Thirdly, the availability of students to participate in the field trip could be an issue, as some may face family or work commitments that may negatively impact on their attendance.

To reduce these inclusivity concerns, there has been a rise in virtual field trips (VFTs) that can complement real-world field trips, which particularly occurred during the COVID-19 pandemic. According to Leininger-Frézal and Sprenger (2022), a virtual field trip provides a learning opportunity to virtually explore the world by using digital tools. The authors identified three different types of virtual field trips that can be used to complement the real field trip:

- Virtual visit: This is the basic type of VFT that resides more in students' observation, with the level of interaction and autonomy being low. This can be seen when students watch a video-recorded presentation about the field trip. The level of engagement on this activity should be accompanied by other tasks, such as answering some questions or reflecting on this activity. Depending on the type of virtual visits, there are free online resources that lecturers can use as part of virtual tours, such as video recorded presentations of field trips in factories, museums, zoos, etc.
- Guided virtual field trip: This type of VFT involves a medium level of interaction, where attendees have to complete some tasks and not only make observations. Meanwhile, there is a medium level of autonomy so that students can make their own decisions on specific activities. For example, attendees can freely manipulate specific tools to explore part of the virtual space. This can be seen in online tours to museums, during which attendees can move in an interactive map.
- Open virtual field trip: This type of VFT involves a higher level of participation and autonomy than the virtual visit and guided virtual tour. The participant can use different tools like videos and photos, or complete tasks, such as quizzes or questions in the virtual space. For that reason, the participant has more autonomy in the selection of the activities that they want to engage with. However, there are some limitations in the virtual field trips, including the number of virtual field trips available, the additional equipment required and cost. Despite its limitations, Leininger-Frézal and Sprenger (2022) suggest that open virtual field trips can be used before the actual field trip to prepare participants.

When selecting and developing the VFT, it is advisable to assess the availability of any of these three options, how it can meet the learning outcomes, the level of complexity in its implementation, the financial implications in its adoption, the level of interactivity (for example, giving a question or series of questions that students should answer after this experience, or the use of supporting tools such as videos, images, apps and maps), and assessing how the virtual field trip can complement the real one.

Regardless of the type of field trip (virtual or not), it is advisable that the lecturer embed this outdoor learning experience in an assessment component, such as reports, an essay, posters or presentations in which students can reflect on their learning during the field trip, the application of concepts learned in the module, and answering the questions that were giving before the field trip. These measures will improve student engagement in the learning activity.

This section has demonstrated that offering field trips and virtual ones improves the level of inclusivity in the learning experience. However, there are other elements of inclusivity that should be taken in consideration during the design of this learning activity. For example, the extent to which field trips can reach more students who are from different backgrounds and have different learning preferences and knowledge needs to be taken into account. To improve further the level of inclusivity of field trips, it is important to understand and apply the principles of the Universal Design for Learning (UDL).

Universal Design for Learning (UDL)

The concept of universal design was developed in the field of architecture so that buildings were designed to be accessible by all users regardless of their abilities (Almumen, 2020), age or any other socio-demographic factor. Then, in the 1990s, Meyer and Rose applied this concept to learning, and it was named Universal Design for Learning (UDL). This is a framework aimed at teaching and learning being more inclusive and transformative for students of all abilities (CAST, n.d.), backgrounds and learning preferences. UDL supports the design of learning spaces that are accessible to a greatest number of users (Kumar & Wideman, 2014) and reduces the level of bias in the methods of expression of knowledge.

UDL offers different advantages in module design, including a positive impact on student outcomes, satisfaction and engagement (Al-Azawei et al., 2016), positive student progress in literacy, maths and science (Rao et al., 2014), and significant gains in reading. Further, due to the collaboration of participants, it mitigates feelings of discouragement, debasement and isolation (Francis et al., 2019). This framework is based on three key principles as follows.

- Engagement (the "why" of learning): This principle refers to the different student motivations to engage with learning, so the learning activities that may work for some students, may not work for others (Hall et al., 2015). To engage students in learning activities it is advisable to use real-life situations (Evans et al., 2010) and develop learning activities and assessments that are aligned with students' personal interests.
- Representation (the "what" of learning): Refers to the representation of what students learn by using multiple methods to present information and learning

content, including, text visual and auditory content (Almumen, 2020). Offering different ways to represent learning is aligned with students' differences in terms of background, mother tongues, and physical and cognitive abilities.

- Action and expression (the "how" of learning): Pertains to how students can represent their learned knowledge (Almumen, 2020). Through this principle, students will be able to select from different assessment components to express knowledge, such as reports, presentations, and technological tools.

These UDL principles improve the inclusivity in module content design by using different learning spaces (for example, indoor and outdoor learning, or synchronous and asynchronous activities), material (for example, text, images, videos, digital tools, etc.) and assessment components (for example, essays/reports, presentations, posters, podcasts, etc.).

The previous sections explored how concepts, such as field trips, ESD and UDL can be used in a cohesive way to develop key competencies for sustainability and improve agency in students' learning. The next section presents a case study that applies these concepts to demonstrate how outdoor learning enhanced the student learning experience in a business school.

Case study: Sustainable City Economies (SCE)

Sustainable City Economies (SCE) is a second-year undergraduate module at the Westminster Business School that has been delivered since the academic year 2021/22 and had 326 participants in the first year and 337 participants in the second. The module is aimed at providing students with theoretical and practical knowledge regarding sustainable cities, acknowledging the importance of the UN's Sustainable Development Goals (SDGs), particularly SDG 11 (Sustainable cities and communities).

The main pedagogy applied in the module is Problem Based Learning (PBL); an active student-centred approach, where a certain problem is posed before students learn new concepts and they find solutions to open-ended, real-life problems (Servant-Miklos, 2020). PBL offers key advantages, such as students becoming agents of their own learning, promoting collaboration (Kay et al., 2000), and problem solving, whilst soft skills enhance students' employability once they graduate.

PBL is applied in this module, where for the learning activities and assessment, students have to critically analyse socio-economic and environmental issues in the city and its causes. They have to evaluate how the city represents a complex network of systems, including energy, transport, housing and governance and find solutions to these sustainability issues by reflecting upon the role of stakeholders and their own role in moving towards developing a sustainable city.

To raise awareness about sustainability and find solutions to these issues, this module has embedded some of UNESCO's key competencies for sustainability in the following four learning outcomes (LOs) that are applied in the learning activities and assessment.

- LO1 meets the critical thinking competency, as students select and apply appropriate techniques for evaluation, with various forms of evidence being collected aimed at investigating the impact of businesses and governmental structures in cities.
- LO2 meets the collaboration competency, as students work in teams and develop communication skills to raise awareness of sustainability issues in the city.
- LO3 meets the integrated problem-solving competency, as students formulate a choice of solutions to sustainability problems in familiar and unfamiliar contexts of various cities across the world.
- LO4 meets the self-awareness competency, as students analyse performance of self and others in promoting a sustainable city and suggest improvements.

The module was delivered through 12 weeks of classes. On week 6 a field trip was organised around the city of London (1 hour 30 minutes), for which students had to analyse whether London was a sustainable city. During the field trip the students had the opportunity to identify sustainability issues and some solutions. The week 7 lecture was organised as a Q&A session of the learning experience in the field trip and a discussion about their role in promoting a sustainable city. The tour guide was invited as guest speaker and a summary of the key learning was discussed with students. For that reason, the field trip meets the LO3 and LO4 requirements. In addition, the field trip experience supported students towards successfully completing assessment 2, for which students had to formulate solutions to sustainability issues in a city of their selection, and to reflect on their learning from the field trip.

Universal Design for Learning (UDL) has been applied in the module design in different learning spaces, materials and assessments to meet students' learning preferences:

- By providing different learning spaces, including the classroom and a field trip, students were able to learn and apply theoretical concepts about sustainability in a real-life situation. This is aligned to the UDL Engagement principle (Guideline 9: self-regulation), as these different learning spaces represent an opportunity to engage students in learning.
- In the classroom different learning materials were used, such as PowerPoint slides, figures, video/audio recorded sessions, padlets, flip chart papers, reading material and discussion boards. This is aligned to the UDL Representation principle (Guideline 1: perception), as students receive information in different modalities and according to their learning preferences and abilities.
- As the field trip was delivered in two modes – walking or virtual tour – students could participate in either of them. This was a suitable solution, given

that some students were concerned about attendance as they were family carers or had work commitments. The two modes of field trip delivery were aligned with the UDL principle of Action and Expression (Guideline 5: expression and communication), as students engage with the learning content in different ways.

- In assessment 2 students develop solutions to the two sustainability issues in the city of their preference and reflect on their own role in the achievement of SDG targets. This is aligned with the UDL principle of Engagement (Guideline 7: recruitment interest), as students have the discretion and autonomy to select the context and tools for developing learning and assessing skills.

Evaluation of field trip impact

The impact of the application of ESD and UDL in the development of the field trip in Sustainable City Economies can be seen in different areas, including number of participants, assessment grades, student module evaluation and written feedback (see Table 15.2).

- Number of participants: In both academic years, there was a trend showing that of students' preference for the virtual tour rather than the walking counterpart. This preference could be related to the difficulties in the student engagement on field trips due to weather conditions, distance, and financial restrictions, as suggested in the literature. It is important to note that, in both academic years, as the walking tour was organised in week 6 when students had to submit an assessment in two different modules, this could be linked to student fatigue and therefore, had a negative impact on attendance.
- Student module evaluation (SME): The SME was slightly lower than for the previous academic year (4.2 and 4.1, respectively), due to student dissatisfaction on assessment 1 grades and some admin issues. However, the written feedback in

Table 15.2 Sustainable City Economies (SCE) – Field trip indicators.

SCE - Field trip		
Category	2021/22	2022/23
Total number of participants	326	337
Walking tour attendance	134 (41%)	130 (39%)
Virtual tour attendance	192 (59%)	207 (61%)
SME	4.2	4.1
Assessment 2 grade	56.93	62.33
Field trip reflection (max 20) grade	11.90	11.38

the SMEs demonstrates a positive perception from most students. The following written feedback focuses on the impact of the module and learning activity and choice of assessment. This demonstrates the importance of agency, as students felt empowered when they could select between the options that were more suitable to their learning preferences. Moreover, the evidence suggests that following the UDL Engagement principle has a significantly positive impact on student experience and learning.

a   "I really enjoyed this module, it was probably my favourite of this semester".

b   "I like that I had a lot of choice when it came to assessments – I could choose the city, problems, solutions".

c   "I liked the field trip and that we had the option to do it online or in person".

d   "The trip video was very good and it was good we had to demonstrate and reflect our knowledge on it in assignment 2".

e   "I mostly liked going on the sustainable London walking tour field trip".

• Assessment 2 grade: This assessment is based on students' analysis, application of concepts and formulation of solutions of two sustainability issues in a city of their selection. It is clear that the average grade of students who submitted the assessment was higher in the second year (62.33) than the previous one (56.93). This could be attributed to, including the use of exemplars in each different section of the assessment, the organisation of Q&A sessions during lectures and the use of the discussion board on Blackboard to support students when working on assessment 2. However, there was a lower average (11.38 out of 20) in the section of assessment 2 about the reflection on the field trip as compared with the previous year (11.90). Despite some exemplars being available for this section, students still need more support about reflection, especially in the analysis of their own role in moving towards sustainability.

Conclusion

This chapter has demonstrated the application of Education for Sustainable Development (ESD) in the form of UNESCO's key competencies of sustainability, and principles of Universal Design for Learning (UDL) in the development of a field trip for a second-year undergraduate module at the Westminster Business School. These concepts complement each other in module design, as seen in the development of the learning outcomes, learning activities and assessment. Having both indoor and outdoor learning opportunities improves student learning and engagement, as they can apply the concepts learned in the classroom to a real-life environment. The written feedback about the field trip demonstrates the importance of UDL principles that promotes agency, where students are empowered to select the field trip mode, and elements within the assessment in ways that allow them to demonstrate knowledge according to their abilities and learning preferences.

Despite the advantages of field trips in the learning experience, evidence has shown that the majority of students (60%) prefer to attend virtual visits rather than walking tours. This highlights an important question as to whether virtual visits should be used to complement field trips (walking tour). The student attendance on the field trips may vary according to factors such as discipline of study, weather conditions, time and finance. Therefore, further studies should be carried out to compare results in different modules at undergraduate and postgraduate level to gain a better understanding of the impact of field trips in learning.

References

Afolabi, P. A. (2019). Assessment of field trip as a pedagogical strategy for teaching sustainable development agenda at higher education level. *International Journal of Advanced Academic Research | Arts*, 5(5), 2488–9849.

Al-Azawei, A., Serenelli, F., & Lundqvist, K. (2016). Universal Design for Learning (UDL): A content analysis of peer reviewed journals from 2012 to 2015. *Journal of the Scholarship of Teaching and Learning*, 16(3), 39–56. https://doi.org/10.14434/josotl.v16i3.19295.

Almumen, H. A. (2020). Universal Design for Learning (UDL) across cultures: The application of UDL in Kuwaiti inclusive classrooms. *SAGE Open*, 10(4), 1–14. https://doi.org/10.1177/2158244020969674.

Andersson, K., & Öhman, J. (2015). Moral relations in encounters with nature. *Journal of Adventure Education and Outdoor Learning*, 15(4), 310–329. https://doi.org/10.1080/14729679.2015.1035292.

Behrendt, M., & Franklin, T. (2014). A review of research on school field trips and their value in education. *International Journal of Environmental and Science Education*, 9(3), 235–245. https://doi.org/10.12973/ijese.2014.213a.

CAST. (n.d.). About Universal Design for Learning. Retrieved June 24, 2023, from https://www.cast.org/impact/universal-design-for-learning-udl.

Evans, C., Williams, J. B., King, L., & Metcalf, D. (2010). Modeling, guided instruction, and application of UDL in a rural special education teacher preparation program. *Rural Special Education Quarterly Thirtieth Anniversary*, 29(4), 41.

Francis, G. L., Duke, J. M., Fujita, M., & Sutton, J. C. (2019). "It's a constant fight:" Experiences of college students with disabilities. *Journal of Postsecondary Education and Disability*, 32(3), 247–262.

Hall, T. E., Cohen, N., Vue, G., & Ganley, P. (2015). Addressing learning disabilities with UDL and technology: Strategic reader. *Learning Disability Quarterly*, 38(2), 72–83. https://doi.org/10.1177/0731948714544375.

Ho, B. Q., & Inoue, Y. (2020). Driving network externalities in education for sustainable development. *Sustainability (Switzerland)*, 12(20), 1–16. https://doi.org/10.3390/su12208539.

Kay, J., Barg, M., Fekete, A., Greening, T., Hollands, O., Kingston, J. H., & Crawford, K. (2000). Problem-based learning for foundation computer science courses. *Computer*

Science Education, 10(2), 109–128. https://doi.org/10.1076/0899-3408(200008)10:2; 1-c;ft109.

Kumar, K. L., & Wideman, M. (2014). Accessible by design: Applying UDL principles in a first year undergraduate course. *Canadian Journal of Higher Education*, 44(1), 125–147. http://www.washington.edu/doit/.

Leininger-Frézal, C., & Sprenger, S. (2022). Virtual field trips in binational collaborative teacher training: Opportunities and challenges in the context of education for sustainable development. *Sustainability (Switzerland)*, 14(19). https://doi.org/10.3390/su141912933.

Lozano, R., Merrill, M. Y., Sammalisto, K., Ceulemans, K., & Lozano, F. J. (2017). Connecting competences and pedagogical approaches for sustainable development in higher education: A literature review and framework proposal. *Sustainability (Switzerland)*, 9 (10), 1–15. https://doi.org/10.3390/su9101889.

Malbrecht, B. J., Campbell, M. G., Chen, Y. S., & Zheng, S. L. (2016). Teaching outside the classroom: Field trips in crystallography education for chemistry students. *Journal of Chemical Education*, 93(9), 1671–1675. https://doi.org/10.1021/acs.jchemed.6b00073.

Pamulasari, H. E. (2017). Outdoor learning model through fieldwork to improve physics achievement in dynamic fluid. *Journal of Turkish Science Education*, 14(3), 73–86. https://doi.org/10.12973/tused.10205a.

Paxton, J. (2015). A practical guide to incorporating service learning into development economics classes. *International Review of Economics Education*, 18, 25–36. https://doi.org/10.1016/j.iree.2015.01.001.

Putz, L. M., Treiblmaier, H., & Pfoser, S. (2018). Field trips for sustainable transport education: Impact on knowledge, attitude and behavioral intention. *International Journal of Logistics Management*, 29(4), 1424–1450. https://doi.org/10.1108/IJLM-05-2017-0138.

QAA & Advance HE. (2021). *Education for sustainable development guidance.*

Rao, K., Ok, M. W., & Bryant, B. R. (2014). A review of research on universal design educational models. *Remedial and Special Education*, 35(3), 153–166. https://doi.org/10.1177/0741932513518980.

Servant-Miklos, V. (2020). Problem-oriented project work and problem-based learning: "Mind the gap!" *Interdisciplinary Journal of Problem-Based Learning*, 14(1), 1–17. https://doi.org/10.14434/ijpbl.v14i1.28596.

Spector, B. (2019). Rethinking field trips. https://blogs.lse.ac.uk/highereducation/2019/09/16/rethinking-field-trips/.

Tal, T., & Morag, O. (2009). Reflective practice as a means for preparing to teach outdoors in an ecological garden. *Journal of Science Teacher Education*, 20(3), 245–262. https://doi.org/10.1007/s10972-009-9131-1.

UNESCO. (2017). *Education for sustainable development goals: Learning objectives.* United Nations Educational, Scientific and Cultural Organization.

Part 5

Crossing educational borders

Chapter 16

Aesthetic harmonies

Nature, technology and holistic learning

Alexander Sabine and Tom Langston

Embodying the ethos of a "Forest Schools" approach, and other initiatives, such as the John Muir Award, outdoor pedagogy has firmly established its relevance in the domains of early years and primary education throughout the United Kingdom (Cont et al., 2023; Stuckey, 2023). Rooted in the Scandinavian educational traditions, Forest School practitioners advocate for nature-immersion, learner autonomy, self-efficacy, personal growth and key skills acquisition in the context of outdoors environments (Knight, 2017; Maynard, 2007). These experiential approaches to learning and living underscore a learner-centred methodology, long-term immersion in natural environments, and pedagogical practice that is entwined with the wilderness, our ecology and communal sense of ourselves, of each other, and the places we collectively inhabit (Gravett et al., 2021).

Tom's reflections spotlight his pragmatic, experiential approach to learning, which has helped to shape his hands-on, creative approach to higher education (HE) teaching, and an interest in outdoor education. Utilising Gibbs's (1983) "Twenty Terrible Reasons for Lecturing", Tom shares his struggle to connect with didactic approaches to teaching and learning in HE, driving him to be innovative in order to adapt. As the HE landscape evolves toward a practical and experiential learning methodology (Gibbs, 1983; Kirschner & Neelen, 2017), new opportunities to review discussions about entrenched and calcified institutional structures are presented (Waite, 2011; Maynard, 2022; Foucault, 1977). Furthermore, rapidly advancing technologies are reshaping the face of Technology Enhanced Learning (TEL) in institutions, adding layers of dynamism to enrich outdoor learning experiences, amalgamating the physical and digital realms (Chai et al., 2022).

The narrative which follows is organised around four thematic cornerstones: "Authentic Learning", "Wellbeing & Resilience", "Creative & Divergent Thinking", and "Collaboration & Teamwork". These four dimensions of enquiry are used to explore the intersection of outdoor pedagogy, TEL, and the pedagogical philosophies of educators in both the primary education sector and HE sector respectively.

DOI: 10.4324/9781003436928-25

Authentic learning

At the core of outdoor pedagogy's value is the underpinning ethos of authentic, experiential learning, a theory rooted in the progressive educational philosophies of Dewey, Piaget, and Kolb (Dewey, 1938; Piaget, 1964; Kolb, 1984). These philosophies emphasise the importance of active learning, where students are encouraged to construct their own knowledge through experiences and interactions with their environments. This is further supported by recent studies on experiential learning, highlighting the significance of in-class experiences and the integration of education theory into practical applications (Steele, 2023). It is already widely accepted that this style of pedagogy presents a unique avenue for constructing knowledge beyond mere information acquisition (Kolb, 1984). Furthermore, the application of knowledge and skills in tangible contexts is not just about understanding theoretical concepts, but also represents a shift toward mastering the ability to apply them in real-world situations, bridging the gap between theory and practice (Morrison-Love, 2023), emphasising active involvement, thoughtful reflection, and an intimate application of knowledge and skills in tangible contexts (Mezirow, 1997; Kolb, 1984)

Outdoor learning, in its various shapes and forms, embeds authentic learning in a tapestry of visceral activities that promote cognition, social interactivity, problem-solving, creativity and overall wellbeing. Experiential learners are embedded in direct interaction with their environment, prone and "rendered raw" to its physical attributes. Over time this has been shown to deepen learners' sense of belonging; shaping self-knowledge and building reciprocity with each other and the world-at large (Jordan & Hinds, 2017). During the interview, Ally described how she creates resonance between curriculum content and practical activities:

> When our year one students delve into the history of castles, I weave whittling into our activities. The children create their own arrows, mimicking the fundamental elements of a castle. This integration introduces intersections of history, science, and design and technology into one activity.

Ally highlights how curriculum content is brought to life for children by tacitly embedding core skills and "ways of being" to enable encounters that bring their learning to life. The authentic learning embedded in these activities exemplifies Bruner's concept of the spiral curriculum (Bruner, 1960), in which young learners are provided with a shared framework for understanding which gradually increases in depth as the content is encountered at later phases of their learning journey. This educational philosophy proposes revisiting foundational concepts at increasing levels of complexity, thereby establishing and expanding students' understanding over time.

Another example of this approach in action is in grasping the functionality of complex interacting systems, both in a natural "ecological" sense and in terms of technological systems. For example, in Forest Schools, children use microscopes to explore natural networks underfoot, forming early schematic understandings of interrelated and mutually beneficial "eco" systems. When children learn, first-hand, about these networks of the forest, and the mycelium strands which "glue" together the "wood wide web" (Sheldrake, 2020; Marshall, 2019), they are primed to better understand the mutual entanglements between humankind and the natural world in which they are subjectively positioned at both individual and societal levels. Simultaneously, they are also equipped with a structural framework to prime a more comprehensive schematic understanding of digital and biological structures, including that of the human brain, communities, the internet and Artificially Intelligent "neural networks" (Petrov & Atanasova, 2020; Voon et al., 2023).

The fusion of outdoor pedagogy with TEL has opened other avenues of innovation in authentic and meaningful learning (Mezirow, 1997; Petrov & Atanasova, 2020; Liao et al., 2022). This approach extends to HE, where new technologies, such as artificial neural networks, require a schematic foundation in order for the learner to integrate novel ways of understanding the world (Voon et al., 2023; Alom et al., 2019). By layering exposure to these intricate systems over time, much like the incremental structure of Bruner's spiral curriculum, the often opaque workings of these digital and biological networks are slowly de-mystified. This process, akin to a kind of digital alchemy, transforms the abstract complexities of technology into tangible, comprehensible knowledge. As Cannon (2023) suggests, the integration of digital media arts into education can be seen as an alchemical process, where creative literacy practices merge with critical media education to produce a richer understanding.

For instance, during collaborations with schools in the Solent region, a drone was used to generate real-time aerial views of the school and its surrounding landscape, fostering a sense of relationality and positionality in the children (Yang et al., 2022). This unique perspective serves as a metaphorical and literal lens to broaden the children's understanding of geography and ecology. This integration of experiential outdoor learning with digital innovation cultivates a distinct brand of authentic learning, nurturing students' understanding of their natural and artificial worlds (Petrov & Atanasova, 2020; Liao et al., 2022).

Authentic learning is not merely a "transmission" process; it encompasses a transformative journey fostering a deeper understanding, refining skills, and shaping attitudes (Mezirow, 1997). By viewing knowledge construction through the lens of a spiral curriculum and integrating this with outdoor and digital pedagogies, both young learners and HE students are provided with robust, integrated frameworks to understand the intricate networks that permeate our natural and digital worlds. Hay (2023) emphasises the importance of nurturing children's artistic identities, suggesting that the fusion of art with outdoor and digital learning can be a powerful tool for holistic development. This synthesis of art, nature, and technology offers learners a multi-dimensional approach to understanding the world, blending creativity with critical thinking.

Wellbeing and resilience

Outdoor education nurtures wellbeing and resilience in both adults and children alike, a benefit that extends beyond direct interaction with nature (Chandrawati & Aisyah, 2022). In tandem, ecopsychology principles highlight the integral relationship between individuals and their natural environments, advocating for a synergy that enhances mental health while promoting greater ecological awareness and sustainability practices (Roszak, 2001; Chalquist, 2009; Thoma et al., 2021; Koger & Winter, 2011). This construction of wellbeing, however, is not emergent only of the act of immersing oneself in the outdoors. To the contrary, these "wild" environments can, at first, be anxiety-inducing for new inhabitants who are unfamiliar with the external forces of nature. When confronted with the raw face of nature we are, perhaps, "rendered raw", and stripped of our intra- and interpersonal defences (Jordan & Hinds, 2017; Kaplan, 1995). As proposed by Ungar (2008), resilience weaves beyond individual attributes, and is kindled through meaningful exchanges between individuals and their environment (Gill, 2014). Overcoming challenges, devising solutions, and gaining new skills within outdoor settings plant the seeds for this resilience. In the context of primary-aged children, Ally offers some further insight:

> Taking calculated risks at a young age is a gateway to developing self-esteem and resilience... Forest Schools offer a judgement-free learning environment... I sincerely believe that it's instrumental in equipping learners with life skills and fostering an affinity for nature and wildlife.

This perspective aligns with Ungar's (2008) proposition that resilience is nurtured through purposeful interactions with one's surroundings in equilibrium, extending our engagement with technology, as explored in relation to authentic learning. The same digital tools – drones, weather stations, and Augmented Reality (AR) – also play pivotal roles in cultivating resilience (Eliasson et al., 2022; Kamarainen et al., 2023). As learners grapple with the complexities of these tools, and their associated challenges, they reinforce resilience initially fostered in their physical interactions (Eliasson et al., 2022). Indeed, hands-on experiences, particularly those derived from interactions with the natural environment, have been shown to foster a profound sense of responsibility and resilience in learners. Sandseter's work on risky play further underscores this, suggesting that challenging interactions, whether with the natural environment or digital tools, can be seen as ethical challenges that bolster resilience and adaptive capacities in learners (Sandseter & Kvalnes, 2023).

For example, the role the children in schools undertook as data collectors with weather stations transcended mere understanding of weather patterns and conditions. It instilled a sense of duty, nurturing their resilience as they confronted these novel challenges (Eliasson et al., 2022). Similarly, the introduction of drones as tools for broadening spatial perspectives further cultivated ecological stewardship, enhancing the overall wellbeing and resilience of these young learners (Kamarainen et al., 2023). In a HE context, immersive experiences, such as those provided by outdoor education, are indeed invaluable. They not only validate the innate curiosity of university students, but spark exploration, deepening their connection with the environment and enhancing their overall wellbeing (Wojciehowski & Ernst, 2018). Such experiences, as highlighted by Wilson et al. (2013), can bridge the gap between students' expectations and experiences in research oriented degrees, fostering a more comprehensive, and transformative, educational experience.

Moreover, interactive AR trails, previously discussed as platforms for local exploration, serve as testbeds for resilience. The challenges faced by children while navigating narratives, such as the "Monkton Merman", cultivate resilience, equipping them to navigate obstacles while delving into their community's history and ecology (Dunleavy & Dede, 2014). Knight's (2017) research underscores the importance of physical environments in bolstering mental wellbeing. The influence of outdoor education radiates beyond the learners, impacting educators as well. A ripple effect of wellbeing and resilience is discernible in those dedicated to implementing outdoor pedagogical practices (Maynard, 2007; Cutter-Mackenzie, 2009; Waite, 2017). Champion (2022) emphasises the reflective experiences associated with immersive learning in higher education, suggesting that a synthesis of outdoor pedagogy and technology-enhanced learning not only fosters knowledge and skills but also promotes a culture of wellbeing. This harmonious blend of hands-on, immersive experiences with cutting-edge technology is, therefore, a catalyst for a more integrated and holistic form of education that places creativity and divergent thinking at its core.

Creative and divergent thinking

Creative and divergent thinking, two intertwined constructs, occupy a central place in educational discourse. Dunker's (1945) seminal work differentiated between convergent thinking, where the goal is a singular correct answer, and divergent thinking, which champions the generation of multiple, potentially effective alternatives. This concept is further supported by the work of Lee and Hwang (2022) who also found that technology-enhanced learning environments can foster creativity and divergent thinking in learners. Promoting this divergent mindset in educational spaces encourages creativity and problem-solving, two outcomes celebrated by outdoor pedagogy. Such environments offer learners the opportunity to explore, experiment, and make meaning of their world through direct experience. Indeed, Robinson (2011) suggests that creativity thrives in environments where learners are empowered to question, make connections, envision possibilities, explore ideas, and critically reflect on their work.

Louv (2008) extends this argument, claiming that exposure to nature can stimulate a child's imagination, thus aiding cognitive development and creativity. This notion forms an integral part of outdoor pedagogy. By inviting learners to navigate natural settings, educators incite curiosity and exploration, fostering a fertile ground for innovative thought and problem-solving. This is reinforced by the findings of Knez et al. (2023) who found that outdoor learning environments can stimulate creative thinking and problem-solving in children. Ally's practice within the forest school setting offers compelling examples. She combines various subjects in real-world tasks, provoking children to think creatively, make connections across disciplinary boundaries, and challenge conventional wisdom. When children engage in such holistic learning experiences, the line between "learning" and "playing" blurs, creating a pedagogical space that emboldens creativity and curiosity (Lee & Hwang, 2022).

Similarly, AR extends the capacity of outdoor education to inspire creative and divergent thinking. As learners navigate the "Monkton Merman" narrative, they delve into the past and present ecological, historical, and cultural dimensions of their community. The integration of the digital and physical worlds offered by AR provokes a myriad of perspectives, inspiring both primary-aged children and adult learners in HE to explore multiple solutions – a testament to the essence of divergent thinking. Within HE, cultivating creativity is key to effective educational delivery and reception. The fusion of outdoor education and TEL in practices illustrates how HE can foster creative and divergent thinking for students across disciplines. Weaving together experiential learning and technological enhancements, this approach offers a robust blueprint for transforming knowledge creation and application. It cultivates not only knowledge acquisition but also vital creative and critical thinking skills, empowering students to become autonomous, lifelong learners ready to tackle the complexities of the 21st century. This potent blend of hands-on, immersive experiences with cutting-edge technology is arguably, therefore, a catalyst for a more integrated and holistic form of education that fosters creativity and divergent thinking at its core.

Collaboration and teamwork

Principles of collaboration and teamwork are deeply entrenched in theories of collectivism and social identity, and are instrumental in constructing students' sense of belonging. As classrooms continue to evolve into diverse, globally interconnected, and digitally-inclined spaces, it is more crucial than ever to nurture teamwork skills that will prepare learners for the challenges and opportunities of a complex world. Within this paradigm, outdoor education, especially when interwoven with TEL, serves as an effective platform for fostering these critical skills.

Drawing on theories of ecopsychology (Roszak, 2001) and ecotherapy (Jordan & Hinds, 2017), outdoor education engenders a profound sense of connectedness between individuals and their environment; a critical component for enhancing both mental well-being and a sense of community. By engaging in shared tasks and challenges within the natural world, students learn not only from the environment but also from each other. This cultivates a spirit of teamwork and camaraderie and provides opportunities to develop key social skills such as leadership, negotiation, and conflict resolution. These skills serve to strengthen social identity and foster a sense of belonging within the group. This shift in leadership dynamics, as observed by Ally, highlights the power of outdoor spaces in recalibrating social relationships:

> When children are outside, you see a different balance... (Those ones that are quiet and timid inside actually have got more confidence when they're outside... Some of them might go, I can't do it. I can't do it. You know, I can't do it and give up. But we encourage them to keep going. Keep going. Let's just try again).

Technology, as we've already discussed, can serve to further enrich the collaborative aspect of outdoor learning. In our collaboration with Solent schools, the weather station project stands out as a model for how outdoor education and technology can work together to facilitate collaborative action and shared problem solving. Children working together to interpret weather data, and connect their findings to broader issues such as climate change, is a powerful example of how outdoor learning can make abstract concepts tangible and personally relevant. Likewise, AR trails brought forth an enhanced layer of collaboration among not just children, but families as well. During themed walking trails, for instance, it was found that children and their families cooperated and problem-solved together to navigate the trail and unravel the different narrative threads. In the process, they developed a deeper understanding of the collective narrative, fostering a sense of shared responsibility and belonging. The need for such collaborative pedagogical models extends into HE as well, particularly in light of increasing concerns about student engagement and self-confidence (Gravett et al., 2021). The blend of experiential outdoor education and TEL serves as a potent strategy to foster teamwork and collaboration skills (Chai et al., 2022; Cont et al., 2023).

Active engagement with real-world tasks in the natural world, enabled by innovative technology, can enhance students' appreciation of diverse perspectives and improve their ability to collaborate effectively (Kamarainen et al., 2023). These skills are invaluable in a multicultural, interdisciplinary, and rapidly evolving global context. Furthermore, this model of education, deeply rooted in the principles of Forest School pedagogy, offers a fresh perspective on how HE can engage and inspire students, thereby addressing the issue of student apathy and building confidence through collaborative, experiential learning (Maynard, 2022; Knight, 2017). In essence, the combination of outdoor learning principles and technology-enhanced pedagogical strategies offers an innovative model of education that places collaboration, teamwork, and a sense of belonging at its core (Liao et al., 2022; Flavin & Quintero, 2018). It provides students with the skills and experiences necessary to thrive in the interconnected world of the 21st century.

By fostering a strong sense of reciprocity and interdependence, outdoor learning is an effective antidote to the increasing atomisation and alienation often associated with our digital age (Jordan & Hinds, 2017; Kaplan, 1995). It is strikingly apparent how the marriage of outdoor pedagogy and technology-enhanced learning can play a significant role in revitalising educational experiences across all educational levels (Gravett et al., 2021; Chai et al., 2022). As we stand on the brink of a socio-technological revolution, this symbiosis holds the promise of responding to the demands of the 21st century while simultaneously rekindling our innate connection to the natural world (Kaplan, 1995; Lee & Hwang, 2022).

In conclusion, sharing our experiences has highlighted the transformative potential of blending technology-enhanced learning with outdoor education, fostering collaboration, teamwork, and a sense of belonging amongst learners. The fusion of experiential learning with technology enhanced tools transcends traditional pedagogical approaches, marking a paradigm shift that emphasises learners' connection with their environment and the effective use of technologies to deepen this connection and enhance children, and students' as beings-in-the-world. As Roszak's (2001) ecopsychology theories articulate, nurturing a relationship with nature is paramount in education, cultivating not only knowledge but also environmental stewardship, producing responsible and environmentally conscious citizens. The insights from our collaboration with Ally and the reflections derived underscore the vast potential of this approach, challenging educators to empower learners with the agency, knowledge, and skills essential for a rapidly changing world. The synergy between outdoor pedagogy and technology-enhanced learning offers a promising trajectory towards an educational model where learning evolves into a journey of discovery, innovation, and transformation. Grounded in experiential and immersive contexts, this journey equips learners to face future challenges and opportunities. It is not merely about comprehending the world but actively participating in it, fostering stewardship and adeptly navigating the intricacies of such an ecosystem and shaping a generation poised to embrace the future with confidence.

References

Alom, M. Z., Taha, T. M., Yakopcic, C., Westberg, S., Sidike, P., Nasrin, M. S., & Asari, V. K. (2019). A state-of-the-art survey on deep learning theory and architectures. *Electronics*, 8(3), 292. https://doi.org/10.3390/electronics8030292.

Bruner, J. S. (1960). *The process of education*. Harvard University Press.

Cannon, M. (2023). Digital media arts and critical media education: an alchemy of creative literacy practices. In *International encyclopedia of education* (pp. 497–502). 4th Edition. Elsevier.

Chai, S., Liu, H., & Ng, E. (2022). Technology enhanced learning acceptance among university students during Covid-19: Integrating the full spectrum of Self-Determination Theory and self-efficacy into the Technology Acceptance Model. *Current Psychology*. https://doi.org/10.1007/s12144-022-02996-1.

Chalquist, C. (2009). A look at the ecotherapy research evidence. *Ecopsychology*, 1(2), 64–74.

Champion, E. (2022). Reflective experiences with immersive heritage. In A. Benardou & A. M. Droumpouki (Eds.), *Difficult heritage and immersive experiences* (pp. 23–40). Routledge.

Chandrawati, T., & Aisyah, S. (2022). *ECE educator training: How to develop literacy and environment education for children?*JPUD. https://doi.org/10.21009/JPUD.161.09.

Cont, S., Rowley, A., Knowles, Z., & Bowe, C. (2023). The perceptions of trainee teachers towards Forest School: Does connection to nature matter? *Journal of Adventure Education and Outdoor Learning*, 1–17.

Cutter-Mackenzie, A. (2009). Multicultural school gardens: Creating engaging garden spaces in learning about language, culture, and environment. *Canadian Journal of Environmental Education*, 14, 122–135.

Dewey, J. (1938). *Experience and education*. Kappa Delta Pi.

Dunker, K. (1945). On problem-solving. *Psychological Monographs*, 58(5), 1–113.

Dunleavy, M., & Dede, C. (2014). Augmented reality teaching and learning. In J. M. Spector, M. D. Merrill, J. Elen, & M. J. Bishop (Eds.), *Handbook of research on educational communications and technology* (pp. 735–745). 4th Edition. Springer. https://doi.org/10.1007/978-1-4614-3185-5_59.

Eliasson, I., Fredholm, S., Knez, I., & Gustavsson, E. (2022). The need to articulate historic and cultural dimensions of landscapes in sustainable environmental planning: A Swedish case study. *Land*, 11(11), 1915.

Flavin, M., & Quintero, V. (2018). UK higher education institutions' technology-enhanced learning strategies from the perspective of disruptive innovation. *Research in Learning Technology*, 26. https://dx.doi.org/10.25304/RLT.V26.1987.

Foucault, M. (1977). *Discipline and punish: The birth of the prison*. Vintage Books.

Gibbs, G. (1983). *Twenty terrible reasons for lecturing*. SCED Occasional Paper No. 8. Birmingham: Standing Conference on Educational Development.

Gill, T. (2014). The benefits of children's engagement with nature: A systematic literature review. *Children, Youth and Environments*, 24(2), 10–34.

Gravett, K., Taylor, C. A., & Fairchild, N. (2021). Pedagogies of mattering: re-conceptualising relational pedagogies in higher education. *Teaching in Higher Education*, 1–16.

Hay, P. (2023). *Children are artists: Supporting children's learning identity as artists*. Routledge.

Jordan, M., & Hinds, J. (2017). *Ecotherapy: Theory, research and practice*. Bloomsbury Publishing.

Kamarainen, A. M., Metcalf, S., Grotzer, T., Browne, A., Mazzuca, D., Tutwiler, M. S., & Dede, C. (2023). EcoMOBILE: Integrating augmented reality and probeware with environmental education field trips. *Computers & Education*, 68, 545–556. https://doi.org/10.1016/j.compedu.2013.02.018.

Kaplan, S. (1995). The restorative benefits of nature: Toward an integrative framework. *Journal of Environmental Psychology*, 15(3), 169–182.

Kennedy, M., & Dunn, T. J. (2018). Improving the use of technology enhanced learning environments in higher education in the UK: A qualitative visualisation of students' views. *Contemporary Educational Technology*, 9(2), 141–158. https://dx.doi.org/10.30935/CEDTECH/6212.

Kirschner, P. A., & Neelen, M. (2017). Stop propagating the learning styles myth. *Computers & Education*, 106, 166–171. https://doi.org/10.1016/j.compedu.2016.12.006.

Knez, I., Ode Sang, Å., Gunnarsson, B., & Hedblom, M. (2023). Wellbeing in urban greenery: The role of naturalness and place identity. *Frontiers in Psychology*, 11, 1241. https://doi.org/10.3389/fpsyg.2020.01341.

Knight, S. (2017). *Forest school in practice: For all ages*. SAGE Publications.

Koger, S. M., & Winter, D. D. (2011). *The psychology of environmental problems: Psychology for sustainability*. Psychology Press.

Kolb, D. A. (1984). *Experiential learning: Experience as the source of learning and development*. Prentice-Hall.

Lee, H., & Hwang, Y. (2022). Technology-enhanced education through VR-making and metaverse-linking to foster teacher readiness and sustainable learning. *Sustainability*, 14 (8), 4786.

Liao, F., Murphy, D., Wu, J. C., Chen, C. Y., Chang, C. C., & Tsai, P. F. (2022). How technology-enhanced experiential e-learning can facilitate the development of person-centred communication skills online for health-care students: a qualitative study. *BMC Medical Education*, 22(1), 1–9.

Louv, R. (2008). *Last child in the woods: Saving our children from nature-deficit disorder*. Algonquin Books.

Marshall, C. (2019, May 15). Wood wide web: Trees' social networks are mapped. BBC News. https://www.bbc.co.uk/news/science-environment-48257315.

Maynard, T. (2007). Encounters with Forest School and Foucault: A risky business? *Education 3–13*, 35(4), 379–391.

Maynard, T. (2022). *Forest schools and outdoor learning in the early years*. Sage.

Mezirow, J. (1997). Transformative learning: Theory to practice. *New Directions for Adult and Continuing Education*, 74, 5–12.

Morrison-Love, D. (2023). Doing: Skills, knowledge, and understanding in conceptual, theoretical, and practical contexts. In D. Gill, D. Irving-Bell, M. McLain, & D. Wooff (Eds.), *The Bloomsbury Handbook of Technology Education* (pp. 122–135). Bloomsbury Academic.

Petrov, P. D., & Atanasova, T. V. (2020). The effect of augmented reality on students' learning performance in stem education. *Information*, 11(4), 209.

Piaget, J. (1964). Part I: Cognitive development in children: Piaget development and learning. *Journal of Research in Science Teaching*, 2(3), 176–186.

Robinson, K. (2011). *Out of our minds: Learning to be creative*. Capstone Publishing.

Roszak, T. (2001). *The voice of the earth: An exploration of ecopsychology*. Simon & Schuster.

Sandseter, E. B. H., & Kvalnes, Ø. (2023). *Risky play: An ethical challenge*. Springer International Publishing.

Sheldrake, M. (2020). *Entangled life: How fungi make our worlds, change our minds & shape our futures*. Random House.

Steele, A. L. (2023). *Experiential Learning in Engineering Education*. CRC Press.

Stuckey, M. E. (2023). *For the enjoyment of the people: The creation of national identity in American public lands*. University Press of Kansas.

Thoma, M. V., Rohleder, N., & Rohner, S. L. (2021). Clinical ecopsychology: The mental health impacts and underlying pathways of the climate and environmental crisis. *Frontiers in Psychiatry*, 12, 675936.

Ungar, M. (2008). Resilience across cultures. *British Journal of Social Work*, 38(2), 218–235. https://doi.org/10.1093/bjsw/bcl343.

Urbina, S., Villatoro, S., & Salinas, J. (2021). Self-Regulated Learning and Technology-Enhanced Learning Environments in Higher Education: A Scoping Review. *Sustainability*, 13 (13), 7281. https://dx.doi.org/10.3390/su13137281.

Voon, X. P., Wong, S. L., Wong, L. H., Khambari, M. N. M., & Syed-Abdullah, S. I. S. (2023). Developing pre-service teachers' computational thinking through experiential learning: Hybridisation of plugged and unplugged approaches. *Research and Practice in Technology Enhanced Learning*, 18.

Waite, S. (2011). Teaching and learning outside the classroom: Personal values, alternative pedagogies and standards. *Education 3–13*, 39(1), 65–82. https://doi.org/10.1080/03004270903206141.

Waite, S. (2017). Making a difference: Learning on a grand scale. In S. Waite (Ed.), *Children learning outside the classroom: From birth to eleven*. 2nd Edition. Sage.

Walker, R., Jenkins, M., & Voce, J. (2018). The rhetoric and reality of technology-enhanced learning developments in UK higher education: Reflections on recent UCISA research findings (2012–2016). *Interactive Learning Environments*, 26(8), 994–1003. https://doi.org/10.1080/10494820.2017.1419497.

Wilson, A., Howitt, S., Roberts, P., Åkerlind, G., & Wilson, K. (2013). Connecting expectations and experiences of students in a research-immersive degree. *Studies in Higher Education*, 38(10), 1562–1576.

Wojciehowski, M., & Ernst, J. (2018). Creative by nature: Investigating the impact of nature preschools on young children's creative thinking. *International Journal of Early Childhood Environmental Education*, 6(1), 3–20.

Yang, B., Wu, N., Tong, Z., & Sun, Y. (2022). Narrative-based environmental education improves environmental awareness and environmental attitudes in children aged 6–8. *International Journal of Environmental Research and Public Health*, 19(11), 6483.

Chapter 17

Found in translation

Developing students' skills and competencies to implement nature-based and place-based outdoor curricula

Heather Prince and Chris Barlow

Outdoor learning embraces 'actively inclusive facilitated approaches that predominantly use activities and experiences in the outdoors...' (Institute for Outdoor Learning, 2024). It usually includes an experiential approach (Beard & Wilson, 2018; Boud et al., 1993; Kolb, 1984) where experience as an educative process is seen by John Dewey (1963 [1938]) as a 'transaction' and is important for growth. Life experience is central and necessary to the learning process (Morris, 2020) and 'knowledge is created through the transformation of experience' (Kolb, 2015, p. 49). Cognitive structures are seen as foundations to the learning process augmented by reflection to promote new learning (Moon, 2004). In respect of outdoor learning, it is the environment and place as well as pedagogy that create challenges and opportunities for creative, innovative and inspiring experiences that are authentic and inclusive and directed in higher education towards professional practice and employability (Thomas et al., 2021).

At the University of Cumbria, UK and its legacy institutions, outdoor and environmental education has been a degree major for more than 50 years, initially for the training of teachers and latterly through degree programmes in outdoor adventure and environmental studies, outdoor leadership, outdoor education, and outdoor and experiential learning at Bachelor and Master's levels. Outdoor learning is an established theme within the Learning, Education and Development Research Centre, and research in this area has international reach and impact. The original move away from initial teacher education was driven by the introduction of the national curriculum of England with relevant content limited to 'outdoor and adventurous activities' as one activity (of six) in Physical Education (Department for Education [DfE], 2013). The range of outcomes recognised by outdoor educators in nature literacy, cognition, care and concern for the environment and personal, social and emotional development in addition to physical and mental health and wellbeing (Jucker & von Au, 2022) were not included in the statutory curricula and thus, could not be justified as routes to qualified teacher status by neoliberal higher education institutions.

However, more recently, and accelerated by the United Nations Climate Change Conference (COP26), there has been an increasing interest in outdoor learning, which includes experiential learning and environmental education, to

DOI: 10.4324/9781003436928-26

address climate change, sustainability, biodiversity and the Sustainable Development Goals (SDGs) as seen in the Department for Education's Sustainability and Climate Change strategy for schools (DfE, 2022). This includes the creation of a National Education Nature Park through mapping the biodiversity of school grounds and the Climate Action awards scheme (Natural History Museum, 2024).

This focus on sustainability now emerging in schools has always been a key theme of the university and of our outdoor programmes. Students are provided with maps, grid references or what3words to enable them to walk, run or cycle to a local site for fieldwork or outdoor activities. This has precipitated rethinking of sessions sometimes constrained by logistical considerations to optimise the student experience with due appraisal of the environment's 'fitness for purpose' including stage of learners' experience, challenge and appropriateness for curriculum delivery. It involves the concept of a 'critical friend' to appraise and challenge the carbon footprint and sustainable intent of curriculum delivery.

Place-based learning

Place-based learning and a focus on developing place identity uses the local community and environment to teach across the curriculum in schools with hands-on, real-world learning experiences (Sobel, 2017). Similarly, in higher education, students' understanding of place influenced by culture and heritage is crucial to conceptualisations of socio-economic and political frameworks manifested in landscapes, framed as natural capital and including the more-than-human (Sitka-Sage et al., 2017). Place-based learning develops skills, knowledge and understanding of local as well as global environmental and sustainability issues. Education and the teaching of authentic, meaningful material build resilience and environmental awareness and consciousness of citizens for a sustainable future.

Learning more about place and the value of the environment supports growth of place attachment – the emotional location 'bond' built on the strength of connection that people feel towards a particular place (Ford et al., 2021). This usually comprises both social and physical constructs and positive anchors and magnets of a place encourage both returning and new inward migration to an area (Clark & Maas, 2015). For children and young people, the attractiveness of a place and their role in shaping it enhances place identity and the resulting employability and life-long learning opportunities

Professional application of outdoor learning

The integration of outdoor and place-based learning is illustrated by the case example of the Eden Project Morecambe in North-west England This project has far-reaching economic, social and environmental ambitions for the area to drive behavioural change within and without the region. Early in its conceptualisation, it stimulated the development of the Morecambe Bay Curriculum (MBC), envisioned as a place-based curriculum to inspire learners to learn more about their place and develop care and concern for it. The MBC vision is to transform the lives of young people in the town and region for enhanced life chances, an understanding of their environment, and health and wellbeing.

These agendas and global environmental concerns have reinvigorated the impetus to train teachers in outdoor learning and provide a focus for higher education students to create meaningful, authentic and time-critical learning experiences and opportunities through professional practice in communities and workplaces. Thus, a new pathway has been created in environmental and experiential learning in the PGCE primary to train educators in place-based learning to work in and with schools in Morecambe Bay as well as a new degree in outdoor education.

With the impetus of curriculum development and professional application, Barlow created a 'Morecambe Bay Curriculum Think Tank' of PGCE students studying a range of subjects (n =40) across the University, exploring learning ideas for themes relating to the environment and geography of Morecambe Bay. This initiative provides the opportunity for students to enjoy involvement in rich and purposeful professional dialogue where they can work with others to share their collective professional skills, knowledge and possibility thinking, all of which will be useful in their future roles. Engaging in a community of practice (Lave & Wenger, 1991) enables students to reflect on their attitude towards their role as professionals and, in this example, promotes the powerful notion of teachers thinking about teaching in collaboration as an enjoyable shared cognitive venture. The outcomes are beneficial for both children's learning and for the professional development and personal professional self-determination of the individual student teacher, not only in relation to outdoor learning but in relation to the ways in which they generally think and act as a teacher.

The Think Tank initiative began during COVID-19 restrictions with online discussions relating to Morecambe Bay Curriculum learning possibilities. The subsequent initiation of bespoke learning ideas related to meaningful nature-inspired, place-based learning in local schools. The Think Tank began by researching themes and resources to contribute to, and construct, place-based best practice templates as developed by the Morecambe Bay Curriculum Geography Leader's Steering Group, such as 'On the spot what have we got?' (celebrating a variety of different learning lenses that can be applied to the child's immediate local environment), 'The Mystery Road' (concerning investigation of the remains of 18th-century sea-trading piers), and 'Our Bay and how it was formed' (a comparison with other bays around the world and travelling across the Bay).

One very successful initiative is Eden Bear, who visits childminder, Early Year Foundation Stage (0–5 years) and Key Stage 1 (5–7 years) settings in the region, exploring local spaces and places. Eden Bear's adventures are recorded through stories and pictures in learning booklets, many of which were created by Think Tank members (University of Cumbria, 2024). This group is also creating a variety of additional place-based sequences of learning utilising ideas generated from the Think Tank, whilst also collecting, formatting and adding to the bank of MBC learning ideas concerning such themes as: Linking with schools across the Bay, village studies, environmental quality, transport, wildlife and investigating 'the beach within reach'.

More recently, a Think Tank hike up Warton Crag, a tree-covered limestone hill near Carnforth that offers stunning panoramic views across Morecambe Bay, allowed for an on-site opportunity for higher education students to discuss possible activities for children for an 'Up on High' place-based best practice expedition. This could offer transferable learning suggestions suitable for other high up locations around the Bay. This visit championed the 'why not?' attitude towards such learning that some teachers might shy away from due to perceived barriers (weather, safety, behaviour management, cost implications, etc.) to actually explore and celebrate the rich situational learning opportunities such an adventure can offer, especially for those children who may have never experienced such a thing.

Think Tank members, inspired by the immediate outdoor learning 'canvas' afforded by the crag itself and the panoramic view, engaged in leg dangling pedagogical discussions perched on Limestone outcrops, suggesting many ways to utilise the 'living breathing map' in front of them to raise questions, identify features, to relate the view to Ordnance Survey maps, to practise compass skills, to consider issues such as flooding, housing development and power generation, as well as identifying transport types, noting routes, what is old and new, etc., whilst also offering interesting art suggestions looking at tidal patterns and the colour and texture possibilities afforded by the view down on woodland, farmland and settlements.

Further discussional 'strolling' led to suggestions for activities such as foraging for and identifying flora and fauna, simulating on-site food chain activities involving children as organisms and creative 'what if?' enquiries regarding the possible siting of a new development or a change in the use of the crag. Post-walk conversation led to the generation of creative writing opportunities with suggestions ranging from writing a Warton Crag Airbnb review from the perspective of a peregrine falcon or a dark-green fritillary butterfly, to creating an expedition notebook packed with comments, sketches and descriptions, to 'what could be down that path?' imaginative writing and stories of trolls (inspired by rock formations that seem to have faces), tales of woodland spirits and 'what kind of dinosaur lives here?' descriptions inspired by the Jurassic-looking bracken glades and dells, and instruction writing on how to care for this place and act responsibly whilst visiting and extended description sentences inspired by the awe and wonder of nature.

Extending interactions

Involvement of students in the Think Tank has also offered opportunities to meet inspirational school-based colleagues, members of the local community and members of the wider learning community and experts in their field. Such engagement promotes the value of networking (Balvanera et al., 2017), the importance of teachers developing their own professional knowledge and understanding, the notion of being actively interested in the environmental teaching context in which a teacher is working and to seek curriculum enrichment opportunities by being curriculum designers and innovators for the benefit of children. Indeed, through such approaches to the profession, children might encounter interesting and inspirational people who might dazzle them with amazing information, allow them to experience new and interesting things as well as opening them up to new positive ways of thinking about their environment, based on direct experience, that might stay with them for life.

Such beliefs about their role as educators promote teacher enthusiasm, professional autonomy, self-advocacy, resilience and a 'can-do' attitude when facing barriers and creativity towards the curriculum to seek opportunities to bring learning to life for children. Engagement in outdoor learning can promote the notion of teachers as curriculum influencers.

Professional identity

Through the 'Being a Teacher' module, students are asked to challenge existing teaching constructs by responding to questions such as: 'what constitutes a learning environment?'; 'how do teachers best cater for the needs of all children?'; 'how does learning 'stick?'; and, 'does learning always have to take part inside within the constraints of four walls supported by a screen?' By asking such pertinent questions, and by reflecting upon their own experiences as a learner, students are developing constructs around the kind of teacher they wish to be, their teacher values and attitudes and their formation of a personal teacher identity, including an avoidance of the 'feared self' (Salli & Osam, 2018) and a delight in the prospect for children of what the 'future self' (Hammerness et al., 2005) might be.

If students can amplify outdoor learning opportunities and develop a sense of professional advocacy and autonomy, they can impact directly on children's attitudes to the world around them, helping to normalise outdoor learning. Indeed, it is powerful for student teachers to recognise that 'small' teacher actions such as sharing a found object, noticing bird song, stopping to point out a dew-sparkled cobweb, recognising an interesting flower, can be supplemented by 'larger' teacher actions such as the willingness to overcome time and planning constraints. Thus, outdoor learning will happen, through cross-curricular opportunities and generally being creative and brave regarding the learning adventures offered to children, and adopting a more activist stance (Sachs, 2001) towards the flexing of professional autonomy based on notions of good practice (Prince, 2020). Schools are places to learn about life and as such can be places of opportunity and inspiration for children, advocating healthy attitudes and choices, including those related to the world around them.

It is therefore long established that teachers (as significant adult role models in children's lives) influence the ways in which children's attitudes and interests develop. Teachers can be agents of change amidst societal concerns such as children's mental health, obesity, the lure of technology and 'disconnection' with outdoor environments. Teacher actions can inspire an enjoyment and willingness to participate in the outdoors and much else. Students need to work out what kind of teacher they aspire to be.

As part of the 'Being a Teacher' module therefore not only do student teachers discuss the ways in which learning can happen, including by being out of the classroom, using the school grounds and through out-of-school experiences within the immediate school location and on fieldtrips, but students are introduced to the idea of subject and area leadership and how leaders can have an impact across the whole school. One activity uses a school improvement plan scenario where all subject areas are asked to review school planning documents and use Kotter's model of change (Kotter, 2012) as a planning structure to create action plans to increase and sustain the use of outdoor learning across the curriculum. Ager's 'CIDIO' (can I do it outside?) construct (Ager, 2019) is applied to review lessons and to consider possibilities and solutions to the overcoming of potential barriers in all subjects of taking learning outside and develop students' interest, confidence and advocacy of outdoor learning. The 'Being a Teacher' module then explores further outdoor learning potential through use of a mock job interview task where students are asked to suggest outdoor learning opportunities for a given subject area and to share their suggestions with their peers.

External accountability instruments have been seen to present a challenge to normative values of the teaching profession (Day et al., 2005) and can devalue or suppress more creative and interpretive aspects of teachers' work (Galton & Mac-Beath, 2008) and the opportunity for pedagogical innovation with their attitude to risk-taking (Howard et al., 2018). Outdoor learning transcends many of these challenges and presents opportunities for creativity, innovation and a re-interpretation of curricula. Without teachers' personal involvement, creativity and commitment, it is likely that curriculum reform will be received half-heartedly and that teachers will be inhibitors to change rather than facilitators. This personal belief termed the 'personality of change' (Goodson, 2003, p. 76) involves teachers' commitments, beliefs, investments and ownership of their work and the balancing of personal and external forces of change is essential to achieve new practices. If teacher values are consistent or identities developed to a 'personality of change' teachers become more accepting of, and resilient to, change and will feel empowered to use their autonomous space to facilitate the learning for children that they value and believe in, and work through any mitigating factors to enable practice to occur.

Outdoor learning for positive educational change and innovation in higher education

The examples above illustrate how direct learning experiences in which students are immersed in the practical possibilities of outdoor learning approaches and thinking contribute to creativity and innovation and powerful professional development for employability. Barlow uses an 'inspire, invest, ignite' approach – *inspire* them to want to do this (through engagement in a variety of practical activities), *invest* in training to support their thinking (through theory, case studies in practice and activities promoting the potential of the immediate outdoor environment), and give opportunities to *ignite* their passion for this form of learning (through engaging their creative abilities in outdoor learning and challenging their curriculum planning potential). These approaches within higher education have applicability beyond initial teacher education, enhancing confidence and capability in our students to take risks and innovate in the workplace, grounded in a clear rationale and purpose.

Teaching in higher education should be creative, innovative and inspiring so that learners benefit from pedagogy which addresses their needs, interests, motivations and aspirations in terms of inclusivity, employability and professional practice. The models and frameworks of outdoor learning described above illustrate these key components through enhanced, flexible and accessible learning. Each student should be enabled to find his or her pathway through learning, which not only prepares the individual for lifelong learning and employment, but also enables personal maturation. Students are challenged through these knowledge exchange projects and outreach to share and celebrate best practice in professional contexts as well as at the university. The cycle of continuous reflection and evaluation with peer feedback and discussion in professional practice triggers feed-forward action and is key to enhancing active and embedded learning (Boud & Falchikov, 2007). The 'Think Tank' approach has rapidly established a 'community of learners' as well as cross-cultural learning and understanding and values a community of practice as 'one of the most important concepts in social and situated learning theory' (Hoadley, 2012, p. 286).

Outdoor learning can involve adventurous teaching by creating an element of surprise (Adler, 2008) or uncertainty of outcome; creative and innovative approaches to teaching, learning and assessment are encouraged. New ways of teaching and learning are critical for educational resilience (Kotter, 2012) and questioning and challenging pedagogy optimises academic practice for both students and staff as a motivational tool and for concrete and professional outcomes. Theoretical understandings of practice in professional contexts are linked to research (for example, Prince, 2019; Prince & Diggory, 2023) so that learners can explore meanings and apply critical thinking to normative contexts.

The greater integration of employability within the curriculum in a progressive framework allows students to recognise their skills, knowledge, understanding and professional values in teaching and learning, and apply them in professional contexts. Practice with its origins at one level of education can be shared to good effect with others and can integrate learning, teaching and research. This is paralleled in higher education in so far as outcomes are often measured in terms of degree classifications, but maturation and the assimilation of many other graduate skills are important.

References

Adler, J.E. (2008). Surprise. *Educational Theory*, 58(2), 149–173.

Ager, J. (2019). Can I do it outside? How to introduce a CIDIO approach in a primary school. *Horizons*, 84, 33–35.

Balvanera, P., Calderón-Contreras, R., Castro, A.J, Felipe-Lucia, M.R., Geijzendorffer, I.R., Jacobs, S., Martin-Lopez, B., Arbieu, U., Spreranza, C.I., Locatelli, B., Harguindeguy, N.P., Mercado, I.R., Spierenburg, M.J., Valet, A., Lynes, L. & Gillson, L. (2017). Interconnected place-based social–ecological research can inform global sustainability. *Current Opinion in Environmental Sustainability*, 29, 1–7.

Beard, C. & Wilson, J.P. (2018). *Experiential learning: A handbook for education, training and coaching*. 4th Edition. London: Kogan Page.

Boud, D., Cohen, R. & Walker, D. (eds.) (1993). *Using experience for learning*. Buckingham: SRHE/OUP.

Boud, D. & Falchikov, N. (eds.) (2007). *Rethinking assessment in higher education: Learning for the longer term*. Abingdon: Routledge.

Clark, W.A.V. & Maas, R. (2015). Interpreting migration through the prism of reasons for moves. *Population, Space and Place*, 21(1), 54–67.

Day, C., Eliott, B. & Kington, A. (2005). Reforms, standards and teacher identity: Challenges of sustaining commitment. *Teaching and Teacher Education*, 21(5), 563–577.

Department for Education (2013). *National curriculum for England: PE programmes of study*. https://www.gov.uk/government/publications/national-curriculum-in-england-physical-education-programmes-of-study.

Department for Education (2022). *Sustainability and climate change: A strategy for the education and children's services systems*. https://www.gov.uk/government/publications/sustainability-and-climate-change-strategy.

Dewey, J. (1963). *Experience and education*. New York, NY: Collier Books. (Original work published in 1938).

Ford, C., Convery, I., Harvey, D., Hallam, S., Loynes, C. & Prince, H. (2021). *Sustainable rural town performance: Place value, attachment and migration*. Research report, Lancaster University and University of Cumbria.

Galton, M. & MacBeath, J. (2008). *Teachers under pressure*. London: SAGE.

Goodson, I F. (2003). *Professional knowledge, professional lives: Studies in education and change*. Maidenhead: Open University Press.

Hammerness, K.M., Darling-Hammond, L., Bransford, J., Berliner, D., Cochran-Smith, M., McDonald, M., & Kenneth, Z. (2005). How teachers learn and develop. In L. Darling-Hammond, & J. Bransford (eds.), *Preparing teachers for a changing world: What teachers should learn and be able to do* (pp. 358–389). San Francisco, CA: Jossey-Bass.

Hoadley, C. (2012). What is a community of practice and how can we support it? In D. Jonassen & S. Land (eds.), *Theoretical foundations of learning environments* (pp. 286–300). Oxford;New York: Routledge.

Howard, P., Becker, C., Wiebe, S., Carter, M., Gousouasis, P. & McLarnon, M. (2018). Creativity and pedagogical innovation: Exploring teachers' experiences of risk-taking. *Journal of Curriculum Studies*, 50(6), 850–864.

Institute for Outdoor Learning (2024). About outdoor learning. https://www.outdoor-learning.org./standards/good-practice/about-outdoor-learning.html.

Jucker, R. & von Au, J. (2022). *High quality outdoor learning. Evidence-based evidence outside the classroom for children, teachers and society.* Cham, Switzerland: Springer. https://link.springer.com/book/10.1007/978-3-031-04108-2.

Kolb, D.A. (1984). *Experiential learning: Experience as the source of learning and development.* Englewood Cliffs, NJ: Prentice-Hall.

Kolb, D.A. (2015). *Experiential learning: Experience as the source of learning and development.* Upper Saddle River, NJ: Pearson.

Kotter, J. (2012). *Leading change.* 2nd Ed. Boston, MA: Harvard Business Review Press.

Lave, J. & Wenger, E. (1991). *Situated learning: Legitimate peripheral participation.* New York: Cambridge University Press.

Moon, J.A. (2004). *A handbook of reflective and experiential learning theory and practice.* London; New York: Routledge.

Morris, T.H. (2020). Experiential learning – A systematic review and revision of Kolb's model. *Interactive Learning Environments,* 28(8), 1064–1077.

Natural History Museum (2024). *National Education Nature Park and Climate Action awards scheme.* https://www.nhm.ac.uk/about-us/national-impact/national-education-nature-park-and-climate-action-awards-scheme.html.

Prince, H.E. (2019). Changes in outdoor learning in primary schools in England, 1995 and 2017: Lessons for good practice. *Journal of Adventure Education and Outdoor Learning,* 19(4), 329–342.

Prince, H.E. (2020). The sustained value teachers place on outdoor learning. *Education 3–13: International Journal of Primary, Elementary and Early Years Education,* 48(5), 597–615.

Prince, H.E. & Diggory, O. (2023). Recognition and reporting of outdoor learning in primary schools in England. *Journal of Adventure Education and Outdoor Learning.* doi:10.1080/14729679.2023.2166544.

Sachs, J. (2001). Teacher professional identity: Competing discourses, competing outcomes. *Journal of Education Policy,* 16(2), 149–161.

Salli, A. & Osam, U.V. (2018). Preservice teachers' identity construction: emergence of expected and feared teacher-selves. *Quality and Quantity,* 52(Suppl.1), 483–500.

Sitka-Sage, M.D., Kopnina, H., Blenkinsop, S. & Piersol, L. (2017). Rewilding education in troubled times; or, getting back to the wrong post-nature. *Visions for Sustainability,* 8, 20–37.

Sobel, D. (2017). *Place-based education: Connecting classrooms and communities.* Great Barrington, MA: Orion Society.

Thomas, G.J., Dyment, J. & Prince, H. (2021). *Outdoor environmental education in higher education: International perspectives.* Cham, Switzerland: Springer.

University of Cumbria (2024). Morecambe Bay Curriculum. Primary digital resource library. https://www.cumbria.ac.uk/study/academic-departments/institute-of-education/morecambe-bay-curriculum/.

Conclusions

Paolo Oprandi

It is hard to know what you will get out of a book until you have read it. The many, varied chapters of this book have been no exception for me. Wendy and I are left inspired. When we put out a call for chapters, we did not know how many people would respond. To our surprise and delight, we were inundated with enthusiastic practitioners wishing to share their methods for applying outdoor learning, their research on it and their love for it.

The book is of interest to educational developers and mainstream teachers whatever the discipline. Through emphasizing the benefits that can be reaped from utilizing the outdoors as a teaching space, it captures the growing awareness of a need for change in many of our educational practices and policies. I wonder too whether this book should be core reading to many of our teaching training courses as it matches the current mood of the educational development community, covering as it does general pedagogic themes such as experiential learning, sustainability, diversity and inclusion, learner autonomy and collaboration.

While the appetite for outdoor learning seems to be huge, its practice in higher education is still low. Many authors in this book make convincing arguments for its use in teaching and learning, but as Jamie Heywood tells us, physical activity amongst higher education students is sadly decreasing, not increasing. Education in its current form is usually one requiring mental calculation, but the authors of this book have made us believe it needs to be more than that. It has made us question whether over the last centuries we have seen a swinging of the pendulum from early adult lives without education that were all about practical work experience but little theoretical reflection to early adult lives with education that are all about theoretical work but little practical experience. The chapters have given us reasons to buck this trend, and find some middle ground.

The arguments for the use of the outdoors in education are wide and varied in this book. Many authors such as Tom Smith and Heather Prince talk of outdoor learning as providing authentic experiences that can be transferred and used outside of the educational contexts. Russell Crawford and Aled Singleton describe the importance of location, being *in situ* where the objects and processes you are studying exist. To these authors, the outdoors serves to take us away from the theoretical and into the real, and thus provides firsthand experiences. Others have

DOI: 10.4324/9781003436928-27

described the importance of the outdoors to the acquisition of important life skills that are more difficult to learn within the classroom. Authors such as Colin Wood and Alex Sabine have identified the requirement for agency in education, Agnes Bosanquet et al. talk of the importance of connectedness to nature in situating our understanding, Suzie Dick introduces the idea of human flourishing and the development of innate capabilities and Patrick Boxall talks of the use of the outdoors in developing the students' creativity.

Jamie Heywood makes a powerful argument for the importance of the outdoors in terms of the mental, emotional and spiritual health of our students. I am reminded that education can cover many gritty and difficult subjects that can bring mental and emotional fatigue to students studying them. Many educational subjects raise tricky and thorny issues which we as a species have some way to go before fixing and which can leave students feeling hopeless, depressed and claustrophobic. It is in this context that Cathy Eliot reminds us that while we cannot overlook these educational issues, it is also our responsibility to provide our students with critical hope. Cathy describes the outdoors and nature to be the lung that allows us to breathe that hope, which she describes as "reconnection with hope in times of despair", while Agnes Bosanquet et al. describe the outdoors as "The most effective learning environment in the university".

While the reasons for using the outdoors in our teaching are strong, the chapters in the book have also been given many ideas on how the outdoors can be used. Aled Singleton introduces us to multiple ideas, such as walking tasks and ethnographic research tasks. Others have cited the use of technologies such as social media. Liam Taylor describes how social media has augmented and improved fieldwork. Andrew Middleton writes of the walking seminar: "As a co-operative social constructivist pedagogy, learning walks mix social purpose and individual agency by accommodating learning through conversation". Jo Peat describes the challenges to providing outdoor learning, such as accessibility and practical limitations and found that unfamiliarity of the outdoors to urban communities can be a barrier to students using it. She talks of the importance of providing safe green spaces for our students and reasons to go and use them. She says the green spaces they have created "helps to induct students into activities that may initially seem alien". Other authors found alternatives to outdoor spaces that could provide some of the same benefits. Gustavo Espinosa-Ramos provided evidence for the successful use of virtual field trips and Beth Hammond introduced location apps that could recreate the places outside of the educational institution.

Chapters such as that by Espinoza-Ramos suggest that some students are resistant to outdoor learning and prefer simulations they can do at their desk. While student voice and preferences are important, it is important we match this with what we know of good pedagogy, hands-on experience and authentic practice. The outdoors can provide deep, lasting memories and learning that can guide our students in the pursuit of their goals. Simulations while efficient cannot provide that same depth of experience. Students might not find outdoor learning easy, but deep learning rarely is.

As with so many discussions about teaching practice, this book leaves me with the question, "What is the purpose of education?" My first response would be rather traditional, "*Education is a means by which students learn through a process of teaching. Learning is the process of acquiring skills to be able to do something or understand a process more fully*". I think this would be a culturally-accepted definition and indeed the goal of many educational institutions, courses and teachers. But after reading these chapters from authors across many disciplines, I wonder if this statement adequately comprises the remit of education. Perhaps education is not only a means of self-improvement through study, but also a means of self-discovery through experience and reflection.

When chatting to my daughter, she said she did not want to go to university because she did not want a desk job and university life seems all about sitting at desks. I did not think I could refute the argument, but I did think of this book and that with the courage and determination of these practitioner-authors, higher education might yet change for the better.

Index

Page numbers in *italics* refer to figures, those in **bold** indicate tables.

Printed and bound by CPI Group (UK) Ltd, Croydon, CR0 4YY

02/09/2024

01031210-0001